THE KING'S ENGLAND

BUCKINGHAMSHIRE
Country of the Chiltern Hills

EDITED BY
ARTHUR MEE

With 206 Places
and 110 Pictures

H
heritagehunter

First published in 1940

This Heritage Hunter® edition published February 2016
Register for free at **www.heritagehunter.co.uk**
for a free ebook every month

ISBN 978-1523999354

Gray's Country Churchyard
Each in his narrow cell for ever laid,
The rude forefathers of the hamlet sleep

The Country of the Chiltern Hills

IT began the fight that made us free. It gave birth to John Hampden and sheltered John Milton. It is at the very heart of history for us all, and yet it is of its natural beauty that we think, for its historic days have passed, but its haunting loveliness goes on for ever.

We do not wonder that in this lovely countryside English poetry took a new turning, from the dull drab world of Alexander Pope to the lively human world of William Cowper. We do not wonder that the Confessor gave one of its villages to the Church, thinking no doubt that he had nothing fairer to give; or that another village was given to Catherine of Aragon in the days when her lord still loved her. We do not wonder that our oldest aristocratic dynasty here made its home, that Shelley could not resist these pleasant ways, that here Gray wrote his Elegy of our countryside. It is not so near to London that our destroying century has ruined it, yet not so far away that we cannot transport ourselves to it on any day we will, finding it, as Milton found it, a paradise regained.

Like a lion rampant as we look at its shape on the map, Nature has made it anything but warlike. It has few great heights to draw the storms about it, no turbulent rivers. We may think it strange that the greatest storm in English history should have burst in such a tranquil scene as this, but true it is that since the Civil War nothing has disturbed the serenity of these 748 square miles. It is as if the English spirit, loving to be quiet and left alone, breaks loose from the cage it has made for itself when it is challenged, and when the battle is won settles down again for another 300 years.

Buckinghamshire does not count in size, for there are 32 counties bigger, but we may wonder if any one of them is more truly English in its landscape, in its human memories, and in its influence on England. It is the county of the Chiltern Hills, with their magnificent beech woods showing Nature at her best from silvery spring to golden autumn. So dense are these woodlands, running down the valleys to the Thames, that in olden days they were the haunts of lawless men, and the stewardship of the Chilterns (still given to an MP who wishes to resign) was far from being the sinecure it is today.

The Chilterns divide the county in two as they run from the south-west corner to pass into Bedfordshire through Whipsnade Zoo. The sheer escarpment so well remembered by all who pay a call on the lions there is characteristic of the range along its north-west face. The slope to the valley of the Thames is much more gradual, and it is on the part with the steepest slopes that we find the highest points—at Wendover, where the grand viewpoint of Coombe Hill rises 845 feet, and near Ivinghoe, where Beacon Hill is 762 feet. Both heights give us superb views.

Through what are called the bottoms, or the folds of the long slopes to the Thames, flow brooks and streams—the Hamble Brook in the west; the Wye flowing nine miles to the Thames and reaching it near Hedsor; the Misbourne, losing itself underground and joining the Colne near Denham, where the river forms the boundary with Middlesex, being joined hereabouts by the lovely River Chess, which has joined the boundary with Hertfordshire at Chenies. Mostly it is the Thames itself which forms the southern boundary of the county, with Berkshire lying along its farther bank, Windsor thus being separated from Eton. The extreme north of the county, over 50 miles from the extreme south, lies in the low hills looking down on the Great Ouse as it sluggishly passes through Olney. From Ivinghoe's Beacon we see the Ouzel on its way to join the Ouse at Newport Pagnell, and the Grand Union Canal running between the Woburn Heights, down which streams flow to join the Great Ouse and the Thames. Those to the Thames include the Thame, which rises at Dunton, and on its 30 miles picks up

THE COUNTRY OF THE CHILTERN HILLS

some streams from the north-west slopes of the Chilterns before it forms the boundary with Oxfordshire and joins the Thames at Dorchester. With Quainton's fine view-point to separate their basins, the Claydon Brook rises north of the Thame among the Whaddon Heights, and joins with the River Bune to enter the Great Ouse near Thornborough. The Great Ouse has entered the county at Brackley in Northants, flowing placidly through Buckingham, and gathers the waters of the Tove, a boundary stream with Northants, before it runs into Bedfordshire at Turvey.

It happens that the Great Ouse is narrow in this county, so that Buckinghamshire has no great river within its borders. Yet it is all very fertile north of the Chilterns, and in the wide Thames Valley, an advantage it owes rather to the shaping of our island than to the layers that build it up. As we journey from London to Wales we can tread down the steps of Time, coming upon the rocks in the order in which they were laid down, and the first of these steps is well seen in this county.

The geologist finds in the extreme south many acres of rich alluvium deposited by the Thames, with London Clay and sands and gravels sometimes 80 feet thick between the alluvium and the chalk. From the ridgeway along the Chilterns we look down upon the layers of strata continuing below the hills, the porous upper and lower greensands with the impervious clay between them. Next come two surprises for the geologist, the Purbeck and Portland limestones, with their huge ammonites, hundreds of which we found built into the wall round Hartwell Park. Brill, where the quaint windmill stands 600 feet up, is surely the farthest north at which this fine building stone has ever been quarried in our island. Beyond to the north lie the cold clays, parted for a brief space by coral strands, and roughly speaking it is the Great Ouse which divides the clays from the older limestones which have meant so much to the builders of the churches whose spires are the pride of Buckinghamshire—Hanslope's challenging from its hill and Olney's from its valley, while Stowe's great school, with its marvellous front, is a perfect example of the precious advantage of building with native material. Finally, the border stream called the Tove cuts through rocks older still, the blue-greys of the Lias, over which the ichthyosaurus may have lumbered.

The good building stone in the north gives the builders fine materials; the gravel, chalk, and sand provide quarrying industries; and, though we may not know it, many of the chairs we sit in and the spades with which our children dig the sands come from Chiltern beeches. The railway has brought to Wolverton great carriage works, and the waterway long ago brought prosperity to Aylesbury, which has also one of the busiest printing works in England; but it is at Slough, with the Great West Road running through it, that industry has grown by leaps and bounds, hundreds of factories having been built on the rubbish heap of the Great War there. Its population has grown apace: altogether there are about 300,000 people in the county.

Here people have lived from immemorial time, with the oldest road in England running along the Chilterns, the Icknield Way, and about it are a few camps older than history. Buckinghamshire has in truth a little of everything, and beauty everywhere. It is the open countryside and the valleys filled with beeches, the broad pastures about the Thames, the Ouse, the Thame, and the Claydon Brook, and the spacious views from the heights which make the county so attractive. It is a wonderful place for the geologist, it never fails the naturalist, and for the lover of wide, rolling prospects it has hardly a dull patch.

If we would choose its typical places we may select almost at random from the map. Amersham has its old houses and watermills. Aylesbury has its medieval square with statues of Hampden and Disraeli, its winding ways and the lovely square in which the old church stands, with a west window of great splendour, and a knight in armour who is believed to have been the far-off ancestor of Robert E. Lee, who led the Southern armies against General Grant and Abraham Lincoln. Boarstall has its

THE COUNTRY OF THE CHILTERN HILLS

14th century gatehouse, a massive survival, and Buckingham has the house to which Catherine of Aragon came, and Charles Stuart. Burnham has the beeches renowned wherever men love trees, and the grave of one of Buckinghamshire's three Prime Ministers. Cheddington has the cultivated terraces the Saxons farmed, and Chenies has the home of the Russells, with their marvellous array of monuments.

Little Missenden has its cottages gathering round the Elizabethan manor, and a fascinating church close by. Long Crendon is rich in old cottages and great houses. Marsh Gibbon has the gabled manor and the thatched barn which Chaucer's granddaughter would know when she was lady of the manor there. Steeple Claydon, given to Catherine of Aragon, has a house given by Mary Tudor to Sir Thomas Chaloner, the scholar and traveller who lives in the glowing pages of Hakluyt. Stowe has established a public school in the marvellous house about a quarter of a mile long through which a great procession of famous folk has passed through centuries. The splendour of Taplow, with the river flowing by its wooded banks, is unrivalled. West Wycombe has been chosen by the Society of Arts as a village to preserve for all time. From Coombe Hill, near Wendover, clothed in all the beauty of the Chilterns, we may stand and see St Paul's about 30 miles away.

The lover of churches will find all he wants to see in this delightful county. At Iver is a church with Roman bricks in Saxon walls, and the handiwork of Norman and Tudor in it. Lavendon has a Saxon tower, and Wing has the finest Saxon church in the county, a wonderful glimpse of England before the Conqueror, with a crypt lost for ages and opened up again. Cublington has a Norman chest, a very rare survival, and Addington has a picture of Christ before Pilate 600 years old. Broughton has the walls of its nave covered with a tableau of life from Chaucer's England, showing the quaint rustic costumes with a scene of Judgment Day looking down on it; and into all this wonder we come by a door five centuries old. Dorton too has a 500-year-old door, swinging on hinges older still, and at Weston Turville we may open a door by which men came into the church to give thanksgiving for Agincourt, and may hear a bell still ringing which rang in the good news. Chearsley has also a bell older than the Reformation. Fingest has a wonderful Norman tower, and Hanslope has a medieval tower and Norman carvings. Stewkley has the crown of Norman churches in all Buckinghamshire, with a tower of splendour, noble doorways, and an enchanting interior.

Penn, the home of the family of William Penn, with its lead font and the graves of the earliest Penns and their portraits in brass, has one of the best Doom paintings that has survived, 12 feet long. Maids Moreton has a church like a little cathedral, a medieval legacy from two sisters. Edlesborough has the finest woodwork in the county, and Clifton Reynes (which has a Judgment Day painting fading on its wall) has four wooden figures on tombs, two 600-year-old knights and their wives. Marsworth has a Jacobean tomb by our first great sculptor, Epiphanius Evesham. Little Hampden has ancient paintings on its Norman walls, and Upper Winchendon has an astonishing pulpit cut 600 years ago from a solid block of oak. Slough still rings the church bells which once rang for Pamela's wedding as the people read of it excitedly in the first English novel.

Buckinghamshire has a famous roll of honour; no small county has contributed more to England's fame. It has given us three Prime Ministers, the two Grenvilles and the romantic Disraeli, who spent his boyhood at the home of his famous father Isaac at Bradenham and lived and died at Hughenden, surrounded by the noble park now belonging to the people. High Wycombe still remembers that it rejected Disraeli three times, but though the county rejected him for Parliament it is entitled to remember with pride that he was a Buckinghamshire lad, that here he chose to make his home, and here he lies. As for the Grenvilles, George and his son William Wyndham, their ministries did two significant things which left their mark

THE COUNTRY OF THE CHILTERN HILLS

upon mankind. The father, by passing the Stamp Act which would have taxed America, sowed the seed of bitterness and cut America adrift from the Motherland; the son was the head of the ministry which abolished the Slave Trade and made it impossible for slaves to breathe in England.

In the pulpits of this county have been heard the voice of the saintly Richard Baxter and the thunder of John Knox, both at Amersham.; and we remember that here the eloquent voice of Edmund Burke is stilled, for he lies at Beaconsfield with the son whose death was a poignant grief he never could forget. Close by the Burkes are the graves of the Grenfells and the grave of Edmund Waller, the poet of the Commonwealth who loved Philip Sidney's cousin in vain and wrote for her Go, Lovely Rose. There are few more pathetic stories than those of the Grenfell brothers, two sets of them, both Jonathans and Davids. Francis and Riversdale Grenfell were the sons of the Field Marshal and both fell in the war, Francis winning the first VC. Julian and Billy Grenfell were the sons of Lord Desborough, who also gave their lives for England, Julian writing one of the finest of all the poems the Great War produced.

There is inspiration for poets in this county, for more than any other county in the land it is Milton's. It was to Horton that he came from Cambridge, to live at his father's house in the early years when his mind was building up his glowing vision. They were the happiest years of his life. When the plague came to London it was to the cottage at Chalfont St Giles that Milton came to escape it, and it is surely something more than mere coincidence that on coming back to these lovely scenes he began his Paradise Regained. It is interesting, too, that long after Milton there came to Chalfont our famous Captain Cook, who would sit here talking with his friend Sir Hugh Palisser on their sailings and chartings. We come upon another explorer at Aston Abbots, for it was the last home of James Clark Ross, who rests here after his Polar adventures.

In the delightful Chiltern valley where Hambleden lies was

born the famous Thomas Cantelupe, now in the calendar of saints, Chancellor of Oxford University and Chancellor of England in the days of our first Parliament. At Fenny Stratford lies the rich man who made himself poor for learning's sake, Browne Willis, and all the world knows that at Olney William Cowper wrote nearly all the poems and letters by which he is remembered. At Gawcott was born a man who left his mark on 500 of our churches, Sir Gilbert Scott. At Chilton is the old house of Sir John Croke, the man who was Speaker in the hour of victory over the Armada, and told Elizabeth that the peace of the realm had been saved by her might, whereupon she said, "No, by the mighty Hand of God, Mr. Speaker." At Castle Thorpe lies Sir Thomas Tyrrell, Chief Justice belonging to a house linked with dire tragedies, for he was descended from Walter Tyrrell whose arrow killed William Rufus, and James Tyrrell who planned the murder of the princes in the Tower.

It is, of course, the dramatic age of the Stuarts that gives Buckinghamshire its immortal place in history. Here was born John Hampden and here he lies; they brought him from Chalgrove Field with arms reversed, drums muffled, and heads uncovered. He had started the Civil War by refusing to pay the Ship Money demanded by the king, but all men honoured him as all lovers of freedom pay him homage to this day. Here at Middle Claydon is still the home of the famous Verneys, and who can forget, in thinking of this noble house, the faithful Edmund who fell at Edgehill, standard-bearer of the king, his right hand severed with a sword but found on the field still clutching the king's flag.

In the village of Milton Keynes the notorious Bishop Atterbury was born, the man whose treachery led him to the Tower in Jacobite days, and at Fawley sleep a fearless judge and his fearless son, Bulstrode Whitelock, who refused to sit in judgment on the king. At Hartwell (where the King of France came in exile with his court during the Napoleon Wars) sleeps Sir Richard Ingoldsby, kinsman of Cromwell who signed the death-

THE COUNTRY OF THE CHILTERN HILLS

warrant, but was pardoned and knighted when the Stuarts came back.

There is a pleasant little scene with which we may close this tragic chapter of the war which made us free. It is in a little country lane, an hour's ride from London, and at the top of the lane and at the bottom is a sight to thrill all Englishmen. At the top is Jordans, the old farm with the Mayflower barn made from the timbers of the ship which carried the Pilgrim Fathers to America; at the bottom of the lane is the old Quaker meeting-place, with a little graveyard in which sleep William Penn, the Quaker friend of a Stuart king, and Thomas Ellwood, friend of Milton. This barn and this meadow are surely among the most significant possessions England has, and it is good that they should be here, in the solitude of a quiet place in as fair a countryside as anyone need wish to see.

Westminster Busby's Family

ADDINGTON. Hidden from the world in a green shade, two houses, a handful of cottages, and a church keep each other company. The older manor house, set in a park of 300 acres, is adapted from a 17th century manor and has some of its original panelling, and in the hall ceiling some 16th century roundels carved with heads. Inside the park gates stand the village stocks. A better reminder of the past is a tithe barn of heroic size, built almost 400 years ago in the form of a cross. It has five bays 12 feet long, and there is not its like in the county.

We come into the church by a doorway set in the handsome tower. The nave arcades, the chancel arch, and the tower are 600 years old. A precious fragment of the old church is a piscina in the vestry, made from a Norman pillar and its capital. A precious picture from Orvieto hangs on the walls, a rare possession for so small a place. Painted nearly 600 years ago, it shows Christ before a red-bearded Pilate, who sits on a dais, the clerk at his feet making notes of the trial. In the windows we see other little realistic pictures in fragments of 16th and 17th century Flemish glass, some plain, some coloured, where the designer put telling details into the story of Abraham and Isaac and the death of John the Baptist. Some colourless marble faces are here in the monuments of the Busbys, who for many generations were lords of the manor. One, a weird head on a wall tablet, is in memory of Elizabeth Busby, who died in 1661; and another wall tablet of 1700 shows a bust of Sir John. The most famous Busby was the headmaster of Westminster School who declined to doff his cap to Charles the Second, on the ground that the boys might think there was somebody more important than the master A memorial with a mourning figure is to Ann Tynte, who died in 1800.

A link with the present day is a medallion to John Hubbard, who became the first Lord Addington and died in 1889. He built St Alban's Church in Holborn and made his name remembered in the House of Commons by his practical advice on the levying of income tax.

THE KING'S ENGLAND

The Three Thomases

ADSTOCK. The suns of 350 summers have cast their shadows across a dial here, set over a porch sheltering a doorway 800 years old in a church which stands on a mound by a charming cluster of thatched cottages. The doorway capitals, with graceful foliage out of which peep heads of demons, are the oldest carvings in the church. Another doorway was once even more beautiful, for it had a carved tympanum; now an arch has been hollowed in it so that only fragments of wings shaped by Norman sculptors are left for us to see.

A solemn little gallery of stone heads supporting a 16th century roof look down on the nave, the lower courses of which are three feet thick, as the Normans left it. Near the tall arch in the 15th century tower is a font of the same age, with roses carved on four of its eight panels and a kind of vase we rarely see, rising from the floor to hold the font in irregular stone waves. Hanging in the tower belfry is a 15th century bell, and a reminder of earlier days is in the 14th century chancel arch and piscina, the fleur-de-lys hinges of the door, and three traceried panels once in a screen and now adding grace to the pulpit.

Four rectors whose names we see on the walls preached in an older pulpit. There was Alexander Burrell who died in 1771, after 50 years in the village, and there were three Thomas Egertons. The first Thomas came to Adstock the year before the Armada, and if we count up the dates we see that these three ministered here during the reigns of eight sovereigns of England and the two protectors. It was while an Egerton was rector here that a great fight between the King's men and the Parliament men took place near the Folly Inn a stone's throw from the village. On the churchyard wall we read the names of 41 men of Adstock who fought in the war of our own time.

Old Folk and Old Houses

AMERSHAM. It has an old street that can never be forgotten, with black and white fronts and watermills at either end. In the middle of it, standing on open arches, is the 17th century market hall with its wooden turret. One of the arches was enclosed to make a lock-up, with a grille and a peephole and metal bars, and in one

BUCKINGHAMSHIRE

corner is the original staircase leading to the meeting-room, which has panelling on its walls and the arms of Charles the Second.

The market hall has had for companions through centuries many gabled houses, too many to remember. It is like a walk through the past to come upon them. Woodside Farm, a tiled 17th century house, has a room in which the Quakers met secretly when meeting was unsafe for them; it was the home of Gulielma Springett, the bride of William Penn. At the corner of a road going over the hill to Beaconsfield is the 16th century Bury Farm, her mother's first home. In one of the old houses not far from the market hall is a remarkable series of wall paintings of great interest to antiquarians. They were brought to light in 1932, and are a rare group representing the Nine Worthies of whom we read in Love's Labour's Lost. They are shown in classical or medieval dress, some in armour, on the walls of a 16th century room. One is Julius Caesar with a double-headed eagle on his banner, one Joshua with a banner of the sun, a third is David with his harp, another is Charlemagne, and another is Godfrey de Bouillon, King of Jerusalem. A little way off is the old timbered grammar school, now turned to other uses, and behind four stunted lime trees is a charming group of almshouses ranged round a courtyard to which we come through a small archway. They were built by Sir William Drake in 1657.

The monuments of the Drakes are in the 13th century clerestoried church, which has an impressive 15th century tower, battlemented, pinnacled, and crowned with a sugar-loaf turret from which a 500-year-old door leads into the ringing chamber; the porch has grotesque faces grinning down on us. It brings us into a nave with heads of men and angels supporting the 600-year-old roof. It was in this church that John Knox (during a preaching tour in the county) preached one of his brave sermons denouncing Mary Tudor during the nine days when Lady Jane Grey was Queen of England, and it was in the same pulpit that Richard Baxter conducted a controversy with the soldiers of Cromwell's army. He tells us that when he was at Amersham he found an "ignorant sectarian" lecturing in the church, and that, thinking it his duty to be there, he took "divers sober officers with me to let them see that more of the army were against them than for them." He took the pew, and Pitchford's cornet and troopers took the gallery, finding there a crowded congregation of poor well-meaning people who came in the simplicity of their hearts to be deceived. Richard Baxter disputed with them from morning until almost night, listening to an "abundance of nonsense."

There is a memorial stone in the town marking the spot where some of the martyrs were burned, one of them William Tylsworth, burned in a fire which his own daughter had been made to light.

The church has a host of memorials to the Drakes, who lived at Shardeloes in the fine park of 700 acres, half a mile away. Seen from the road across the wide lake formed by the river, the house is charming; it is one of the countless places at which Queen Elizabeth was entertained, this time by William Tothill, who lived here with his wife and presumably with some of his 33 children. There is a monument to one of them who married an unknown Francis Drake, Sir William's son, and Francis has a bust in a niche.

Sir William died in 1699 and lies in a shroud on an enormous tomb reaching from the floor to the roof of the chancel, with golden cherubs weeping for him. There are medallion portraits of Montague Drake of the next generation, a wall monument of Elizabeth Drake kneeling with eight children in 18th century costume, a fine tomb by Scheemakers with white marble figures of a woman and a cherub in memory of Montague Drake of 1728, and two reliefs by John Bacon, one of a woman kneeling in memory of William Drake of 1796 and one of Thomas Drake of 1810, sitting. There are two 19th century Drakes, one sitting with a Bible in his hands and John Drake, an old rector who was here for 50 years. Also in memory of the family are several windows, the one over the altar with ten apostles glowing in colour and the four Evangelists writing in the tracery. The glass is 18th century, and came from a Hertfordshire manor house.

There is a tiny brass of this ancient family on which is engraved the portrait of chubby John Drake, a boy of four dressed much as little Charles Stuart would be dressed, and kneeling on a rich cushion. He has these charming lines engraved about him:

> *Had he lived to be a man*
> *This inch had grown but to a span;*
> *Now is he past all fear of pain*
> *Twere sin to wish him here again,*
> *View but the way by which we come*
> *Thou'll say he's best that's first at home.*

Three other brasses of the 15th and 16th centuries show Henry Brudenell armed with a dagger, and his wife; Thomas Carbonell, his 15th century neighbour, also with his wife; and the 16th century John Penne with his wife, she tall and slim.

While little John Drake was still alive at Shardeloes in 1623 little Henry Curwen was born. He came here to study at the rectory and died as a pupil, and he lies in a big tomb decorated with cherubs and angels, with doors opening to reveal the figure of a woman leaning on a globe. Kneeling on an altar tomb of a hundred years later is Elizabeth Bent in widow's garb, with her son George.

The 18th century rectory has in its garden a timbered well-house with a well which was worked within living memory by a horse; it has on the floor the enormous double-grooved drum and the turning-post. A little way off stands the hamlet of Coleshill, with a few timbered houses and a splendid windmill; it was the home of Edmund Waller, the poet, whom we come upon at Beaconsfield, where he lies.

The Knight in Armour

ASHENDON. Crowning a hill in the Vale of Aylesbury, it is set in a delightful pastoral scene, with the Chilterns looking romantic on the horizon. Below and around the Norman church cluster thatched cottages shaded by trees. The church tower, its little windows shuttered with old oak, is 15th century, but a deeply splayed window and a doorway which no longer opens are Norman. So is the font, with a 17th century cover. There is a handsome arcade 700 years old, and an exceptionally wide chancel arch. Five big corbel heads of varied features hold up the medieval roof of the aisle. In a medieval recess, over which are two oak shields from the old rood screen, lies a 13th century knight clad in chain armour, still about to draw his sword. He is believed to have been one of the Cheyndutt family. The pulpit with its raised panels, the altar table, a high chair in the chancel, and a long oak chest are all Jacobean, and in the vestry is a carved stand at which parsons have washed their hands for 300 years.

Last Home of a Great Explorer

ASTON ABBOTS. Its attractive old cottages, some timbered and thatched, gather about the village green, looking up to the 16th century tower of a 14th century church remade in Victorian days. Children have been christened at its font for 500 years. Near the modern oak screen, with an iron grille and a ringers gallery, is a 17th century chest. The east window, with scenes from the life of Christ, is in memory of Sir James Clark Ross, the Polar explorer whose heroic career was rounded by peaceful years in the old house of Aston Abbots which was for centuries the home of the abbots of St Albans, to whom the village once belonged. In the shadow of this ancient church sleeps this man whose life was passed amid the tumult of great seas and the thunder of toppling bergs and splitting icefields.

Descended from a family of soldiers and sailors, he was in the Navy at 12, three years before Waterloo, and at 18 began his apprenticeship to the Arctic, sailing with his uncle, Sir John Ross, in quest of the North-West Passage, which they missed by mistaking clouds for mountain barriers. He went with Sir Edward Parry on three great expeditions, and in 1837 reached the farthest North then known. With his uncle he was imprisoned four years in the ice, during which time he explored a great area of unknown land and discovered the North magnetic pole.

Having won glory in the Arctic and made a complete magnetic survey of the British Isle, he sailed in the Erebus and Terror on a magnificent four-year voyage to the Antarctic, where he discovered the sea which bears his name, traced the icebound continent for 700 miles, and found, towering amid the ice, a volcano 12,000 feet high, which he named after his ship Mount Erebus. It was in Ross's old ships that Franklin sailed to his doom. Ross led the first expedition in search of Franklin, but without success, and this concluded his sea career, after achievements unparalleled in North and South. He was called the handsomest man in the Navy; he was, at any rate a brave leader and a gifted writer.

He Captured Delhi

ASTON CLINTON. Far-spread on the escarpment of the downs, it has many Jacobean thatched cottages and an inn which has been receiving travellers since John Hampden's days. In a big churchyard bordered by trees a modern tower rises over the 14th century church, which has its original chancel with a fine arch, three beautifully carved seats for priests, an Easter Sepulchre with

Amersham — Church and High Street

Amersham — The Old Market Hall

Aylesbury — Old Church with Curious Spire

Beaconsfield — The Medieval Church

heads of medieval knights, and fragments of glass 600 years old. The bowl of the Norman font once served as a garden urn. The roodloft doorways are still here, older than the Reformation, and there is a Jacobean chair. Here lie many members of the Lake family, whose manor stood where now stands a handsome house of the Rothschilds. The most notable member of the family to sleep here is Viscount Lake, who entered the Army at 14, fought in the American War of Independence, and, being appointed to the command in India, bore the chief share of the Mahratta War of 1803 and captured Delhi.

The Three Scotts

ASTON SANDFORD. To these remote water meadows on the Thame may be traced an influence which made its mark on many of our churches and buildings last century.

Here in 1801 came as rector the father of Sir Gilbert Scott, leader of the Gothic revival of last century, who built or restored (not always wisely) 26 cathedrals, about 500 churches and chapels, 16 colleges, and many other buildings, and 57 monuments. From this tremendous worker descended genius in a pure flame to his grandson Sir Giles Scott, whose cathedral at Liverpool, which worthily links our century with the glorious achievements of medieval Europe, stands at the head of a long list of distinguished buildings.

Thomas Scott the rector lived for 20 years and died here, in the big stone house in lovely grounds near the little church. He was a man of literary gifts with a remarkable career. The son of a Lincolnshire grazier, he spent some years as chemist's apprentice and then, taking orders, succeeded the austere John Newton in the living at Olney and in the friendship of Cowper, who helped him with an autobiographical book called The Face of Truth. Scott became a great Bible scholar, and a thoughtful writer whose essays attracted the attention of Cardinal Newman. His great work was a Bible Commentary issued in weekly parts, now a classic, and he is known as Scott the Commentator to distinguish him from all the other Scotts.

His stone is under the altar, where he lies with a little grandchild. The two bells which tolled at his death were cast in Woking 500 years ago. This humble church, 700 years old, has no chancel arch, its place being taken by a modern beam which rests on capitals, one a

13th century stone head with gaping teeth. The choicest treasure of the village is the little piece of old glass showing Christ enthroned, a precious fragment in the top of a lancet window, glimmering in green and gold. It is one of the oldest fragments which have survived the years, for it was put here in 1280. There is very little glass of that period still left in England.

Dovecot and Cottage

ASTWOOD. The county's Farthest East, it has Jacobean timbered cottages, and, a mile from the church, a curiosity in Dove Cottage, a house which was once the manor dovecot. In the churchyard, with a little avenue of limes to the porch, is a fragment of an ancient cross, and on the stone of a window is a mass dial. The embattled tower, with its handsome stair turret, has Norman stones, though much of it is 16th century. The font is 14th. There are Tudor brass portraits of Thomas Chivnale, with his two wives in fur-trimmed gowns. The roofs are 400 years old, and there is a 17th century carved chest, and seats on which the villagers sat in medieval days.

Two Squares in a Country Town

AYLESBURY. It lies at the heart of this beautiful county, a pleasant country town high above the fertile vale to which it gives its name. Had ever an English town more curious winding ways and narrow passages? They are everywhere about its market square which in itself is rich with ancient inns and courtyards, with a clock tower looking down on it and three bronze statues—an impressive company for a market square. They are three of Buckinghamshire's familiar figures, two of them famous the world over. The two stand at the top of the square by the cross in memory of the men who did not come back. Magnificent in bronze, a spirited figure with his sword drawn, is the man whose brave defiance of Charles Stuart started the Civil War, John Hampden; and near him stands that strange contrast to our great Englishman, the romantic Disraeli, modelled in bronze by Sir Francis Grant, the sculptor friend of Sir Walter Scott. Looking up to these famous men from the bottom of the square, standing in bronze between two lions is a man who owned 12,000 acres of this county, the third Lord Chesham. At night the top of the square is floodlit for the peace memorial, on which are bronze tablets with over 200 names. There is a second memorial at a cross roads in memory of 63 men who went out from the great Hazell printing works at Aylesbury and did not come back, and a third memorial is in the churchyard—a Calvary with the two Marys at the foot of the cross.

Gone are many of the old inns which in medieval times used to stand in picturesque array round this old market square offering a warm welcome and refreshment to weary travellers, but the Bull's Head still has a 300-year-old barn for a garage, and the King's Head remains as one of the great sights of the town, and one of the most interesting buildings in the county. The King's Head has been here since the 15th century and has a rare distinction among English inns, for it belongs to the nation, having been given to the National Trust so that future generations may see a medieval inn as it was. It has been the guest house of a monastery, and its foundations were probably laid down in 1386. We pass into it through a medieval gateway and sit in a lounge which was the old refectory and still has a magnificent leaded window older than the Tudor dynasty, with its original heraldic glass still glowing in it. Two panes of glass from the windows of this room have been built into a window of Westminster Abbey and three more are in the British Museum, but here still we see the arms of Prince Edward who was killed at the battle of Tewkesbury. Angels bear shields with the arms of Henry the Sixth and other heraldic emblems. It is claimed that Oliver Cromwell sat in one of the chairs in this lounge when the inn was occupied by the Parliament troops in the Civil War. Long before then priests hid in the hiding-hole still here.

The clock tower at the top of the square is 70 feet high with the clock set in four gables above which rises a slender spire.

This is the curiously interesting old square of the town and we pass through it to a square more charming, in which the great church stands. The square is closely built round with the old grammar school (now the museum), the Prebendal School (home of John Wilkes), and the fine almshouses rebuilt last century with the style of their twisted chimneys preserved. The museum is charmingly housed in the quiet little way leading to the church, and has collections of objects from prehistoric ages and representative of the

Roman period in Britain, with Egyptian antiquities and a variety of miscellaneous exhibits. There are local birds, mammals, and plants, and many interesting domestic bygones, such as candle-snuffers, leather bottles, the flail used for threshing and the notched sickle used in reaping. A gilded bronze figure from a crucifix found in Aylesbury church keeps company with a 700-year-old crucifix found at Coleshill. A case of much local interest contains 193 trade tokens used in the county, and another case has in it a number of decorations given by Louis the Eighteenth to British officers in Paris as part of the Army of Occupation when he returned to the throne from his English exile.

The church was restored by Sir Gilbert Scott, but it has much of its medieval interest. Its central tower is 13th century; but it would seem to many that it has been a little spoiled by the odd little spire built on to it. The spire is something of a curiosity, for it rises not directly from the ancient tower but from a smaller tower with an open parapet and slender pinnacles set without the old tower's battlements.

The church has preserved the ancient charnel house below its lady chapel; it is believed that it has been here as long as the chapel, which is 14th century, and it is now the crypt, a low place 21 feet by 13 feet, reached by a trapdoor. The clerestory has admitted light into the fine interior of this church, its nave, transepts, and chancel, for 500 years, and all this time the Madonna and Child have been in their canopied niche above the richly traceried west window, perhaps the finest thing to see in the town. It is a mass of brilliant colour and has something of a history, for it won a prize at an international exhibition in 1862. Its figures are free and unconventional, 8 major prophets above with 20 minor prophets below, and in a space under these 6 panels with scenes from the early days of the Old Testament. They bring us from the serpent which brought all this woe into the world by tempting Eve, to the serpent Moses held up in the Wilderness, the first panel showing us Adam and Eve in the garden, the second their expulsion, followed by the passage over the Red Sea, the offering of Isaac, the Passover, the holding up of the brazen serpent before the children of Israel.

The oldest and best piece of stonework we remember in Aylesbury is the Norman font. It has been broken in three pieces but is whole

BUCKINGHAMSHIRE

again, a masterpiece of carving, once more with its round base, its moulded stem, and its arcaded bowl, round which run bands of foliage.

The church rose under the hands of English master masons who must have had serfs among their workmen. They made a spacious building with a central tower and built the chancel as we see it; it has an Easter Sepulchre, a double aumbry, canopied oak seats for priests, and a roof now made new borne on stone angels. The 18th century altar table is mahogany, carved with cherubs, and on the eastern wall are wooden figures of St Peter and St Paul fashioned by craftsmen of Oberammergau.

The 14th century lady chapel, entered through a richly carved oak screen, has a roof made by the men who talked the language Chaucer was then beginning to fix for us in his poetry. There are handsome stone seats with leafy canopies and two carvings in wood and stone—a stone Madonna on the north of the altar, and a wooden carving of Christ and the children on the south.

In the transepts are two fine monuments which have survived the centuries. Under a recess lies a knight in the armour and chain mail of 600 years ago, his head resting on his helmet and his feet on a lion. His face is worn away by time and his name is gone, but it is believed he may be Robert Lee, a knight whose descendants were to make history in a continent of which he never heard, for one of these descendants would be Robert E. Lee, who led the Southern armies against the policy of Abraham Lincoln in America's Civil War. On a canopied monument near him are two charming figures believed to be a Lady Lee and her daughter, both kneeling in the dress they wore before the Spanish Armada. At the mother's feet are two tiny babies in swaddling clothes. On the tomb are some 16th century verses asking that crimson flowers may be placed here in memory of Lady Lee, and there was a bunch of crimson carnations in front of her when we called; we understand that there is always a bunch of red flowers here.

The transepts have moulded arches, and set in one of them is a door with a remarkable old lock. The door leads us into the vestry, where we find an old chest and an old cupboard. This interesting door is 700 years old; made from oak and hung on ornamental hinges, it is studded, and has an iron boss in the middle and an iron bar on a pivot. The iron bar is raised by a winch-key, which passes into the middle of the boss and lifts the bar so that it swings into a catch on the jamb of the doorway. The roofs over the transepts and the chapels are 15th century, and the timber roof of the 13th century porch is probably by the same craftsmen. There are some fine medieval poppyheads and a few misereres carved with foliage and grotesques. In the north aisle is a Book of Remembrance for Buckinghamshire men who fell in the war, a new page being turned over every day. The fine west doorway and the doorway of the south transept are modern copies of 12th century work, and the transept doorway has small statues of St Peter and St James given by Sir Gilbert Scott when he was restoring the church.

At the west end of the town is a fine range of buildings housing the county hospital. It is about 220 feet long and we pass through a pillared portico into an entrance hall with portraits hanging on the walls and a bust of Florence Nightingale. A few years before the building of this hospital there were found in a field hereabouts 200 skeletons, believed to be those of soldiers who fell in the battle here when the Parliament men defeated Prince Rupert and his Royalists.

The Old Bells

BARTON HARTSHORN. Beautiful among low-lying pastures on the Oxfordshire border, it is a little place of many graces. The green has the churchyard on one hand, and on the other the manor house wall. Two bells which have been ringing for 600 years hang in an open bellcot over the 13th century nave of the church. One doorway is 700 years old and another a century younger, the younger one with remains of its original door. On a wall of the vestry are six 15th century yellow tiles with brown wheel pattern. The altar table was carved by a Jacobean craftsman. A transept window of St George and a red-winged angel is a peace memorial to Archibald Trotter, who died for us in 1914; and a brass tablet records that Edward Smith was for 55 years of last century pastor and friend of the people here.

Happy Man and Hopeful Pastor

BEACHAMPTON. It is close to the county border by the River Ouse, and has a church begun 600 years ago and finished last century. It has the brass portrait of a blacksmith who died in

Shakespeare's day, William Bawdyn, a fine bearded figure who looks what his inscription calls him, for it begins "Behold I happy am." Another brass shows Alice Baldwyn in Jacobean costume, and close by is a delightful little group of her four children.

The oddest monument of the church is one of Sir Simon Benet, who left a legacy to University College at Oxford which the college remembered 100 years later, when it decided to put up a marble bust to him in this church where he lies. So the college did its good deed for that day, but it is a little comical that it should have dressed the good Sir Simon complete with a wig and lace cravat he could never have worn.

Bishop Wilberforce kneels in a rich blue robe in the east window, which reminds us that he was bishop of the diocese, and on a chancel wall are a death's head and an hourglass, decorating an address to his flock by Matthew Pigot, who was 20 years pastor under Elizabeth and here declares his hope that he will meet his people later.

The First VC of the War

BEACONSFIELD. Its name is famous in the world, but Lord Beaconsfield is here no more than a name; he lies at Hughenden. Beaconsfield is famous for other men and for the charm the centuries have given it. The road to Oxford widens into its very heart with the road to Windsor crossing it in front of the big churchyard. A charming place the great square is to wander in, with handsome timbered inns, a broad green with the memorial to those who live for evermore, and the splendid church which even the 19th century did not spoil. Its fine flint tower with leafy pinnacles is a great delight, the arcades are not unworthy, and there are still a few medieval treasures which have survived rebuilding.

Between the chancel and the chapel is part of a 15th century screen, and in the chancel is a handsome altar tomb of those days richly carved under an arch flanked by round columns. Like the 16th century tomb in the chapel, it has lost its brasses, but the brasses remain of John Warren and his wife, who died in Shakespeare's day, and chiselled in stone are the 17th century figures of Thomas Waller and his wife, kneeling, both holding hearts. There are three beautiful old chairs, a fine tapestry, and a heavily bound chest with a series of

Dutch paintings, one showing a ship being loaded by a primitive crane.

Nor can we escape the feeling of age and history as we walk about these walls so new, for we are in the presence of names that stir the feeling of the past. Here lie the Grenfells, the Lawsons, and the Burkes—the Grenfells of so high repute in courage and service; the Lawsons remembered for their association with the Daily Telegraph, represented here by Lord Burnham whose distinguished life was spent in Fleet Street; and the Burkes whose name lives in politics and literature, for they are none other than Edmund Burke and his only son. There is a portrait of the father in relief on the wall, and in the vestry is a writing desk made from the pew in which Edmund Burke sat. Here he lies with the son whose tragic death broke his heart, perhaps the saddest memory in this place.

There is a wall tablet in memory of Field Marshal Grenfell and a window to his two heroic sons, the window showing David with his sling and Jonathan with his bow. It is happily conceived, for David and Jonathan these two boys were. They were Francis Octavius Grenfell and his brother Riversdale; they grew up together and in death they were not divided, for they gave their lives for England. Rivy, as his friends called him, began a business life in the City after leaving Eton and joined his brother's firm, but a collapse just before the war left him almost penniless, and it was with a feeling of relief that he joined up as a civilian and embarked on the greater adventure which was to end for him so tragically and so soon. He fell during the Retreat from Mons.

Francis, who had chosen a soldier's life before the war, was a captain of the 9th Lancers, and in those first desperate days in France he won the first VC of the war. The charge of the 9th Lancers, brought up against double lines of barbed wire, has been compared to the charge at Balaclava, and in that terrific onslaught Francis Grenfell was shot through his coat and his boot and was wounded in three places. The call went out to them to save the guns, for all the gunners had fallen and the guns were still under fire. Captain Grenfell called for volunteers and went with them, though his wounds were still undressed; they slowly turned and lifted the guns and saved the battery, and, despite his wounds and weariness, Grenfell rode nearly ten miles back with the squadron before he fell from exhaustion. He lived another year and went back only to fall during the second attack on Ypres, and he left his VC and his medals to the Lancers, for he said he owed them entirely to his regiment.

The churchyard itself has something old and beautiful, for a 16th century arch in the wall leads to the old rectory, a charming black and white building with oriel windows in its overhanging storey. Under a huge walnut tree at a corner of the churchyard is a pyramid-shaped tomb in which lies a poet whose home was a few hundred yards away, at Hall Barn; he was Edmund Waller, who wrote poems to Philip Sidney's cousin and plunged into miserable plottings for Charles Stuart. Son of a wealthy landowner, he was left fatherless at 10 and became a kinsman by marriage to Cromwell. He took the Parliamentary side in the Civil War. His wife died when he was only 25 and he fell in love with Lady Dorothy Sidney, a girl of 18 living at Penshurst in Kent, and though she slighted him and married an earl he immortalised her in his poetry; it was to her he wrote the charming lines, Go, lovely rose . . .

Unhappily the poet turned conspirator and brought himself within sight of the gallows. Famous as a Commonwealth orator, he was one of the commissioners sent to Oxford in 1643 to negotiate with Charles, and the king won him over and sent him to seize London while the Royalists advanced on the city. The plot miscarried, and the poet, to save his life, incriminated his associates and two men were hanged. He was sent to the Tower and declared incapable of serving in Parliament, being finally banished. While he was in exile his poems were published without his knowledge, and the favour with which they were received paved the way for a reconciliation with Parliament. On payment of a heavy fine he was permitted to return, when he wrote his famous Panegyric on Cromwell:

> *Heaven, that hath placed this island to give Law*
> *To balance Europe, and her States to awe,*
> *In this conjunction doth on Britain smile,*
> *The greatest Leader and the greatest Isle.*

At the Restoration he was equally complimentary to Charles the Second, to whom he said, "Poets, sire, succeed better in fiction than in truth." His poems are marked more by polished simplicity than passion or spontaneous feeling.

Round about Beaconsfield are magnificent woods, one of which belongs to us all, for it was given to the National Trust in memory of one of the most generous Englishmen who ever lived, George Cadbury. There is a garden here also which attracts every boy who knows of it, and every man too, for it has been laid out as a Lilliputian village with a toy railway set among low hills and fields and woods. Mr Callingham has laid in his garden on the Warwick Road 1200 feet of railway, and calls it Bekonscot, and he has devoted this child of his enthusiasm to charity, raising for many good causes a sum of over £5000 in seven years. The village is all modelled on a scale of an inch to a foot, and covers about 1000 square yards.

We have had the pleasure of exploring the village, walking along its miniature roads, up and down hills, across tiny bridges, past the fine church with pointed arches and stained-glass windows designed by Edmund Dulac, through the High Street with its pretty timbered shops, its town hall, post office, and hotel. In the street the smallest children have the advantage, for they see better into the shop windows than the grown-ups. On most of the shops are written the names of Beaconsfield shopkeepers. Scattered about among the fields and woodlands are pretty houses. Signposts on which are printed names such as Lane's End point the way to alluring places. There are street lamps, traffic signals, and even a wireless station. In the fields are sheep and cattle. It is a pleasure to hear the little chiming bells from the church, and as we pass the pavilion on the pier there is a sound of concert music. In the evening the village is a picture with its illuminated streets and buildings. The railway, which is controlled by electricity, is a work of art, with an intricate system of points and double lines of rails passing through deep cuttings. The village is more than a model, for its maker has tried to show how buildings may be made to harmonise with natural surroundings.

Edmund Burke and His Only Son

EDMUND BURKE, lying in Beaconsfield with his son, has been called the greatest thinker who ever devoted himself to English politics. In the last decade of the 18th century he probably had more influence on the world of political thought than any other man.

He undertook to expound to all the principles of human government on the widest scale. He held kings and nations in the hollow of his hand while he told them what to believe and do, and gave them reasons why. And yet in his personal affairs he could never manage his own finances, and he could thrill men by lofty idealism and passionate sentiment on such subjects as Justice and Freedom without having any grip of the facts determining justice in a particular case.

The most remarkable witness of his failure to see plain facts was his attitude to his only son. In his eyes Richard was fit for any position in public life, yet everyone else who came into contact with Richard Burke saw that he lacked capacity, personality, and manners for public service. Yet his father's faith remained unshaken.

Richard was sent to Dublin in 1792 as adviser to the Roman Catholic Committee there, and was welcomed with great respect and high hope. He was old enough to have acquired discretion, for he was 32. But the committee found that he was utterly without tact or judgment; that he was arrogant, impertinent, and vain. He went home, it is said, with 2000 guineas in his pocket, a price they cheerfully paid to get rid of him. When Edmund Burke, at the age of 64, had brought to an end the impeachment of Warren Hastings, he decided to retire from public life and make way for his son. He arranged that Richard should go to Ireland as secretary to the Viceroy. Within a month of his election Richard was stricken with rapid consumption. Burke knew of the danger only a week before his son's death, and both parents broke down with grief. As the hour of death approached Richard heard the cries of his parents in another room as he lay in bed. He got up, dressed as if he were well, and appeared to them, declaring that he was feeling better. To convince them he posed and recited a favourite passage of his father from Paradise Lost, and then, baring his head as if in worship, he fell into his father's arms and passed away.

It was the bitterest hour of Edmund Burke's life. So broken was he that he never passed by the grave where Richard was laid in Beaconsfield. Writing to the Duke of Bedford, who had objected to a pension given to the stricken father, Burke spoke of the science, erudition, taste, honour, generosity, humanity, and many liberal accomplishments of his son, and then his poignant grief poured itself out in a few of the most tragic words ever written with a pen, these:

But the storm has gone over me, and I lie like one of those old oaks which the late hurricane has scattered about me. I am stripped of all my honours; I am torn up by the roots and lie prostrate on the earth.

I am alone. I have none to meet my enemies in the gate. Indeed, my lord, I greatly deceive myself if I would give a peck of refuse of wheat for all that is called fame and honour in the world.

Prime Minister of England and Discoverer of Nineveh

BIERTON. It has many thatched cottages built in Cromwell's time, one behind the modern school particularly charming; it has a Roman past, and memories linking it with a lost city of the Bible.

On a little hill stands a big church with a 13th century tower, capped by a small lead spire and carved with a corbel table of grotesque heads and gargoyles. The lofty appearance of the 14th century nave arcades, with their grim and humorous faces, is enhanced by the height of the arches carrying the tower, under which are tiles older than Chaucer. In a nave wall are two 14th century figures, possibly the Madonna and St Anne. The chancel, glorious with light from plain gold glass, has a piscina and two niches of the 14th century. Here is a quaint slate and alabaster monument to Samuel Bosse, who passed out of life in the time of Shakespeare. He kneels with his wife in black and ruffs, four sons behind him and three daughters behind her, all on cushions, while six babies lie in six cradles. There is a Norman font with fine cable ornament, and one of the rare 14th century patens. In the lady chapel, with the remains of fine carved arches over two doors, is a lovely blue altar, and on an old bracket carved with two Crusaders is a modern Madonna. The nave roof is by 15th century craftsmen. In the chancel is a backed chair carved when Shakespeare was writing, and a table about as old. The canopied oak pulpit is modern.

Henry Peter Layard, the father of Henry, the immortal discoverer of Nineveh, is remembered on a tablet in the nave. He sent his son to an Uncle Austen to learn law in London, there to make the acquaintance of "a foppish young man, who wore waistcoats of the most gorgeous colours and the most fantastic patterns, with much gold embroidery, velvet pantaloons, and shoes adorned with red rosettes." It was young Benjamin Disraeli, then writing Vivian Grey, and submitting it page by page to the criticism of Henry's Aunt Austen, from whose dinner table Uncle Austen rose one night explaining to his nephew that Benjamin was in money troubles again and that he must go and release him from a debtor's prison. Doleful letters came to the man who lies in this nave from Uncle Austen, complaining that young Henry, instead of studying law, was studying the Arabian Nights; while Benjamin Disraeli was devoting himself not to legal treatises but to Chaucer. So forth the two erring students went, each to fame by his own way; and the sad thing is that the man who sleeps at Bierton cannot have guessed that he was the father of one whose fame and praise were to be in all men's mouths or that young Benjamin was to be Prime Minister.

The Cross on the Hill

BLEDLOW. With its back to a steep northward spur of the Chilterns this beautiful village lies shaded by elms, looking out on the vale and hemmed in by the historic Icknield Way. A huge cross cut into the chalk of the hillside stands for its landmark. The cross is of Greek shape, 25 yards wide; and this and Whiteleaf Cross, its neighbour, are the only turf-cut crosses in the county. A fragment of another cross, built in the 15th century, is in the churchyard, which is a curious place, fenced in because of the chasm at one side of it, in which the little River Lyde flows on its way to the mill.

A group of charming timbered cottages, with bricks laid in herring-bone pattern, have stood near the church for 400 years, sharing the pride of its ancient beauty. Except for its 14th century porch and windows, this lovely old place is almost as the 13th century masons left it on refashioning the Norman church. Its tower rises in three stages and keeps its original line of corbels, with grotesque heads; the lowness of the tower is in striking contrast with the length of the nave and chancel. The nave is aisled and clerestoried with a noble group of arches on round columns with foliage capitals. There are 15th century beams in the aisle roof and 17th century beams in the nave. The chancel arch, built about 1260, has sacrificed something of its beauty to the modern screen, with a very heavy canopy.

We pass beneath a sundial into the porch (which has a perfect stoup), and come through an admirable doorway with carved capitals to be greeted by St Christopher, a colossal figure that has looked down from the walls for 600 years. He is carrying the Child and has apparently just had a little conversation with a hermit in a medieval fastness. Over the south door, painted in strong lines by a 13th century brush dipped in red ochre, are two kneeling figures, and a hand blessing them. Coloured lines define the arches of the nave and draw the eye to the heavy round pillars and the capitals, all beautifully shaped with groups of leaves. The 13th century men who put the lovely group of lancet windows in the chancel built into another wall one of the Norman windows and set the Norman font, boldly carved with leaves, on its inverted capital. Fragments of the original church (a group of carved stones set on a window ledge) have labels put on them by Mr Clement Skilbeck, scholar, antiquary, and artist who was churchwarden when we called, lovingly watching over the church enriched with his gift of his delightful picture of Christ calling St Matthew. Another painting of the Descent from the Cross, is by Samuel Wale, an 18th century RA.

One of the most charming things in this rare old church is the oak eagle, shaped so that the head helps the wings to support the Bible. A Latin Bible it was when the eagle was new in the 15th century, before the English Bible came. Medieval bosses and corbels look down from the roof of the aisle, and another piece of 15th century work is a richly canopied niche, with pinnacles at each side.

The plain north and south doors with strap-hinges are among the oldest things in the county, being 700 years old, and there are fragments of ancient glass in some of the windows, two 13th century piscinas, and a 17th century communion table.

Four vicars are remembered here. One is William Herun, shown in a small brass portrait wearing robes of Tudor days; another is Timothy Hall, a historic character who left Bledlow to preach at All Hallows in London, and pleased James the Second by reading from the pulpit the Declaration of Indulgence, which gave liberty of conscience to Roman Catholics. As a reward the king made him Bishop of Oxford, and he was consecrated at Lambeth; but after the flight of the king he fell into great poverty. Two hundred years later William Stephen died after preaching here for 60 years; he was the son of James Stephen, a pioneer for the abolition of the Slave Trade. The most recent memorial is to John Cruikshank, a vicar who died in 1916; it is a window showing a beautiful picture of the Annunciation. A touching reminder of the past is a tablet on a buttress of the chancel telling of John Williams who died of smallpox in 1745, his master, whom he had served for 20 years, putting up this simple memorial.

The saddest thing we heard of at Bledlow was the murder of a superb group of elms which were the admiration of the countryside, beloved by artists from near and far. They grew in a little dell, and their disappearance was one of those tragedies which are the constant bewilderment of lovers of our countryside.

The Cathedral Antiquary

BLETCHLEY. The railway has not destroyed its rural charm. Could the Romans resume their march along their Watling Street a mile away they would find much here in the natural scene that they would recognise.

On the village green is a massive block of granite as a peace memorial. From the magnificent battlemented church tower a wolf glares across the meadows. Tall poplars grace the churchyard, and fine yews lead us to the porch, in which is the richest possession of the church, the great doorway the Normans built. For over a century it admitted Norman and Saxon to the nave; for 600 years it has been in the position to which it was removed. The English builders pointed the round Norman arch and gave it a boldly carved head as keystone, retaining the beak moulding and heads of Norman patricians and Saxon peasants. On a buttress close by is a scratch-dial. The capitals of the nave piers have carvings of flowers and ornaments, and there is a decorated arcade between the chancel and the 13th century chapel, while in a 14th century aisle grotesque stone heads support the far-descending arch timbers of the medieval roof. The splendid tower arch was built 500 years ago, with the bell-ringers' gallery open to the nave.

Most of the beautiful things in our fine churches, like many of our loveliest poems, are of unknown authorship, but the man who built this tower, and at least one of the arches of the aisle, has been for 500 years proclaiming his name, for he cut it on one of the stones of this arch, so that we may all honour the 15th century Mr Kemsey. It must have been another hand that carved the low relief of a chalice and a wafer high up in a chapel.

In this chapel is a coffin lid with a floral cross and something like a bugle. It is believed to stand for Sir John Grey, ancestor of the barons Grey de Wilton. A judge under Henry the Third, he incurred his master's displeasure by marrying the lady of his heart without the royal consent; and he was fined and deprived of his offices. He joined the seventh Crusade and returned home, to die here in 1266. On an altar tomb lies a superb alabaster figure of one of his descendants, a 15th century Baron Grey of Wilton, the features beautiful, the figure suggesting perfect repose, as, his head on an elaborately wrought helmet with water-lilies, he sleeps with his feet on a lion. The panels have shields with 18th century colour, and over the tomb hangs a 17th century helmet, in black and gold.

In the chapel with the Crusader's stone sleep Thomas Willis and his wife who, crushed by grief, followed him to the grave within two months. They were the parents of the famous 18th century antiquary, Browne Willis, who spent lavishly on the church in which they lie. Born to a rich estate, a scholar of high attainments, Willis was one of the first men to study original charters and documents at our cathedrals. A man of boundless generosity, he gave to college, church, and chapel, endowed his children beyond his means, and reduced himself at last to poverty, wearing clothes so old and shabby that he would be mistaken for a beggar. Yet he was able to leave Oxford a rich collection of manuscripts. His wife sleeps here in an elaborate altar tomb with coloured shields.

There is a quaint portrait brass of Thomas Sparke, a rector who died in the same year as Shakespeare, showing him with two daughters and three sons, all kneeling with church towers in the background. On the rector's right is a group of his friends and congregation, and above are figures grimly symbolising fame and death, with inscriptions explaining each device. Near the rector's brass is a plainer tablet to his wife Rose, with a florid poem on her virtues beginning with the conceit, "68 years a fragrant rose she lasted"; and above it is an alabaster fragment in black, red, and blue, showing a kneeling man in Tudor armour with five sons and three daughters. The Jacobean font cover is elaborately carved, and on a stout round column of good design is a Jacobean poorbox.

The Norman doorway has admitted congregations to acclaim the coronation of over 30 sovereigns; in the altar frontal is part of a robe of the Order of the Garter worn at a coronation of our time.

Beaconsfield   The Broad Highway

Beaconsfield   The Model Village of Bekonscot

Brill   The 17th Century Mill

Boarstall   The 14th Century Gatehouse

BUCKINGHAMSHIRE

In Thirteen Parliaments

BOARSTALL. Crossed by an 18th century bridge, a moat 60 feet wide protects three sides of what was the famous Boarstall Castle. Only the massive 14th century gatehouse survives, but a magnificent survival it is, still apparently one of the strongest places in the county. Three storeys high, defended at each corner by an octagonal tower pierced by slits for archers, it has 17th century balustrades running between the battlements of the towers. Below the parapet is a gargoyle to which travellers have looked up for 600 years. A Royalist stronghold held by Sir William Campion, the castle fell to Fairfax in 1646 after a long resistance; but it survived for more than a century to shelter generations of Aubreys.

The grounds are separated by a 17th century wall from the churchyard, into which we pass by a Jacobean doorway with the original door still on its hinges. The church was built soon after Waterloo by Sir John Aubrey, who saw a Stuart Rising as a boy, sat in 13 Parliaments, saw Louis the Eighteenth a fugitive in this countryside, and died Father of the House of Commons. Reaching almost to the roof of the chancel, his tomb declares his two wives to be women of such excellence that he regarded them as "the choicest blessing of Providence, and the peculiar felicity of a long life." There are two memorials to them, a rich east window and a monument in blue marble, with angels guarding their shields. There is a canopied Jacobean pulpit from the old church, a 17th century altar table, and a silver cup engraved with the Annunciation and the Nativity, and inscribed with a record of its weight.

Peace

BOVENEY. It is a peaceful hamlet at the end of a lane which leads to nowhere else. Its hard-to-find church is in a field almost hid by elms, with the tranquil waters of the Thames flowing by towards Windsor's noble turrets. It is a humble place with a wooden bell turret and Norman walls over three feet thick, darkened by trees.

The church has a big 13th century font, a few 16th century benches, and 17th century panelling on its walls. The low screen is made up of ancient woodwork, the pulpit of 17th century panelling. Treasured in a glass case are fragments of alabaster sculpture with scanty traces of colour; it is thought they belonged to a 15th century reredos.

From the churchyard can be seen the pleasant gables of Boveney Court, whose oldest corner has sheltered in this abiding peace since the days of the Civil War.

The Village Choir

BOW BRICKHILL. It rises steeply from the River Ouzel, to pines and far-spreading heath. In the woods is a prehistoric entrenchment within a ditch, which at one point is 55 feet wide and 18 deep. It is called Danes Borough, but it was old before the first Dane came this way.

The 15th century church, with its embattled parapet, stands a hundred feet higher than the village and may occupy the site of a lookout of primitive men such as first peopled our hilltops, making this their guard and the entrenchment their home. They would see far, as we do, for from here is one of the finest views in the county.

In niches over the modern porch are figures of Christ, the Madonna, St John and St Paul, with Stephen holding three stones to remind us of his martyrdom. The simplicity of the interior throws into relief two medieval treasures, an oak-panelled pulpit, dark with four centuries of service, and a font as old as the church, its bowl carved with heraldic devices and supported by angels with outstretched wings.

A 17th century tablet in the chancel wall records that William Watson "of yeoman race" was parson here for 36 years. To see the church as he knew it we must see Thomas Webster's painting of last century, for his delightful picture of a Village Choir, now in the Sheepshank Collection at South Kensington Museum, was painted here before the old gallery was removed. It is one of the quaintly precious pictures of the rural life of the early 19th century, and it has given a wide repute to the choristers of this little village, with their pitch-pipe, cellos, and clarinets.

Here Sleeps a Prime Minister's Father

BRADENHAM. It is Isaac Disraeli's village, the boyhood home of his famous Benjamin, Lord Beaconsfield. He loved this place and brings it into his novel Endymion, under the name of Hurstley. He lived in the 17th century manor house with the churchyard over the garden wall. In front of the house spreads the great green with a view as fine as any for miles around.

The lychgate bringing us to the church has on it the names of those who live for evermore, one of them Albert Leslie Stephen, who won the DSO in South Africa and won his immortality on the anniversary of the day he was gazetted.

The medieval tower is snugly set among lofty fir trees at every corner of the churchyard; it has a little pyramid roof in which still ring two of the oldest bells in England, bearing the name of Michael Wymbish, who was making bells in Norman England and was still flourishing about 1300 when these were made. The modern porch has the oldest doorway in the county, built about 1100; the great stone forming the lintel is supported on moulded brackets, and above the lintel is a solid tympanum. One of the nave windows has a little 13th century glass with flowers in it, and the east window of the chapel has brightly coloured coats-of-arms. The chancel has a brass portrait of Richard Redberd, a rector who died in 1521 and wears his elaborate vestments. There is a great wall monument over the projecting tomb of Charles West, with lifesize symbolical figures of the 17th century, posing in easy attitudes with their legs crossed. At each corner of the tomb is a little cherub's head. The chancel has been made new and is divided from the nave by an effective screen with a roodloft, stretching from wall to wall. It has elaborate tracery in its four bays and at the gateway, and traceried panels on its gallery.

A plain marble tablet is all the village has in memory of Isaac Disraeli, though he sleeps here. Father of the Prime Minister, descended from Levantine Jews who reached England from Italy, he was born in London in 1766, when panic and commercial jealousy had compelled a timorous Government to repeal an earlier Act conferring freedom on English Jews. Resisting his father's wish that he should follow him in commerce, he devoted himself to literary studies, mastered languages, sought the favour of Dr Johnson and other men of letters, and, inheriting a fortune from his grandmother, was at last able to do as he pleased. He was a member of the Jewish community in London for over 40 years, but drifted away and had his children baptised in an English church. Hence Benjamin Disraeli, although proud of his race, was by baptism a Christian.

For many years a diligent student at the British Museum, Isaac Disraeli, before he was 30, published the first volume of the work that made him famous, his Curiosities of Literature, adding five further volumes during the next 40 years. These volumes were supplemented by others on Literary Amenities, the Calamities of Authors, and the Quarrels of Authors, works which threw a searchlight into the dark corners of a romantic subject. He wrote poems which died as they were born, novels with hardly more life, and histories long since forgotten, although his original researches won him high commendation. When he came here to spend the last 30 years of his life his son Benjamin was already 13. Here with a wide circle of friends Isaac lived and worked. Seven years before his death he was stricken with blindness, but he went on with his work. Scott, who was one of his admirers, delighted him when they met by repeating a poem Disraeli had written. He derived inspiration for his Stuart novels from the old man's writings. Disraeli lived to see his son a Member of Parliament and a novelist, and died in 1848, the year of European revolutions.

Built During the Crusades

BRADWELL. Standing by a stream flowing to the Ouse, it has old cottages along its winding way, a 17th century inn, and two magnificent chestnuts near the gates of the big churchyard. In its 14th century tower, with a later saddleback roof, hang two bells bearing the name of Michael Wymbish, who cast them 600 years ago.

A 14th century porch and doorway admit us to a church built during the Crusades. The nave capitals have 13th century carving, and from their foliage peeps the head of a 13th century man. The capitals of the chancel arch have a great rarity, inscriptions cut in the capital letters used 700 years ago. Carving of the same century survives in the inner arch of the modern east window, and the same masons may have carved the font, which they reshaped from one the Normans made. The reredos has a painting of the Adoration, in which a youth is blowing a trumpet as he runs.

Across the fields, beyond the railway, a farmhouse occupies the site of the 12th century Bradwell Abbey, where are a doorway, a window, and the ballflower ornament of a chapel 600 years old.

BUCKINGHAMSHIRE

Thomas Becket as a Witness

BRILL. It crowns a hill over 600 feet high, where our ancient kings had a palace. Here, with Becket as a witness, Henry signed a deed which still exists.

On the hill is a red brick mill which has been working for 300 years. The wide streets glow with the colour of their local bricks and tiles, and are pleasantly relieved by two greens. On one is the peace cross; by the other are quaint green-shuttered almshouses, each of a single storey.

Set in a wall in the main street is a barometer "in grateful recognition of Sir Edmund Verney's devotion to the welfare of the people of Brill"; not, of course, old Sir Edmund, the peerless standard-bearer who fell fighting for Charles Stuart in a cause which he loved not, but the gallant Crimean veteran who died in 1910.

At the end of the village is a Tudor manor house, with handsome gateposts to its courtyard, and still with its old chimneystacks. In a field near the church are earthworks thrown up in the Civil War.

Above the low 15th century tower of the church rises a small lead spire. We come into the wide church by two narrow Norman doorways, each with its original shafts, and, above the pointed tower arch, is a Norman window which serves no more. In one of the doorways swings a medieval door, and in the other a modern door with a curiously shaped handle fashioned in the Middle Ages. The chancel is 14th century and the arch a century older, and on either side of the arch are traces of medieval paintings brought to light after being hidden for centuries; they were in their prime when the fine 14th century font was carved. The plain seats in the chancel, probably 14th century, are the oldest woodwork, but the finest is the Jacobean chancel roof, which has ornamental arches resting on massive tie-beams, the central arch having five pierced posts tapering to meet in a boss with a carved pendant. On the walls of the sanctuary are the badges of nine regiments and the names of thirty men who gave themselves for England in the Great War.

The Doom

BROUGHTON. We come to see an ancient village church, and remain to wonder at one of our oldest picture galleries. A tributary of the Ouse winds between willow-clad banks through the fields, by which we find the rectory with a noble chestnut in its garden, and the churchyard with two great yews, their domes trimmed like mushrooms, looking down on an 18th century font with a sundial, and, close at hand, a medieval coffin lid. The 14th century church appears to rise from one much older, for its walls are of great strength and substance, notably in the tower's foundations, through which runs an old stairway. The south door, which has been letting people in and out for 500 years, has the ironwork and hinges of its ancient predecessor, still perfect.

Six hundred Christmases have been kept here since the village folk first passed under this chancel arch, and the same modest nun holds up one side of it, while a grim ruffian has all the time been grimacing at her from the other side. On either side of the arch is a chained book, their pages little worn. The chancel window, a Crucifixion, is in memory of John William Irving, curate and rector for half of last century.

But it is the paintings which enchant us. Covering both walls of the nave, they are for the most part splendidly preserved, and show us how moral and religious teaching was imparted to an England where the rural poor were serfs, unable to read or write in the days before printed books. The oldest of the pictures is simply an abiding lecture for that time, with figures outlined in red and filled in with blue and green, a tableau of life from Chaucer's England, with quaint rustic costumes. The subject is an allegory, supposed to denounce the practice of taking oaths by parts of our Lord's body. Supported in the arms of the Madonna, Our Lord is surrounded by nine men, one of whom holds His severed foot, another His heart, and a third a sacred wafer; while in the foreground sit two gamblers over a roughly ruled board, playing for wagers. Here is the Gothic spirit preaching a cautionary sermon to unlettered sinners in forms and characters to stimulate their understanding, and to move them to recognition of a second Crucifixion by their misdoing.

A Doom picture of the next century is conceived in the spirit of the famous wall paintings of the Campo Santo at Pisa, with terror and beauty blended. On the right a sturdy archangel sounds the Last Trump, while in the corner below him glow the flames into which the condemned are to pass. In the centre the Recording Angel holds a huge pair of scales, and the Madonna with her left hand presses down one side of the scales in favour of mercy, and with her right opens wide her cloak to shelter timid souls. Above her is enthroned the Judge, with two towers, the mansions of the blessed. The angels have halos from which rise wings that seem to soar.

Over the South door St George has lost his head, but the cross glows on his breast, his white horse is noble in gait and gear, and his spear still finds its way down the red monster's throat, but has not yet prevented the dragon from using the second head in which his tail ends to thrust out a barbed tongue at the princess and her dog. Finally there is a square panel showing St Helena with a cross on Calvary, accompanied by St Eloi with his crozier on shoulder.

Of such were the lessons pondered in rustic English when there was no teaching except for monks and lay priests, when our great folk spoke Norman-French, lawyers and clergy spoke Latin, and simple people, left to speak the much-despised English, had only pictures such as these to point a moral and adorn a tale.

The County Town

BUCKINGHAM. It has a proud past and proud names that live in Shakespeare. When Alfred divided England into shires in the year 888 he chose it as the county town, but its ancient glories have declined.

Yet nothing can destroy the charm of a little town lying amid great meadows, with a river embracing it on three sides, wide views over the valley, and storied buildings to dignify the present and stir the memory of the past. The marketplace, running through the centre of the town and embodying the ancient bull-ring, is a reminder of the days when Buckingham was very rich in wool. Its chief feature today is the battlemented 18th century castle which long served as the county gaol, and the red brick town hall, in which is a mace designed before the Commonwealth and altered after the execution of the king to suit the Protectorate, having what is called the Cromwellian bauble-top. Close by the marketplace is the town's oldest building, now in the keeping of the National Trust—the little Norman chantry which became a class room of the school founded by Edward the Sixth. Here, with zigzag moulding on its capitals, is a deeply recessed doorway which was as old to Royalists and Commonwealth as the Civil War is to us. One window has grimly carved heads; there is an old piscina; and in a gallery are six bench-ends with elaborate heads and shields carved in the 17th century. The ancient chantry is linked to a delightful timbered house.

Up the hill stands the storied Castle House, with four centuries of history in its annals. To it in 1514 came Catherine of Aragon, to be entertained as the still happy queen; a generation after the royal feast Buckingham was named in an Act of Parliament as one of the 36 necessitous towns of England. Its wool trade had gone. But the old house remained unshaken by misfortune, and in the 17th century was still so notable that here came Charles Stuart presiding over a council of war under the roof that had welcomed the proud daughter of Spain. The great traceried beam across the ceiling of the room in which he sat and talked is still in its place. In the same room is the fireplace by which Charles would sit, its magnificent oak mantelpiece reaching to the ceiling and showing its date, 1619. After Charles came Cromwell, staying, it is said, in a house facing that which had sheltered the king.

There is a fascinating black and white house whose timbers were put together in Tudor days; and another is the manor house, with 16th century twisted chimneys recalling those at Hampton Court. The house has witnessed melancholy scenes. Fronting it stood the old church which, first losing its crumbling spire, next lost its tower, and at last altogether lost itself in ruin. Only its ancient churchyard remains, with tombs overgrown by ivy and cherubs on forgotten stones, forlorn amid flowers growing wild in the shade of pines and cypresses. The stump of the old cross moulders in this solitude.

Between the old church and the new are the almshouses founded 500 years ago by John Barton, renewed under Queen Anne, and rebuilt in our time. The new church, surrounded by limes and wide green verges, is on the site of a Saxon castle whose stone-lined well has been found. A striking building, the buttresses and windows of the church are richly carved. The ribs of the vaulted roof rest on pillars of stone and marble alternately. Over the west door is a great shield carved with a swan (an emblem we see in gold on the clock tower of the town hall).

The east window, put up in 1890 by the Buckingham Needle and Thread Society, represents the Te Deum, and its great pageant of life

Buckingham   The Market Place

Buckingham   The Norman Chantry

Chesham

Bradenham

TWO FINE MEDIEVAL CHURCHES

Calverton   A Row of Thatched Homes

Cuddington   A Corner by the Green

TWO BUCKINGHAMSHIRE VILLAGES

Chesham Bois — Quiet Flows the Chess

Burnham — Gray's Beech with its Fantastic Roots

and colour shows in finely balanced groups the apostles, prophets, martyrs, and other figures in the great hymn of praise and jubilee. For half a century this admirable society, parent of many fellowships friendly to cathedrals, has existed solely to enrich the church. They can do nothing finer than their window, which, apart from historic buildings, is the pride of the town; but they have added a charming reredos showing the Nativity, some excellent panelling, and a beautiful altar frontal, all harmonising perfectly with their chief gift.

A literary treasure of the church is a Latin manuscript Bible, written 600 years ago in beautiful characters, the rich reds and blues of the capital letters standing out brilliantly against the quieter red of the text. It was presented to the church in 1471 by John Rudying, a remarkable man with a remarkable brass at Biggleswade in Bedfordshire. Formerly chained to a desk in the old church, the Bible was stolen and long lost, and was recovered at last by Browne Willis, the 18th century antiquary. It is now preserved under glass.

There is a good copy of Raphael's Transfiguration in the chancel, and in the Children's Corner is a duplicate of a Raphael Madonna. From the old church little was saved—four bench-ends with tracery and poppyheads by Tudor craftsmen, one bench of 1626, and two 17th century chests. The Buckinghamshire Hussars have a stone memorial on a wall, and below it is the Book of Remembrance, with the names that live for evermore.

One of the natural glories of this lovely countryside is the famous avenue of elms and beeches which leads from the town to the great arch of Stowe Park, a three-mile royal way to one of our ancient homes transformed into one of our great public schools.

Knight and Lady at the Door

BUCKLAND. It lies in the meadows, shady with elms, and with the Chilterns on the skyline. Griffin gargoyles look down on the village from the tower, and as we enter the church a 14th century knight and lady look down on us from a beautiful doorway, with flowers cut on its arch. Restoration has hidden much of the history of the church, but there is work of all the medieval centuries, and also of the 16th, left in windows, arches, arcades, roofs, and doorways. The low Tudor roof of the nave has three bays with traceried spandrels, the wall brackets resting on amusing stone corbels. The aisle roof with four bays is of the same time. The entrance to the lost roodloft is still here, and there is a 15th century piscina, a 16th century chalice, and a sanctus bell; but the most precious relic of the past is the charming 13th century fluted font with a band of foliage in deep relief round the top. Over the priest's doorway is a crudely carved figure with upraised arms, and in the south wall of the nave outside are fragments of old corbels and window tracery.

One of Nature's Wonderlands

BURNHAM. Its noble beeches are known to millions, and one beech tree by the Swilly stream must have been noticed by Thomas Gray when staying with his uncle at Burnham Grove, for he introduced it into his Elegy, and

> *There at the foot of yonder nodding beech*
> *That wreaths its old fantastic roots so high*
> *His listless length at noontide would he stretch,*
> *And pore upon the brook that babbles by.*

Burnham Beeches, one of our natural wonderlands, is a scene of splendour surviving from primeval England. The area known as the Beeches comprises nearly 600 acres, of which 374 acres are national property. Formerly belonging to Burnham Abbey, the woods remained in private possession from the Dissolution until 1879, when the Corporation of London bought the part which is now public.

Many of the trees appear almost to defy botanical laws. The normal life of a beech is little more than two centuries, but here some are believed to be nearly 1000 years old. The secret of this long life is held to lie in the fact that the trees have been not only lopped but pollarded again and again. A tree stripped of its boughs, its head sawn off, would survive to produce another crown, which in turn was claimed by saw and axe. The age of many of the existing boughs, some of them two centuries old, is proof that the pollarding and lopping ceased when coal came into general use in the county, making trees no longer essential as fuel.

Gnarled and weird to look at, the trees are an amazing sight, brought into literature by Thomas Gray. During one of his visits he wrote to Walpole describing it as a "little chaos of mountains and precipices, mountains, it is true, that do not ascend much above the clouds, nor are the declivities so amazing as Dover Cliffs; but just such hills as people who love their necks as well as I do may venture to climb, and crags which give the eye as much pleasure as if they were more dangerous."

With its drives and walks, its ponds and dells, Burnham Beeches seems still a forest, although its area, apart from the two private woods, does not exceed that of Hyde Park. But it is unique for the antiquity of its trees, and with the beeches are immense oaks, birches, hornbeams, maples, yews, hazels, ash trees, willows, and flowering shrubs as fine and varied as any in England.

The Grove, where Gray would stay on his visits here, is a dignified white building behind a high wall. A white house also is East Burnham Cottage, where Sheridan brought his young bride after their honeymoon. Here George Grote and his wife came to live, and in this house he produced the first volumes of his History of Greece. They sold so well that he was able to build East Burnham Park out of the profits, and in this History Hut, as he called it, he finished his great work. It is a long house shaded by a tall cedar, and in it Grote was often visited by his friend Mendelssohn. Another house of much repute for the great library once housed here is Britwell Court, on the road to the Beeches; it is now the home of a Protestant Community known as the Servants of Christ.

Another famous visitor to Burnham was John Evelyn, who stayed with his cousin at Huntercombe, a creeper-covered 17th century house with a beautiful fanlight in its dignified classical doorway. Opposite is all that remains of Burnham Abbey, which has been a farm but is now the home of the sisters of the Society of the Precious Blood. In the chapel here is a fine portrait brass of Arnold Pinchard, founder and first warden of the Society, showing him in his vestments and biretta. A few old windows and walls remain, and with them the doorway of the chapter house, which has detached shafts and moulded capitals. The abbey was founded by King John's second son, Richard of Cornwall, after he had been shut up in the Tower of London by Simon de Montfort. He signed the foundation charter at Cippenham Palace, which stood on a green grassy plot out in the fields. Willows grow in the dried-up moat, and there is little to show that here lived the kings of Mercia and some of our Norman rulers.

But Burnham still keeps its 700-year-old church, by which stands the peace memorial on a raised turf bank; it has a bronze soldier in front of a stone cross. The church tower has an oak-shingled spire, and below the modern belfry is a clock which has been telling the time since three years after Trafalgar. The south aisle has pillars and pointed arches, and on some of the columns are old inscriptions stating that "the Pope is a knave" and "the Pope is a villin." On the transept wall is a wonderful collection of 50 old oak panels, mostly foreign and nearly all carved with Bible pictures. Still older panels form the desk in front of the pews in this transept, for they are 15th century, and belonged to the lost chancel screen. They have traces of colour and are pierced with four groups of round holes. Three finely chased old helmets hang on the wall above, and under them is an ancient hatchment showing the arms of the Hastings family with no fewer than 100 quarterings. It was a common custom to show arms on a sheet of canvas above the tomb, but this hatchment must be almost unique in its intricacy.

The massive altar rails have five big oak panels magnificently carved with foliage; they bear the date 1663 and were once in Eton College Chapel. Near by is a heavy iron chest of the 16th century, with foliated ironwork round the lock, and huge handles. In the modern safe is an old leather-covered box containing 16 parchment documents mostly 600 years old and all dealing with property in the village.

On the wall at the end of the nave are brass figures of exceptional interest, most of them engraved by London craftsmen on the backs of brasses ruthlessly torn up from Flemish churches. A fragment belonging to one of these brasses is in Northiam church, Sussex, the Flemish work having been cut up and sent all over England. At the top of the group we notice the Elizabethan figures of Edmund Eyre and his wife, with two sons and three daughters. Below is their kinsman Thomas Eyre, with three wives and seven solemn-faced children. Under the pews in the north aisle are unusually small brasses of Giles Eyre, with a big purse hanging at his girdle, and his smiling wife in the long dress fashionable about 1500. Standing in a row above them are the 15 daughters of William Aldriche, their hair falling down their backs.

Near the south door is a handsome white marble wall monument by John Bacon, who won the first gold medal the Royal Academy ever awarded for sculpture. The monument shows a seated woman holding a medallion of Judge Willes in a long wig, while the scales of justice fall from her hand. On the chancel wall is a stone to Paul Wentworth of Burnham Abbey, who was buried in the church at the end of Queen Elizabeth's reign. It was he who began the daily prayer before the opening of Parliament. There are vigorously carved busts of George Evelyn and his wife, who lived at Huntercombe, George, a bearded figure holding a book, his wife with a long hood falling over her shoulders. Below kneel two armoured figures of their sons, wearing wigs. In a niche opposite these is a bust of John Wright, an Elizabethan vicar in ruff and gown, his finely chiselled head full of character. He followed Richard Davies, who once lost this living by seditious preaching, though he was restored by Queen Elizabeth; he helped to translate the Bible into Welsh. In the churchyard lies old Matthew Tate, who was vicar for over half a century. In accordance with his request he has no gravestone, but the elm tree he planted is his memorial, flourishing after two centuries.

Father and Son in History

IN this church lies William Wyndham Grenville, son of a Prime Minister and Prime Minister himself, who succeeded to his father's old seat for Buckinghamshire and followed Edmund Burke as Paymaster-General. A staunch supporter of his cousin Pitt, he had a brief term as Speaker, and, created a peer, was Foreign Secretary at 32. When France was in the throes of Revolution Grenville staunchly maintained the policy of Pitt, and earned the gratitude of the country. A man of broad sympathies, he earnestly advocated Roman Catholic emancipation, and, finding Pitt unsympathetic, declined to join his last ministry.

On the death of Pitt he and Fox formed the administration of All the Talents. Hated by the king, and not greatly esteemed by the country, the Government had a brief career, during which it abolished the Slave Trade; and, having done this notable thing for the world, Grenville went into opposition, and never again accepted office. His heart was in his home at Dropmore, which he had bought in 1782, and transformed from a wilderness into a paradise. There he found a scholar's solace in the company of books and of men who loved them as much as he did. An eminent classical scholar, he produced excellent translations from Greek and Italian, and from English into Latin. He edited Chatham's Letters to his nephew, and brought together a valuable collection of family documents forming the volumes of the Grenville Papers.

It is remarkable to reflect on the historic significance of this rare case of a father and son becoming Prime Minister, for the father, by his Stamp Act, sowed the seed of division between the two English-speaking nations, and the son, by abolishing the Slave Trade, established freedom for ever under the British flag.

A Prime Minister's Death

CALVERTON. A tragic incident in Parliament has left its mark on it by a set of curious circumstances linked with the church. The church, refashioned last century from the materials of the old church, stands on a rise from which it looks down on the River Ouse winding through a richly wooded park, on 17th century cottages, and on one of the finest cedars in the county. The church keeps its old chancel arch, the old south arcade, and the tower which rose in its pride before the days of Queen Elizabeth. From the old church also come brass portraits of John Roky and his wife in their Tudor robes. The modern work includes a pulpit with painted panels of four saints (Paul, Peter, Barnabas, and John the Baptist), and a reredos by Italian artists, with the Adoration of the Wise Men.

The manor house, built when the newly-found America was thought to be India, is a fine type of the house which preferred domestic comfort to embattled security. The six almshouses near the church, each with a hooded doorway looking out over wide grassland, carry the mind from this quiet country to a sad chapter of our history. The houses were built by Charles George Perceval, who was rector here for 38 years from the early part of last century. He was a boy of 16 when his Prime Minister uncle, Spencer Perceval, was murdered in the lobby of the House of Commons. A younger son of a younger son, the rector was grandson of the second Earl of Egmont, of whom the Prime Minister was the fourth son. The death of the Premier and the dying out of the elder line made the rector heir, and his son became the seventh earl, erecting in the churchyard here a beautiful cross to his mother.

BUCKINGHAMSHIRE

Tragedies of the Throne

CASTLETHORPE. It has its roots in history, recalling great days and sinister figures, and keeping alive the memory of children of long ago. The field behind the church hides the remains of a stepping-stone to Magna Carta, a fortress built by William Maudit against King John.

The Norman church which stood here then was remade in the 14th century with the old material; one of the original nave pillars remains, with its foliage as clean-cut as when the Conqueror's masons carved it. The font came with the clerestory in the 15th century; on the bowl are the carved heads of a man and a woman, one at each side, turned as if to watch the priest. The 17th century brought the very fine screen, with two arches on either side of handsome iron gates, the whole only four feet high. The tower is 18th century. There is a splendid black and white tomb with marble curtains drawn aside to show us, carved in alabaster, Sir Thomas Tyrrell in his robes as Chief Justice, with a scroll in his hand, his head on his wife's knee. He was descended from the family of Walter Tyrrell whose arrow killed William Rufus, and of Sir James Tyrrell who planned the murder of the princes in the Tower—the first of these deeds acclaimed by the people, the second "the most arch deed of piteous massacre that ever yet this land was guilty of," as Shakespeare makes him say, remorsefully. The Thomas Tyrrell sleeping here served with the Parliamentary forces, but at the Restoration was forgiven and appointed one of the Commissioners to try the men who tried the king. He lived to see his heir married to the granddaughter of Sir Walter Raleigh, and it seems probable that a baby who lies here by the altar (Eyre Tyrrell) was Raleigh's great-grandson. Another child's memorial is a window with the Madonna and two saints, to Alice Trower, aged nine.

Milton's Country Cottage

CHALFONT ST GILES. It is the little paradise John Milton found but never saw. Here in the lovely valley of the River Misbourne, over the hill from Jordans with its Mayflower barn, is the cottage which has become a sacred shrine for those who

speak the tongue that Shakespeare spake
The faith and morals hold that Milton held.

THE KING'S ENGLAND

It is the "pretty box" which Thomas Ellwood found for Milton in the Plague Year of 1665, the cottage in which he found a little peace. He had seen what he had seen, had lived through the wondrous days of Cromwell and the Commonwealth, had been a hunted man, had seen his books burned by the common hangman, and was growing old in loneliness and blindness in the City of the Plague; and then it was that Thomas Ellwood thought of this "pretty box" for him. Here the blind poet came with his manuscript of Paradise Lost. We may picture him sitting in the little lattice windowed room, or out in the sun in the tiny garden by the lane, enjoying the fragrance of the flowers he could not see.

The brick and timbered cottage with the dormer window in its roof is still as it was then, except that from being a simple home it has become a shrine, a Milton museum, with priceless editions of the book he sold for five pounds, and with prints and portraits of the poet and odd little things of the England of his day. We found a vine creeping up the walls and the garden gay with old-world flowers, much as it must have looked when Milton sat here dictating to his daughter. There was no Thomas Ellwood here to welcome him, for that ardent Quaker had been put in Aylesbury Gaol, yet a day was to come when they sat together discussing the manuscript of Milton's unpublished masterpiece, and here it was that one day Thomas Ellwood said, "Thou hast said much here of Paradise lost, but what hast thou to say of Paradise found?" So it was that another dream began in Milton's mind, and here he found his paradise.

Often he must have sat in the shade of the great elm of which only the stump remains in the street. Often he must have passed by Stonewall Farm and talked to the people at the gates of these timbered cottages. Under the upper storey of one of them is a lychgate revolving on a post, at the top of which are to be seen the grooved wheels for the rope which worked it long ago.

We come through the gateway into the medieval church with the 600-year-old ballflowers round its doorway, a rich array of 14th century paintings, and 15th century angels looking down from the roofs.

It is the picture gallery that catches the eye as we come in. By the doorway is the Crucifixion with figures of Mary and John, and there are pictures of the expulsion from Eden which had been there cen-

Chalfont St Giles   The Medieval Church

Chalfont St Giles   John Milton's Cottage

Chenies   The Tudor Manor House

Chenies   Old Cottages by the Green

turies before Milton came with his own great picture of the scene. There is a Jesse Tree adorned with fruits, St Anne teaching her daughter, kings and prophets with scrolls, animals in the act of springing, St Catherine rescuing someone from darkness, and scenes of the tragedy of John the Baptist, the executioner in a quaint hat, Salome waiting with a charger, and then again bearing the head to her father at the feast.

The church was much refashioned in the 15th century when the tower was built, and all the roofs and some of the bench-ends were carved with fleur-de-lys. There is a Jacobean almsbox, and lovely foliage of that age on the altar rails, which are said to have been in St Paul's, given by Dean Hare who lies here. He was Chaplain to Marlborough in his campaigns, and not far from his mausoleum lies a humble dispatch carrier of the duke, with lines on his gravestone telling us that the grave was his chief friend, for,

> *Italy and Spain, Germany and France,*
> *Have been on earth my weary dance.*

There lies in this churchyard a man known widely to his generation for the delight he gave to millions, Mr Bertram Mills, the circus man. He was a member of the London County Council and a man greatly beloved for his widespread charity.

Under a recess adorned with a little Norman carving lies a Tudor lady whose portrait is engraved in brass, and there is a brass portrait of a 15th century priest, and a group of a 16th century civilian with two wives and three sons. Of the next generation is William Gardyner, an armoured figure in brass with his wife and their nine children, and a generation later still is the family portrait of Thomas Fleetwood, he in armour with his two wives and their 18 children grouped about them, all kneeling. He was Treasurer of the Mint and lived on the great estate here known as The Vache, a park across the river. The house has the old fireplaces by which Thomas Fleetwood would sit with his great family; and here in the days when Sir Hugh Palliser lived at the house came another immortal to John Milton's village, no less a figure than Captain Cook, who would sit here talking with his friend Palliser of their charting of the coast of Newfoundland in days gone by. It was as a compliment to his friend that Cook named an island Ile Vache, and, perhaps to return the compliment, Palliser put up in these grounds the first monument ever set up to Cook, "the ablest and most renowned navigator this or any other country has produced." So we read on this column, to which a fine yew hedge leads us behind the house, and we feel that it is not unfitting that there should have passed this way two of our towering heroes, he who opened for us the gates of another continent and he who opened for us the windows of Paradise.

Master and Captive of the Tower

CHALFONT ST PETER. Milton must have known it, for his friend Thomas Ellwood came here as tutor to the children of the Peningtons. They lived at the Grange, which was rebuilt last century although much of the old brickwork and flint foundations remain. In medieval times it had been a farm belonging to Missenden Abbey. In 1559 the Grange became the home of the Penington family, notable among whom was Sir Isaac, Lord Mayor of London. He was a Cromwellian and presented a monster petition to the Commons against the innovations of Archbishop Laud, whom he led to the scaffold, being then Lieutenant of the Tower. He raised huge sums for the Parliamentary Army, and was a great power in the cause of the Commonwealth while he was lord mayor, but was arrested at the Restoration, when he languished to death in the Tower he had once ruled. In 1654 Sir Isaac Penington gave the Grange to his son Isaac, who married Mary, widow of Sir William Springett and mother of Gulielma who became the wife of William Penn. It was in their time that Thomas Ellwood was constantly here, and George Fox was also a visitor. In 1666 the Grange was confiscated because of Lord Mayor Penington's part in the Civil War, and the family went to live at Woodside Farm, Amersham, where Gulielma first met William Penn. The only other important name in the history of the Grange is that of the infamous Judge Jeffreys who lived here for a time while his mansion was being built at Bulstrode Park.

The church, with its red brick tower, has been made new since Stuart days and is one of the few completely Georgian churches. It has three brass portraits from the older church, two of them portraying William Whappelodes and their wives, both in armour and as much alike as twins, but with a generation between them. The first

William has a little dog looking up to him, the second William is interesting because he was a steward to Cardinal Beaufort, Bishop of Winchester. On another brass is Robert Hansom, a vicar of 1545, shown in vestments which had just been forbidden by the Reformation. In the vestry are two 17th century chests and a funeral helm.

Ringing Before the Reformation

CHEARSLEY. It lies on the slopes above the valley of the Thame with a simple memorial cross facing the green. Not far away is a farmhouse in whose walls live all that remains of famous Notley Abbey, founded in 1162 by the first Earl of Buckingham. The house built on the site of the old guest house is a reminder of the haunting past, with its traceried windows and pointed doorways, and its medieval stone dovecot surrounded by thousands of iridescent wings. The church the monks watched over till the Dissolution is set below the village, near the river, its 15th century tower rising sturdily above the 13th century nave, which is roofed with timbers 600 years old. The font bowl, beautiful with fluting and foliage, has been here for seven centuries. It is about the same age as the piscina which the 15th century masons set back in the wall when they rebuilt the chancel. We see dim reminders of medieval frescoes over the chancel arch, and in the figure of a woman over a window which was once a doorway; and there is a reminder of what a townsman looked like in the 15th century in the brass picture of John Frankeleyn, with his wife and their seven children. The roof of the chancel is 500 years old and the little sanctus bell is older than the Reformation.

The Saxon Terraces

CHEDDINGTON. It has something older than its Norman church, for here still are Saxon farmlands, permanent witnesses to the rural practices of Alfred's England, history without words, an integral part of the landscape. Here we are in a fertile valley of the River Ousel, but the Saxons preferred the hills, and there they grew their crops, leaving their rustic testament behind. On the chalk hills are the very terraces they farmed. They ploughed the hillside in horizontal strips, unbroken land dividing each ploughed strip from its neighbour. At each ploughing the soil of the first furrow was turned over from the upper to the lower side, so that in time the downward trend of the earth removed changed these hillside strips into level terraces. Three of these terraces remain as they were left, to show us where crops were grown by hill-keeping Saxon farmers short of implements for felling the immense trees of the valleys.

Neither Saxon nor Norman nor those who came after spoiled the sylvan charm of the quiet scene, for this is a village full of trees, among which towering pines and chestnuts dwarf the massive 15th century tower of the church. But great timber has been cut here, for one of the two doors opening into the tower for five centuries is made up of a single plank.

Much of what the Normans built has been remade, but the south porch has parts of their chevron-moulded arch and carved columns. Within and without we found stones worked by Norman chisels, some with flowers in relief, and one with a grotesque little figure.

The finest architectural feature added to the Norman church is the chancel arch, sweeping without a break to the ground, a splendid example of 14th century building. It is to the magnificent Jacobean pulpit that we are chiefly drawn, however, a wonderful piece of oak carving, the panels rich with decoration, the reading desk borne by cockerels, the standards of the canopy clasped by dragons, the panelled canopy itself ornamented with beautiful cresting, pendants, and pierced pinnacles. Between the pinnacles dragons lie back to back with their tails curled, the picture of dubious benevolence. More admirable carving is found in the Jacobean altar table, enriched with faces and arabesques.

Fragments of glass 500 years old, one showing a skull, are in the window of the vestry, which has a panelled oak chest made by a carpenter who may have had to lay aside his tools for the Civil War.

We came here upon a remarkable record of long service, a chorister (Mr W. Welch) having been singing in the choir more than 80 years.

The church rests on a rise, its great churchyard commanding wide views in all directions, with the heights of Whipsnade to the east; but it is to the Saxon hillside farmlands that we turn here first and last.

The Chapel of Great Splendour

CHENIES. A perfectly delightful corner of this lovely county, it is a fitting home and resting-place for one of the most powerful dynasties of our English aristocracy, the House of Russell, Earls and Dukes of Bedford. Yet in spite of all this stir and splendour Chenies remains a picture of simplicity. Beautifully set by the wooded valley of the River Chess, it has a snug little green shaded by elms, with a red-roofed well in the centre, with the mellow brickwork, high pitched roofs, twisted chimneys, and dainty oriels of the Tudor manor looking down on it, and the medieval church close by. From the green the lawns slope up to the manor house, suggestive of the intimate touch that has existed between the house and the village for many generations. The house is shorn of its ancient splendour, but its walls are those built by the romantic young man of Long Bredy farmhouse in Dorset who founded the fortunes of the house and married Anne Sapcoate, a Chenies heiress of four centuries ago.

The church in which this young man sleeps, surrounded by his descendants arrayed in glory, joins the house in which they lived, and from its tower a griffin among the gargoyles looks down on the manor. The church has much interest, but it is for the superb splendour of the Bedford Chapel that we come. The chapel is unfortunately locked, but may be seen through glass. The church itself was entirely rebuilt in the 15th century, and has since been much restored. It has kept from its predecessor a 12th century font with a band of foliage round it; and a 14th century tomb with the battered figures of a knight and his lady. Lying loose in the south aisle is a carved capital from the old church, with a medieval angel corbel beside it. There is a little 16th century glass in the central light of the east window showing a man kneeling. There are several brasses, one having, like another at Beachampton, a portrait of the village blacksmith, John Waliston, shown in 15th century costume with two wives. Two other medieval brasses have portraits of Richard Newland, a tiny man in his rector's robes, and Edward Molyneux, in armour with a great sword, his feet on a greyhound, and beside him his wife in a mantle. Finest of all the brasses is one with a splendid buttressed Tudor canopy under which stands Lady Ann Phelip, holding a heart and two scrolls. By her is the stately figure of Agnes Johnson, mother of Robert Leyff, a 16th century rector. Finally there is the brass portrait of Elizabeth Broughton with flowing hair, who died just before the first Russell appeared at the manor.

All who come will wish they could see the full splendour of the Bedford Chapel, gay with banners and magnificent with marble. Filled with light and colour, it has a pavement of black and white tiles and is divided by a modern arcade. There are angels and helmets on the walls, small oak statues of St Peter and St Andrew on elaborate marble brackets, and beautiful modern glass in the windows in memory of the Russells, who have no monument, each window having in it an angel sitting with a scroll or a book of heraldry. The statues of St Peter and St Andrew are interesting because they were carved in wood by French craftsmen 400 years ago, and have been brought here from a church in France. The oldest tomb in the chapel, on which two 14th century figures lie, is supposed to be that of Sir John Chenies and his wife, who were here before John Russell came to the manor to take away a bride.

Many great chapters of history have closed in these Russell tombs. Here lies the romantic John in his mantle and collar of the Garter, his feet on a lion and his sword at his side, with his Chenies heiress in her robes as a peeress, her feet on a heraldic goat. It is a stirring thought that here is a man who came up from his farmhouse near the sea, rose in favour to be knighted in company with Sir Thomas More, conducted the funeral of Catherine of Aragon, was present at the trial of Anne Boleyn, brought Philip of Spain to England, and stood by Mary Tudor when she married Philip at Winchester. Ann was his third wife, and when he found her was in the household of Catherine of Aragon, little dreaming perhaps that she was to be the mother of the proud Russells. Francis the second earl, lies with his wife Margaret, noble figures in alabaster, he in armour wearing his coronet and the collar of the Garter, and she in her robes. The third earl is missing from the group, but in coloured alabaster on a black marble tomb lies the second earl's daughter Ann in her coronet and ruff, and near her on a tomb with armed men kneeling in the panels lies Bridget, the second earl's second wife, whose mother was sent to the Tower and whose father was beheaded. She is wearing her robe and coronet as a peeress, with a ruff. Francis the fourth earl and his wife lie in a blaze of colour on a tomb above which are arched niches with figures of a girl and an infant in its shroud; the father is in a mantle and collar of the Garter, and the mother in her robes.

The most striking of all the monuments is the fifth earl's and the first duke's, which fills the west wall and shows the first Duke and Duchess of Bedford sitting under a cupola with columns on each side and curtains open to reveal them clasping their bowed heads in anguish. There are medallions of nine children, and the centre medallion is a portrait of their son William, whose tragic fate they are lamenting. He grew up to be Lord William Russell who was judicially murdered for his supposed complicity in the Rye House Plot. It is believed that he was innocent, and his death sounded the doom of the Stuart dynasty. It was as consolation for his execution that his father was granted a dukedom.

The House of Russell

THE RUSSELLS, who have furnished the country with soldiers, sailors, and statesmen, and, by royal gifts and wealthy marriages, have acquired immense estates, sprang from a farmhouse at Long Bredy in Dorset, where young John Russell's knowledge of languages served him well during a shipwreck, took him to court, and set him on the way to rank and fortune.

Francis the second earl inherited vast monastic properties at Tavistock in Devon, at Thorney in Cambridgeshire, and at Woburn in Bedfordshire, with Covent Garden and Long Acre in London, where the family property was increased by a later marriage which brought the Bloomsbury estate into the House. The earl entertained on so princely a scale that Queen Elizabeth told him he made all the beggars. His youngest son fought by the side of Sir Philip Sidney at Zutphen. His grandson Edward became the third earl. Francis, cousin of Edward, was fourth earl, and played a prominent part in developing the London estate and draining the great Fen Level. Clarendon, the Royalist historian, held that had not this earl died too soon his mediation between Charles and the Commons would have averted the Civil War. The fifth earl fought first for Parliament and then for the Royalists in the Civil War, and was the father of Lord William Russell, a sturdy patriot, who, regarded by the Crown as dangerous owing to his opposition to the Roman Catholicism of the future James the Second, was executed on a spurious charge of complicity in the Rye House Plot. After the Revolution his aged father was created Duke of Bedford.

The fourth duke, leader of the Whigs, was for many years foremost in politics, and the fifth built Russell Square on the site of Bedford House. The sixth duke was the father of another Lord William Russell, murdered as an old man by his valet, and of Lord John

Russell, who served his country in Parliament for 66 years. He introduced the Reform Bill to the Commons in 1831, was one of the first Free Traders, and rose to be Prime Minister. On being defeated after a second Premiership, he resigned and never resumed office, though until his death he continued an active figure in the national life. As he lay dying he said to his wife: "I have made mistakes, but in all I did my object was the public good. I have sometimes seemed cold to my friends, but it was not in my heart."

The Imperturbable Ambassador

THERE rests in Chenies church an urn containing the ashes of Sir Edward Malet, son of an ambassador and an ambassador himself. At Washington during the Civil War he knew Abraham Lincoln, whom he remembered seeing in company with a group of Red Indians. Lincoln was showing them a globe of the world, and said, as he pointed to England, "We white people all come from that little spot."

Driven from Paris during the Franco-Prussian War, Malet followed the Government to Tours, where for a time he was stranded, with the official archives, shelterless in the street. During the Commune he had charge of the Paris Embassy, which was shattered by shellfire, but he took his papers and valuables into the cellars, and there he dined with his staff in evening dress while the guns were roaring, an Englishman unperturbed.

It was at this time that he had one of the strange little experiences of his career. A French boy of about eight sought him out and explained that his mother was under shellfire, friendless, and penniless. He must remove her to safer quarters, he said, but he needed 500 francs. The bewildered ambassador lent the unknown boy the money and expected to see him no more; but in a month the little man appeared, wan and starved, explaining that the new home had been more exposed than the first, and he had been kept prisoner by gunfire and illness. Nevertheless an allowance had arrived, and he repaid the loan. As to his mother, she was much shaken and in need of change and he had decided to move her to Wiesbaden. The hero of eight gravely bowed himself out, having paid his debt and astonished an imperturbable Englishman by the sight of an imperturbable French boy.

BUCKINGHAMSHIRE

Sir Edward Malet's duties took him to Peking, Athens, Rome, Constantinople, Egypt, and finally to Berlin. Wherever he went there was war or threat of war, but always he was the trusted counsellor of conflicting interests and ambitions, and, wherever possible, a peacemaker, regarded at last as one of the most trustworthy elder statesmen of Europe. For over 40 years he served his country and humanity, aware of international dangers, but believing some good of all men. He died at Chorley Wood in 1908.

The Tale the Old Cross Tells

CHESHAM. It has beech woods on its hills and the River Chess running through its valley. Much of its business is to do with its beeches, and a mighty multitude of children owe something to them, for from these beeches Chesham makes the wooden spades with which our children play on the sands.

We come to it through country with many ancient buildings scattered about, and past the striking watercress beds of Waterside. There are half a hundred historic monuments round about, the oldest of them a shop and a cottage side by side in Church Street with a 14th century roof, windows with wooden tracery, and a timbered gable.

An avenue of 80 limes brings us through a park to the church, which has been much as we see it for 700 years. It stands in a corner of the park overlooking the town, and about us in this pleasant scene is a tragic reminder of the bitter days before an Englishman was free to think the thing he will. It is the cross in the churchyard in memory of Thomas Harding. Persecuted for his faith, he was sentenced to do penance and condemned to wear a badge of green cloth embroidered with a faggot for the rest of his life; but all undaunted he would go into the woods to pray alone, and in secret he would sit at home and read Wycliffe's Bible. The book was found in his house, and for possessing it he was tried and condemned. They took him into "the dell going to Botley at the north end of the town" and burned him at the stake; it is recorded that he loved Wycliffe's Bible and was willing to suffer joyfully some pain for it at the last. There is a quotation from Wycliffe on the churchyard cross.

The oldest possession of the church is a fragment of a Norman arch in a transept wall. The church itself is 13th century, with a chancel made new in the 14th, and with rich tracery of the 15th in its windows. The porch is 15th century and has a room over it, four mass dials on its walls with a rare carving of a Crucifix above a 14th century niche. Above the old central tower rises a lead spire of the 18th century. The doorway is enriched with the little ballflowers so popular with the 14th century sculptor, whose work is also seen in the piscina in the chancel. The seats for the priests are now of wood, the arm-rests carved with the symbols of the Evangelists.

An old vicar of Charles Stuart's day looks down with his solemn face and his white beard from the chancel wall; he was Richard Woodcoke. In a small window is an armoured knight in memory of Francis Dent who was drowned in the South African war, and another window has four scenes from the life of Christ in memory of a brave vicar here for 25 years of last century; he was A. G. Aylward, who died from fever caught while visiting his flock in an epidemic.

We noticed that the Baptist Chapel has been here for more than 200 years, and that one of its proud records is that Thomas Sexton and his grandson preached in it for 111 years.

All Chesham knows the story of its Mad Hatter, Roger Crab, one of the most extraordinary characters of the 17th century. He kept a hat shop at Chesham but sold his estate and gave it to the poor, then going on to live near Uxbridge in a mean cottage he built for himself. He would eat no flesh and drink no wine, and lived on roots, herbs, cabbages, and grass, with bread and bran. In all this he felt he was practising Christianity.

He lived through the middle 60 years of the 17th century and witnessed the dramatic events of that time; and he made himself known through all England by a life such as would have filled the front pages of every stunt paper in London today. He wrote his own story, which he called The English Hermit, or the Wonder of This Age:

Being a relation of the Life of Roger Crab, living near Uxbridge; taken from his own Mouth; shewing his strange, reserved, and unparalleled Kind of Life, who counteth it a sin against his Body and Soul to eat any Sort of Flesh, or living Creature, or to drink any Wine, Ale, or Beer. He can live with three Farthings a week. His constant Food is Roots and Herbs; as Cabbage, Turnips, Carrots, Dock, and Grass; also Bread and Bran, without Butter or Cheese; His clothing is Sackcloth.

Crab begins his story by saying that, seeing he is become a gazingstock to the nation and a wonderment to his friends, he will indite a few lines as the Most High shall direct him, and he goes on to describe his ideas and experiences, telling us that once, when in prison, his keeper brought him nothing to eat, but "a dog brought him a bit of bread." In explaining why on moral grounds he would not touch meat, he declared that butchers were excluded from juries, and it was agreed that as the receiver was worse than the thief the buyer was worse than the butcher.

The Church in the Meadow

CHESHAM BOIS. It crowns a beautiful wooded crest above the valley of the Chess. Its church is set in a meadow with a great oak, by a churchyard with a spreading yew. It is mainly 14th century, with a 15th century tower. The handsome east window has in it flowers that have not faded since the 14th century, and 15th century shields of the Cheyne family. The nave and chancel have roofs put up by craftsmen of 500 years ago, resting on stone corbels carved with angels and heads, some with forked beards, some painted red, black, and gold. The finest example of woodwork is the Jacobean pulpit, carved with satyrs, the original canopy now serving for its base. There are two 16th century brasses, one of Elizabeth Cheyne, standing on a mound wearing a loose gown; and beside her Robert Cheyne in armour. Hidden under the organ is one of the rare chrysom brasses, showing Benedict Lee, who died nearly four centuries ago within a month of baptism, so that according to custom, his baptismal robe became his shroud. In the sanctuary is a 16th century Cheyne tomb carved with shields enclosed in a garter and wreaths, books, and an hour-glass. Above it a tablet has a Latin inscription, meaning, He did not die but went away.

In this quiet village was born Sir Arthur Lasenby Liberty, son of a Nottingham lace manufacturer, whose name has gone all over the world, he having built up the proud London house of Liberty, with as lovely a collection of things for sale as any shop in the world.

Glass Older than English Books

CHETWODE. It has its share of the architectural riches of the county, some ancient glass, and a manor house belonging to a family which, taking its name from the village, has been here since Thomas Becket was at Canterbury. The great house, built in

Shakespeare's days, has its original gables and some Tudor chimneys.

Of the 13th century priory about which life here long centred there remains little outside the church, with the chancel in which the old monks chanted mass. Five splendid lancets fill the sanctuary wall, their great shafts rising to support the deep mouldings of beautiful stepped arches. On either side of the chancel are triple lancets with corbels of foliage, animals, and grim creatures of old fancy. High on a wall are stone heads and delicately carved angels, corbels of an earlier roof which the monks must have seen.

The richest treasure is the wonderful glass before which Sir Gilbert Scott used to sit enchanted as a boy. The oldest was made before Dante wrote his Divine Comedy; the latest is older than our first printed book. In precious panels 700 years old we see John the Baptist in a golden robe starting back in rapture as he gazes on a holy lamb. There is part of a Crucifixion, a Crowned Madonna, and an archbishop robed for mass.

By raising a trapdoor we may see the decorated cross cut on the tombstone of Sir John Giffard, 600 years old. The only other old monument is a Jacobean urn, with weeping women.

The Rare Brass

CHICHELEY. The pretty cottage gardens under the great roadside trees, the white gabled rectory, and the church in the park close by the fine 18th century hall, would still charm William Cowper could he come back to them. Here he spent many happy hours in the days when the Chesters owned the hall. He wrote the epitaph of one of them:

> *Tears flow and cease not where the good man lies,*
> *Till all who knew him follow to the skies.*

Built in Italian style, with fluted pilasters, magnificent windows, and a sculptured cornice of masks and cornucopias, the house is rich in marbles and panelling, with carved woodwork worthy of Grinling Gibbons. The old moat is dry, but there are still four fishponds, and in a field crossed by a fine avenue of limes is an ancient dovecot.

The 15th century tower of the church rises with its gargoyles between the low chancel and the battlemented nave, the walls so thick as to suggest that they must be Norman. There was much refashioning here 600 years ago when the aisle was added. There are many memorials of the Cave family, 16th century lords of the manor. It is believed that in all England not 20 brasses were laid down in the troubled reigns of Edward the Sixth and Mary Tudor, and here is one of the few, showing Anthony Cave in armour, his wife in a veiled headdress, and, on one of the shields, the arms of Calais, of which Cave was a merchant. His son Anthony is twice depicted in the morbid style then at its height, once as a shrouded skeleton engraved on a brass, and again as an undraped corpse on a wall monument, with his eight children kneeling above, and grotesque figures standing on either side to support the frieze and cornice over his tomb.

Sir Anthony Chester, a 17th century ancestor of Cowper's friend, kneels in armour with his wife in a cloak, on a panelled tomb with Corinthian pillars and a beautiful frieze. There is a Jacobean Bible box, and Jacobean panelling and Tudor painting on the walls.

The Five Generations

CHILTON. It has a setting of rare splendour, with the heights of Brill and the stately avenue of Wootton to the north, and the Chilterns grouped like magic ramparts across the south horizon. The site of the church, on a wayside rise, was chosen by the Normans, and their stones are in the wall of the nave and the arches of the tower. For the rest the work is 13th century and after.

The 14th century tower, with its menacing gargoyles, is balanced by the 13th century transept. Erect on an outer wall of the nave is a crosslegged knight in chain mail and a loose coat, a strange place for a Crusader. The 15th century porch has over it a priest's chamber, reached by a doorway in the church. The chancel is 13th century, and has a double arch with the roodloft doorways beside it. Stone corbels of heads and angels support the fine 16th century roof of the nave. Between the chancel and the chapel is an oak screen with finely carved balusters and heads on Tudor panels. In the chancel, roofed with 15th century timbers, are Tudor poppyheads and two elaborate chairs. Under a big marble monument lies Richard Carter, the 18th century judge who rebuilt the great house by the church. A wooden cross from the battlefield is from the grave of Colonel Egerton of the Coldstreams.

On a Jacobean altar tomb with elaborate pilasters of coloured marbles is a remarkable group of the Croke family. Sir John is in armour with ruff, his wife in a black dress, and kneeling below are 11 children, one as a child in his chrism robe, two as boys, three as women, and five as men, two of the men (including Sir John Croke, Speaker), being in the scarlet robes they wore as judges. On a transept wall is a monument with the kneeling figure of a daughter of the house, Elizabeth Tyrrell, her baby beside her swathed in a red robe which covers her head, beneath which is a skull.

Separated by a wall from the churchyard stands the home of the Crokes, a handsome three-storeyed house with two old doorways through which came and went five generations of Crokes, all learned and honourable but the last. The line was established here in the time of Henry the Eighth, when John Croke, enriched with monastic lands, bought the estate and built the house. He and his wife sleep in the church.

The younger John, red-robed on the monument, was the Speaker of the House of Commons who told Elizabeth that the peace of the realm had been defended " by the might of our dread and sacred queen," Elizabeth cutting him short with, "No, by the mighty hand of God, Mr Speaker." He refused to vote for compulsory attendance at church when he might have brought it about by his casting vote. His brother Sir George, the other red-robed figure in the group, was a brave judge who firmly resisted encroachments by the Crown on the administration of justice. He opposed Ship Money and vindicated Hampden at his trial, stoutly affirming the sole right of Parliament to levy taxes. Sad it is that a house so brave should end in ignominy, but the last Sir John, for his corruption, had to sell the estate and (descendant of scholars, lawyers, legislators, and judges) died beggared by his own rascality.

Twenty Centuries Old

CHOLESBURY. Here on the high land are the marks of a work 2000 years old, traces of a British fortification, oval in shape, enclosing 15 acres inside the ramparts, which are about 10 feet high and vary from 30 to 40 feet wide. Tall beeches now grow in the ditches, sheltering a little house of God, and in the middle of the plateau is a pond which has mirrored the sky since the days when the Saxons took possession of the camp and gave it a Saxon name. Tradition tells that they set up a church here and baptised their converts in the pond. In the 13th century the Normans built a little church of nave and chancel. During the last century it was taken down and rebuilt with loving care, stone by stone. The 600-year-old piscina remains. We can see where the new is blending with the old in the decorations on the arch of the deeply moulded 13th century doorway, in the new font made in imitation of the old (a fragment of which is in the churchyard), and in the new windows set inside 13th century shafts. The west window, where we see a figure of Alfred among the saints, is in memory of Henry Jeston, who died in 1889 at the great age of 92. He had served the church for 50 years, one of the most familiar figures in the village, which stands outside the camp, its cottages edging the common.

The Four Oak Figures

CLIFTON REYNES. Amid its quiet charms we look across the meadows to the graceful spire of Olney, and remember the bright eyes and quick wit which, about two centuries ago, set that old village stirring and added famous chapters to our literature.

Here came Lady Austen, the beautiful and cultured widow of a wealthy baronet, to visit Mrs Jones, the rector's wife. Chance brought about a meeting with the poet Cowper, then a man of 50 living at Olney, and, friendship ripening into affection, Lady Austen inspired the poet to write songs for her harpsichord. She suggested his masterly poem on the Loss of the Royal George; she told him the story of John Gilpin; she urged him to a more sustained effort than he had yet essayed, setting him to work on The Task, with the sofa on which she was sitting as a text for it.

The rectory to which she came stands unchanged in the trees near the fine church, in which lies a unique group of four oak figures. No other church in England has as many, and no other church in Buckinghamshire has one.

The Norman tower, with some of its original window openings, rises above a building remade and enriched 600 years ago. The 15th century added the clerestory, the floral stringcourse to the nave, and the south aisle's stringcourse with beasts among the flowers; but it was the 14th century builders who remade the fine tower arch, raised the nave arcades in slender beauty, built the chancel, carved the piscina and sedilia with men's heads and the priest's doorway with heads of apes, and shaped the font with its worn figures of God holding His crucified Son, the Madonna, and six graceful saints.

It is the north chapel, older than Chaucer's poems, and now a sanctuary in memory of the Fallen, which contains the four wooden figures. Two lie together in a canopied recess, a 14th century woman with her husband, and a knight whom the villagers call Simon Borard, but who represents more probably Sir Ralph Reynes, who died in 1310. He is in mail; his left hand on his scabbard, his right sheathing the sword with which he fought his last fight 600 years ago. His wife wears an elaborate dress with veil and wimple. Their heads rest on pillows; their feet on dogs. Slightly later is the 14th century tomb, carved with shields and flowers, on which lie the other two, believed to be Roger Reynes and his wife. He is in mail with a short surcoat, his handsome face turned towards his wife whose hands are clasped in prayer. Once she had a red kirtle, and his armour was bright, but, time has faded their colouring and wearied the dogs at their feet. Through a hole we see that the figures are hollow, for the medieval craftsman filled his statues with charcoal to absorb all moisture and so preserve them. To have four of these rarities is a proud possession for any village, for there are not a hundred of them in all England.

Another Reynes, Sir John of the later 14th century, lies in stone with his wife on a magnificent tomb cut round with 16 niches for a little band of medieval mourners, men and women alternately, a fascinating study of costume in the days of the Black Prince. He is in armour with chain mail round his neck; the lady has her face framed in an elaborate, stiff headdress. Two puppies snuggle together at her feet, and at the knight's is a dog obviously modelled from life. On its flowery collar we trace the letters BO, but are left wondering at its full name. Over the tomb hang a breastplate and a vizored helmet, such as were carried in funeral processions. Close by is a brass, small and broken, portraying another Sir John who was in his prime when Agincourt was fought, and still smaller brasses show the shrouded figures of a man and his wife, also members of the Reynes family, who died about 1500. On the wall is the bust of Alexander Small who, born under James the First, lived through the Civil War, the Com-

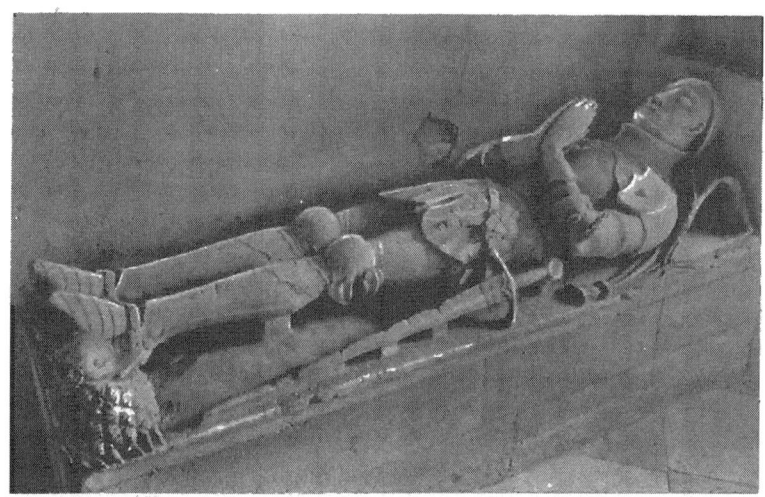

Thornton — John Barton of the 15th Century

Clifton Reynes — A 14th Century Knight on his Tomb

Chenies 15th Century Tower   **Dinton** Medieval Tower and Porch

Ellesborough   Church in the Chilterns

monwealth, the flight of James the Second, outlived Dutch William and Mary, and saw Queen Anne on the throne.

A tombstone in the chancel bears the surprising inscription, "Samuel Pepys, died 1703, most faithful rector of this church." While he served here his namesake was writing his immortal Diary, and it is strange that both died in the same year, the great Pepys and the lesser one.

We lift our eyes to the windows and the fine timber roofs, the roof of the narrow nave raised so high that its 300-year-old beams are almost lost in shadow. A little of the 14th century glass remains to show us a mitred bishop, roses, a leopard's head, and fragments of tracery; and glass from the 15th century, with small figures, fills the window over the chancel arch, where we may make out a Doom picture painted on the wall when Joan of Arc was listening to her Voices.

The Duke's Clock

COLNBROOK. Bestriding the main Bath road, it has a medley of architectural styles in its old houses and older inns. History has halted from time to time to add a footnote to its pages here. It was here that Edward the Third met the Black Prince returning from victory with the King of France as his prisoner; here, at the George Inn, Queen Elizabeth stayed a night as a prisoner on her way from Woodstock to Hampton Court; and here Charles received deputations from Lords and Commons during the Civil War.

The fine modern church, modelled on a 13th century predecessor, has beneath its bell gable the clock given to the old church by the Duke of Marlborough on leaving here for his new palace at Blenheim. The church, peaceful in its secluded corner, has good windows, that in the sanctuary having the Adoration of the Shepherds and the Wise Men, while others have saints, among them Boniface, Walburga, Elizabeth, Hugh of Lincoln, and Edward the Confessor. An oak reredos is carved with the Crucifixion, the Resurrection, and the Ascension; with saints, prophets, and apostles between the panels. The oak screen is elaborately traceried, has linenfold panels, and, in red and gold, keys of St Peter, the scallop shell of St James, the arrow of St Sebastian, and other emblems. The altar is of cedar of Lebanon, and we were told that in wet weather its scent fills the church.

THE KING'S ENGLAND

The Norman Chest

CUBLINGTON. Lying amid the pastures of the Vale of Aylesbury, it has from its churchyard a splendid picture of undulating country. The 15th century church is a simple building with a tower of only one stage. The chancel arch, reaching to the plain roof, has a crouching man and a monkey on it; on either side of the altar is a niche with embattled cornice; and a wall bracket has in it a woman's head. The oak lectern arrived before the Civil War; but the oldest thing in the church is a truly wonderful survivor, a chest made by Norman craftsmen, whose carved cable ornament remains. There are two old books and the desk to which they used to be chained.

The Unknown Soldier

CUDDINGTON. The River Thame runs past the charming groups of cottages, and the roads fork at the village green. Near the ancient church stands a stone house, once Tyringham Hall but now the village club, which bears the date 1609 over the door and keeps its original windows in moulded oak frames. The village has two pathetic crosses: a fine granite peace memorial in the churchyard, and in the church a tiny cross which once stood in Flanders Field, with its original metal plate stamped *Unknown British Soldier*.

The church, many times enlarged in the 13th century, has an interesting variety of 13th century work in the nave arcades. We enter by a 14th century porch and a doorway beautifully moulded with free columns, a century older. The arcaded font and the low chancel arch bear the stamp of 13th century work; above the arch is a bearded man who has been watching over the church since the 15th century, when the tower was built, and above the arch leading from the aisle to the chapel is a very queer head. Two 14th century angels in green and gold look down on the chapel from the tracery of the windows which light up the altar. The altar itself is modern, with carvings of flowers, and there are beautiful altar rails which have the strange sight of a muzzled bear cut on one of the posts. There is a 14th century piscina, and much-worn medieval tiles in the tower.

A Ducking for a Braggart

DATCHET. Shakespeare must have known this lovely place within sight of Windsor, for here he gave Falstaff his ducking in Datchet mead. In fancy we may recall Robert and John staggering under the burden of the great clothes basket in which the braggart knight is stowed away by Mistress Ford and Mistress Page, on his way to the river to be soused with the linen.

The 14th century church, largely remade, is a dignified building near the green. It has a portrait brass on the sanctuary wall showing a London goldsmith kneeling in prayer with his wife and two daughters, two books open before a charming Tudor group.

A mile away is Ditton Park, once the home of Sir Ralph Winwood, ambassador under James the First. An ardent Protestant, he had a leading part in organising resistance to Spain and Austria in their attempts to stamp out the Reformation in Europe, and, all unwittingly, he helped to bring Sir Walter Raleigh to the scaffold, for he was mainly instrumental in securing the prisoner's release from the Tower, and in promoting the expedition to Spanish America which failed so sadly, and incited the ignoble king to sacrifice to Spain the noblest man of his realm.

The Knight and His Sons

DENHAM. The village street of our dreams, the village street of novel, film, and play, is here. Its cottages are mostly old and its houses have great charm. Wistarias and creepers cover the walls, and at one end are the clear waters of a silver stream. Though but a mile or two of fields separate the village from ever-spreading London, we found no traffic disturbing Denham's calm repose. Not even the great film studios a mile away have broken its rural tranquillity.

At the end of the street is Denham Place, hiding behind a high brick wall. It is a delightful building set up in Restoration days, and we look across the lawn to the dormer windows in its high-pitched roof. Within are fine tapestries and old woodwork, and below the ceilings are some remarkable friezes of coloured plaster showing country scenes. Captain Cook was a visitor here, and Lucien and Joseph Bonaparte lived here a century ago. Another 17th century house is Denham Court, surrounded by a moat and approached by a grand avenue of lofty limes. John Dryden described the garden as "the most delicious in England," and here he wrote his famous Ode on St Cecilia's Feast:

> *From Harmony, from heavenly harmony,*
> *This universal frame began.*

At the gate of the drive is Denham church, surrounded by trees. Tower, nave, and aisles were built about 1460, the arcades with pointed arches on tall clusters of round pillars. The roofs are original, and the stone corbels are carved with heads of a king, a bishop, and some ladies. In a 500-year-old wall painting of Judgment Day we can distinguish the winged figure of an archangel sounding the Last Trump, while below him are shrouded figures rising from their graves.

The oldest thing in the church is the 13th century font on slender round pillars, a pair of pointed arches on each of the eight sides of the bowl. The chancel is 14th century, and in the sanctuary is a pair of old chairs with richly carved backs.

On the floor in front of the altar is a splendid company of brasses. There is sour-faced Walter Duredent in armour, with a long sword, and by him his two wives in the stiff headdresses fashionable about 1500. In two groups below them stand 12 sons and 14 daughters. About 40 years later is the brass of Dame Agnes Jordan, last Abbess of Syon, one of the only two brasses of abbesses remaining in England. Her solemn face looks out of a hood hanging over her shoulders, and a long dress falls in folds at her feet. Near by is Leonard Hurst, an Elizabethan parson in his gown, while below him are four figures of 16th century children. In a frame by the sanctuary window is a brass of John Pyke, a gloomy-looking monk and schoolmaster of 400 years ago. On the back is a later inscription to a lady, showing that the brass was used again, having been stolen. On the wall near by is what at first seems to be another brass, but is actually a stone finely engraved with a kneeling figure of Philip Edelen, who died during the Commonwealth. He wears a skullcap and a beard, and rests a hand on a book.

On a table tomb lie battered figures of Sir Edmund Peckham in armour, and his wife in an uncommon embroidered cape with a high collar. Sir Edmund died in the year Shakespeare was born, and was Master of the Mint to Henry the Eighth and his successors, receiving £200 as executor of Henry's will. He restored the purity of the gold coinage, and was a staunch supporter of Queen Mary. His eldest son Robert was a great student, and partly for health and partly owing to the triumph of the Protestants he exiled himself in Italy. His body lies in Rome, but his heart was brought home to this church, and all his manifold virtues are recounted on a tablet here.

A son of whom he can hardly have been so proud was MP for High Wycombe, but for conspiring to rob the Exchequer he was hanged at Tower Hill eight years before his father was laid to rest in this tomb.

On the wall of an aisle is a sumptuous white marble monument 200 years old. It is capped by a festooned urn, and shows curtains drawn back to reveal a bust of Sir Roger Hill, an aristocratic-looking man in a long curly wig.

There are many old headstones in the churchyard, from where we can see a beautiful house built as a charity school 200 years ago. Half a mile from the church is Savoy Farm, a medieval timbered house surrounded by a natural moat fed by the River Colne. Parts of the house are 600 years old, and within are 16th century mural paintings. It was here that Lady Cynthia Mosley spent some of her happiest hours with her children, and it was in the wood that she was buried by her own desire. On a sunken lawn is her white marble tomb, designed by Sir Edwin Lutyens and inscribed:

A little space was allowed her to show at least a heroic purpose and attest a high design. Cynthia, my beloved.

Cromwell Rides Triumphant

DINTON. Here came Cromwell riding triumphant from Naseby, where, seeing the enemy draw up and march in gallant order towards them, and his a company of poor ignorant men, he could but smile out to God in praise "because God would, by things that are not, bring to naught things that are—and God did it."

He was riding to visit Simon Mayne at Dinton Hall, and here he left his sword of victory, which is still, we understand, in the house. The house is divided from the churchyard by an ivied wall, and has a handsome porch and a great array of Tudor chimneys and dormer windows. There is stone corbelling in the cellar 600 years old. It was the home of the Maynes, the mistress of the house being sister of the first Lord Lovelace and mother of Simon, who fought with Parliament in the Civil War. He signed the king's death-warrant, and at the Restoration was sentenced to death but died in the Tower, his body being delivered to his widow for burial at Dinton. He had a faithful servant named John Bigg, who lived out the sad years after his master's death as a hermit in this village, being wrongly believed to have been the masked man who executed the king.

Simon Mayne's father has a brass in the church, showing him in riding-boots and ruff, with his wife and two children, one of whom is the boy who grew up to judge the king. The brass is one of a fine group of portraits belonging to three centuries. One of the 15th shows William Lee and his wife; three Tudor brasses show Francis Lee with his wife in a veiled headdress, Thomas Greneway and his son with both their wives, and John Compton and his wife with their eight children at prayer. Under a marble stone sleeps Richard Beke, who married a much-loved niece of Oliver Cromwell, Lavinia Whetstone. A Jacobean altar tomb with marble columns, pediment, frieze, and cornice is in memory of Richard Sarjeant and his wife, and near it is a monument with weeping cherubs to an 18th century Richard Ingoldsby.

The massive 15th century tower of the church rises with its turret over the clerestoried nave, under whose parapet lurk grim gargoyles. In the tower is a doorway built when the county was still sending out Crusaders, but the chief glory of the church is in the porch, with stone heads supporting timbers 500 years old. Here is a magnificent Norman doorway with a chain of hearts between the pillars and the door. On the massive stone lintel is an immense dragon with a gaping mouth into which a valiant little Michael is about to thrust a cross. The elaborately carved tympanum has a tree whose fruit is being eaten by two fierce-looking animals, each with tail erect and tapering into what seems to be a fleur-de-lys.

The nave arcades are borne on stately pillars carved with bell capitals 700 years ago. The font is but a century younger. Three big medieval stone heads and three Jacobean wood corbels support the modern roof. Behind the finely carved Jacobean pulpit is a long peephole into the 13th century chancel. A chest with Tudor panelling has a lid carved by a Jacobean craftsman.

The village has many beautiful pictures, the noble church seen from under the chestnuts, pretty houses seen through an archway in the churchyard wall, and the hall to which the Protector came. On the village green are the stocks, and the old whipping-post with iron manacles still attached to it. Surrounded with firs by the roadside is an 18th century architectural freak, a summerhouse like a mock castle ruin. In the churchyard, which has the shaft of a 15th century cross with a bronze sundial, are two 19th century stones with odd inscriptions. One is to Samuel Paine, 80:

> *I have plodded through Life's weary way*
> *In various callings of the day*
> *A ploughboy first in Suffolk born*
> *I turned straight furrows for the corn.*

The other is to Henry Wootton, who lived 89 years:

> *I have ploughed my land and sown it too,*
> *I have grown it, dressed, and drained it through!*
> *My landlord sends me word to quit*
> *To Him in duty I submit.*

The Elizabethans in the Norman Church

DORNEY. It lies in the Thames valley not far from Windsor's proud battlements and Eton's playing fields. It has timbered cottages carrying their 300 years with an easy grace, a grand Tudor manor house, and an ancient church in a shady lane. Dorney Court, half hidden by the trees near the churchyard, is a grand 15th century house with tall chimneys and many gables. It has several original doorways, stone fireplaces, and a great hall with panelled screens. It is said that the first pineapple produced in this country was grown at Dorney Court and given to Charles the Second, a record of the event being made by a woodcarving of a pineapple in one of the rooms.

The nave and chancel walls of the church are Norman, and although most of their windows belong to later centuries traces of a Norman window can still be seen. The chancel arch is 14th century, the brick tower with its castle-like turrets is Tudor, and the porch and the chapel were built in the days of Wren. There is a Norman font, much old woodwork, panels of the medieval screen, a traceried 15th century chair, 16th century seats, and a 17th century pulpit which used to grace a church in Somerset. The screen between the tower and the nave is partly 17th century, and above it is a low musicians' gallery of the 17th century. The window under the gallery has a portrait of Charles Stuart with orb and sceptre. One grand monument has on it an Elizabethan family kneeling at prayer—Sir William Garrard in armour with his wife in a hood and cloak, and below them are their 15 children, five holding skulls to show us that they passed away in infancy.

This tranquil village gave London a lord mayor in 1458, and in the next century the name of another of its sons, Robert Rave, was added to the imperishable roll of martyrs who died for their faith.

The Ancient Door

DORTON. The past speaks here with a quiet voice from Norman and Jacobean days. Grouped together are the little old church, the manor, and a farm shaded by fine trees. We came to them by one of the loveliest walks in the county, a long path skirting a brook, the hedge aglow with wild roses, and with branches of ash, oak, larch, and beech meeting overhead. The dormered Dorton House is a charming Jacobean building round three sides of a courtyard, with graceful chimneys of moulded brick. Carefully restored on lines harmonising with the original, it looks today as it did when John Hampden was in the saddle. It has two of its original staircases, fine ceilings, a magnificent screen with elaborate cresting, and many rare treasures. One of these is a finely illuminated vellum volume of all the charters referring to Boarstall from Norman days to 1444; it has a quaint picture map of Boarstall when it was the strongest fortified manor in the county. The other relic is an interesting medieval symbol of land tenure, a 15th century cow's horn, with silver mountings.

The little church has kept its Norman walls in nave and chancel, and from the nave floor rise two ancient posts supporting the round timber arches which carry the bell turret, capped by a tiled pyramid roof. A 15th century base supports the bowl of the Norman font, over which, beautiful with elaborate cusps and pierced work, is a cover made in 1630, inscribed " a gifte to butyfie the House of God." The 17th century pulpit is plain, but the altar rails, from the same time, are handsomely designed with classical arches. There is much fine woodcarving here, but nothing impressed us more than the grey, battered, medieval door, studded with 15th century nails and swinging on hinges 700 years old.

The Scholar and His Sheep

DRAYTON BEAUCHAMP. It lies amid green pastures at the foot of Tring Hills. Here Richard Hooker, the brilliant scholar, was rector for a year, living in the house set down in the fields. One day in 1584, Izaak Walton writes, two visitors, George

BUCKINGHAMSHIRE

Cranmer and Edwin Sandys, rode up to the gates and asked for the rector. They were told they would find him keeping his sheep, and, going into the fields, they saw a man reading Horace, with one eye on the flocks: he had been sent to look after them by his vixen of a wife. They thought he was wasted at Drayton, and soon had him moved to the Temple. The pulpit with five angels is his memorial here.

The little church he had watched over for a year was at that time already both new and old. It had the Norman font which we see today, with its lovely little arcade unharmed. The 15th century men had been there restoring and strengthening the old place, putting in some plain pews, of which five are still left, setting in the bright glass in the east window, which by a miracle remains to this day the village's great treasure. Skilfully patched by modern hands, there are figures of ten Apostles in two rows, with a background of red and blue. Each face is different, and each man carries his symbol. We see Peter with a book and two big keys, Andrew with a book and a big yellow cross, Jude carrying a little ship, John (the only figure without a beard) holding a golden cup, James with a sword, and another James and Bartholomew each with a knife, Thomas with a spear, Philip with a cross, and Simon with an axe. Other fragments of old glass are in the north and south windows of the chancel.

Next to these lovely glass portraits the villagers prize two 14th century brass portraits, Thomas and William Cheynes, both about four feet long and of great value to students of armour for details. There are only seven years between them but the details vary. Thomas the elder, who carried Edward the Third's shield in battle, has a curly-headed lion at his feet. Another little brass portrait, its head broken away, shows the beautiful vestments, chalice and wafer of Henry Fazakyrley, who died in 1531.

The Cheynes, who were lords of the manor in Chelsea and have left their name on one of the most renowned streets in London, have another huge memorial in the chancel. Made to fit from floor to ceiling, it reflects a delightfully pompous spirit. Here is the wigged figure of Lord William Cheyne, Lord Lieutenant of the county for Queen Anne. He lies on his side, and sitting solemnly regarding him is his young wife, wearing a gorgeous dress with lace-trimmed sleeves, her coronet on a little cushion.

Fourteen Orphans in One Day

DRAYTON PARSLOW. It stands on a ridge looking to the pines of Woburn across the Ouzel valley, with the soft line of the Chilterns against the sky. A green mound marks where a Norman castle stood when the first church rose. Some 17th century thatched cottages stand by a road running down the hill, remnants of the older village. The tower has been a landmark on the ridge since the church was refashioned 500 years ago, stones from three churches of three centuries being embodied in its walls. Some delightful carvings remain—four heads in the 14th century chancel arch, and one of the finest fonts in Buckinghamshire. It is a gem of 15th century workmanship, with canopied, sunken panels divided by rich buttresses. It has an embattled rim. Among fragments of glass which have been gleaming in the windows for 500 years is the figure of an angel coming down, carrying a gold crown. The altar table, with fluted rails, was put here in the 17th century. There is a sanctus bell.

A poignant little story is told on the brasses in the floor near the font, where we see a group of three boys and another of 11 girls in Tudor dress—14 children who were orphaned in one day by the tragic death of their parents, Benet and Agnes Blakenolle. The portraits of the father and mother have been lost, but the sad tale is told in an inscription let in the stone.

The Scholar's Friend

DROPMORE. It owes the beauty and splendour of its 600-acre park to Pitt's Foreign Minister, Lord Grenville, who made it his delight in the stress and strain of the days of Napoleon to plant trees. Here he found a waste and made a paradise. He built the house in the park and cut down a hill in front of it so that he could see Windsor Castle. He planted it all year after year, and the magnificent cedar he set on the lawn is still flourishing, with 400 more in the park. There is a noble avenue of them, and about it are pines and other trees, and in due season a blaze of rhododendrons and azaleas. It was the proud boast of Lord Grenville's gardener, when showing these trees, to say that he had carried the biggest of them in his waistcoat pocket.

The common, with the cottages clustering about it, is part of the old waste land, the wilderness Lord Grenville turned into a heritage of beauty. It is fitting that he should have been keeper of London's loveliest green spaces, Hyde Park and St James's.

The church, a simple brick structure, was built last century, and has in its pulpit four 18th century Flemish panels, boldly carved with cherubs and monsters. In the churchyard sleeps Sir John Aird, whose splendid engineering career ended in 1911. Son of the man who built the Crystal Palace for Sir Joseph Paxton, he was responsible for some of the greatest enterprises of last century, at Amsterdam, Copenhagen, Berlin, and various cities in Russia, France, Italy, and in South America and India. He built docks and railways for London, and crowned his work by constructing the great dam at Assuan, the pioneer dam in the transformation of modern Egypt.

Not far away from this man of action, in the shade of a splendid cedar, sleeps a man of learning who left a name dear to us all, Dr Paget Toynbee, brilliant scholar, our foremost authority on Dante, and a man of singular beauty of character. He was born at Wimbledon in 1855, a brother of Arnold Toynbee. After taking his degree at Oxford he became a private tutor, but in 1892 began that career of scholarship which lasted the rest of his life. His first contribution to the study of Dante, the work which brought him fame, was an index of names. He wrote papers for English and foreign magazines, published a Life of Dante, and undertook the colossal task of collecting all references to the poet in English literature from the time of Chaucer. He also did much important work on the text of Dante's letters.

He was a keen gardener, and made a strange little friend at his home at Burnham, a robin who went with him on all his walks. Robin shared in every meal, and slept in his host's chamber. He even peered over the reader's shoulder at times when Dr Toynbee was perusing proof-sheets dealing with Walpole, Dante, or Gray.

Once this privileged guest met with sad disaster, when rashly one morning hopping from a toast track on to a scalding tea urn, collapsing instantly from shock as if dead. Hearing his cry of distress, the doctor glanced up from The Times and hurried to the rescue. The patient was revived, but lay helpless for several days in a basket lined with cottonwool until his feet were healed after the burns. When, a little later, and himself an invalid, Dr Toynbee was away from home for three or four months, he did not expect to see his friend again, but only a few hours had elapsed after his return home when the faithful robin appeared to greet him, then briefly disappeared and returned again, this time a little shyly with a companion to introduce, Mrs Robin.

Norman Doorway and Medieval Tower

DUNTON. It has a medieval tower of rugged white stone set against a Norman nave made new last century. The Norman doorway has a door no more, but here it is for us to see, under an arch with chevrons, and a lintel adorned with the chisel of the craftsman. The sculpture is much worn after its 800 years, but at one end are three small figures with angels looking out of the clouds above; it is said to represent a miracle. At the other end is something like the outline of a horse. On the stonework of a tiny window near the priest's doorway into the chancel is a mass dial from the days before clocks. The chancel is 13th century, but the arch was made new in the 15th, when the woodcarvers set up here the angels at the end of its hammerbeams. The font is Norman; the piscina is 13th century. There are three brass portraits, two small ones of a man and a woman of the 15th century, and a Tudor lady with a child holding her dress.

Old-World Beauty

EAST CLAYDON. It has old-world beauty, charming black and white cottages, and a high place in our countryside, but our call is short and sweet. Close by the church stands the White House, the old manor farm built at the end of Elizabeth's reign, with the lovely porch half a century younger. The fine medieval tower dominates the village, with 15th century battlements and a 14th century corbel of an angel worked into it. The chancel arch has rested for 600 years on two winged figures with faces a little unpleasing; the plain font is 15th century.

EDGCOTT. Its small church stands on a little hill with its tower rising like a beacon above miles of grasslands dotted with cottages and farms. The church goes back for 800 years, one of its nave walls built by the Normans; the other is 15th century, the work of the men who built the embattled tower. In that medieval restoration the doorways were rebuilt, the roodloft steps laid down, and the font was shaped with its panelled sides sweeping gracefully down to the pedestal. The chancel arch is 14th century and was left intact in the 15th. Fragments of the medieval screen have been used again in the chancel, and there is a 16th century poppyhead bench-end among the modern seats. On a wall in the tower is a queer head with an open mouth. The church has kept its ancient sanctus bell, and the studded door in the south doorway has 17th century hinges.

By the church is the Manor Farm on the south and Rectory Farm on the west, Rectory Farm preserving the old rectory with its timbered brick walls and its central chimney stack.

The Finest Woodwork in the County

EDLESBOROUGH. High on the bare western slope of the Chilterns, its handsome church a landmark for miles, it looks across to Ivinghoe's proud beacon and to the great lion cut in the chalk at Whipsnade. It has a 15th century barn and a dovecot, and two splendid sycamores at the foot of the mound crowned by the church. The tower, with embattled parapet and a turret 70 feet from the ground, has been here since the days of Crecy. There are quaint figures on the outer walls, where a bearded head seems to watch our coming.

The church, with a low 15th century roof supported by its original corbels (on which are carved a demure old lady and a man who snarls over his task) must have echoed to prayers for men fighting in the last Crusade. The font is 16th century, its modern cover having a finial borrowed from the superb pulpit, which is one of the treasures that bring us here.

It is the woodwork of the church, among the finest in Buckinghamshire, which makes the village famous; it has a richness and splendour worthy of a small cathedral. With one exception it is all 500 years old. There is a beautiful oak screen, painted red and blue, with a frieze of gold leaves, a crest of fan-vaulting, and rich tracery above the panels of the door. There is the daintiest little three-tiered canopy over the pulpit, carved with foliage and finials. The six sanctuary stalls are a treasury of carving, the misereres are delightful with frogs, eagles, a lizard and a bat, a griffin, and a mermaid mothering a lion. The arms are guarded by angels, a monkey, a bearded man, a bishop, and by harpies.

One small 15th century window keeps its original glass, a gem showing a pilgrim ten inches high, with his Bible, his staff, his red cloak, and the pilgrim's scallop-shell in his bright yellow hat. Some of the stone figures carved to keep the pilgrim company here are now in the vestry, a flying dragon, a crowned head, a skull, a chalice, and two angels. On the chancel arch in its iron bracket is an hourglass whose sands were running out as Queen Elizabeth's life was ebbing.

There is a portrait brass of John Swynstede, engraved while Chaucer was riding to Canterbury. It is magnificent, showing him in flowing vestments and loose curly hair. The brass of John Killingworth, who died just before Agincourt, has vanished, and all that is left behind is a lovely rose. John Rufford, wearing plate armour and skirt of mail, and armed with sword and dagger, has all his three wives with him after 400 years, but less fortunate is the 17th century Henry Brugis, whose monument knows him no more, though his wife in her fur gown remains perfect in brass.

Among the vicars here we noticed one remarkable man, Henry John Todd of the beginning of last century. One of the most industrious writers of his age, he added thousands of words to a new edition of Johnson's dictionary, and catalogued a great number of cathedral charters, books, and manuscripts.

A Gift to the Nation

ELLESBOROUGH. It has become a place of imperial consequence, for here in its beautiful park stands Chequers Court, the Prime Minister's country house, the unique trust which, by the romantic beneficence of Lord Lee of Fareham, affords our Premiers a country home, a staff of servants, and funds for the enjoyment of leisure and luxury in idyllic surroundings far from the stress of Downing Street.

The 15th century church, refashioned last century when its fine tower was added, stands on a spur of the Chilterns among high hills, and has magnificent views. In the churchyard, dedicated to all who sleep here, is a beautiful sculpture of the Crucifixion. Among those who rest in this peaceful scene is Thomas Edwards, an 18th century lawyer-poet, who, inheriting his father's fortune, bought an estate and devoted his retirement to writing sonnets, the only man of his day to preserve this form of poetry. Here also lies Sir John Lawson

Walton, an earnest reformer and Attorney-General who was laid here in our own century.

In the vestry are some fragments of 15th century glass, one showing the head of Our Lord with the crown of thorns. Reset in the porch is a fine 15th century bearded head, and on the arcades and windows in the nave are corbels carved 500 years ago. The chancel has a beautiful example of 15th century work in its embattled piscina, carved with flowers.

It was the Hawtreys who gave Chequers its present form, and a portrait brass here shows Thomas Hawtrey in Tudor armour, his wife beside him, with their 11 sons and 8 daughters. Another member of the family (Bridget, who died as Lady Croke) lies on one of the most imposing tombs in Buckinghamshire, her head resting on one hand, the other holding a book. Four black columns support the splendid arch above her, the panels carved with flowers and cherubs, with a background of coloured shields and emblems of mortality.

There is a tablet to Sir John Russell, great-great-grandson of Oliver Cromwell. The Russells were descendants of Cromwell's daughter Frances by her marriage to Sir John Russell. On inheriting Chequers in the 18th century they brought to it a unique collection of Cromwell portraits and other relics, now among the heirlooms secured for Chequers by Act of Parliament.

The Prime Minister's Country House

IT is fitting that the Prime Minister should have an estate mentioned in Domesday Book and a house built through the centuries. Chequers belonged in the 13th century to the Chekers, then for 350 years to the Hawtreys, then to the Crokes, one of whom was Speaker. After that it passed to John Russell, whose father had married Cromwell's youngest daughter Frances. In our own time Lord Lee of Fareham lived in it and bought it and gave it to the nation, as recorded on two panels in one of the windows:

> *This house of peace and ancient memories was given to England as a thank-offering for her deliverance in the Great War and as a place of rest and recreation for her Prime Ministers for ever.*

It is one of the most notable gifts ever made to the English people. The house lies in a dip in the hills 630 feet above the sea, with heights in its grounds reaching to 800 feet, from which is one of the widest views in England, with the Berkshire Downs, Salisbury Plain, and the Cotswolds all in sight, and at times even the peaks of the Welsh mountains 80 miles away.

What profound decisions have been taken in this house no man knows, but it was at a conference in the Long Gallery at Chequers, sitting round the fireplace with Cromwell's sword hanging there, that the British and French Prime Ministers with General Smuts and General Foch decided on the principle of a Single Command which ultimately won the war.

Entering Chequers by the new porch built by Lord Lee to replace what he considered a battlemented atrocity of 1820, we come to a small hall with windows of 16th century heraldic glass, a medieval oak chest, an old porter's chair, and an oak box in which the rush-lights were kept. On the walls are portraits of Charles and Henrietta Maria and one of Sir Edmund Verney, his standard-bearer, whose right hand was picked up on the battlefield still clutching the king's flag. In the Little Parlour an 18th century bird-cage hangs at the window, and on the walls are portraits of Richard Cromwell as a youth and Henry Cromwell as a child. The Hawtrey Room has a portrait of Shakespeare's patron the Earl of Southampton and another of Francis Bacon, a clock which belonged to Oliver Cromwell, chairs and tables of those days, and original heraldic glass recording the marriages of the Hawtreys up to 1540. Historic flags hang in the Great Hall, where there is a Saxon helmet picked up by Lord Lee after the battle of Ypres; and there is a splendid chest which James the Second kept at the Admiralty. The Study has a frieze recording the marriages and arms of the chief owners of Chequers, and the Dining Room has a frieze of sheepskin. In the little room over the porch, which has the windows dedicating Chequers to the nation, the curtains are Stuart needlework, and just inside the door are two small portraits, one of Mrs Cromwell and one of her little son Oliver, aged two. In the Great Parlour the 16th century panelling is believed to have been made by Dutch refugees, and is elaborately inlaid with holly and bog oak. In the Long Gallery, where Cromwell's sword is hanging by the fireplace (believed to be the one he carried at Marston Moor), there hangs on the wall the original letter he wrote from the battlefield saying " God made them as stubble to our swords."

Ellesborough   Chequers, the Premier's Country House

Dorney   Dorney Court, 16th Century Manor House

TWO TUDOR HOMES

Denham 15th Century Tower   **Gayhurst** Tower Built by Wren

Denham   The Village Beautiful

Among the many other relics in the house are Cromwell's slippers, a mask made in his life for the family, his wife's watch and Bible, Queen Elizabeth's ring (a gem of great beauty), Nelson's watch, and Napoleon's pistols. The pictures hanging everywhere are of very great value, and include The Armourer by Teniers, a lovely portrait of Brigetta Hawtrey by Mark Gheerarts, Rembrandt's Mathematician; a Raeburn portrait and a Gainsborough landscape; a Hoppner and a Reynolds; a wonderful portrait of Lady Jane Grey's sister Mary, and many miniatures. The Prime Minister's country house has rightly one of the most historic of all national collections.

There is a sunken garden made by Lord Lee and in the grounds are trees of immense age—a yew tree looking like a group but springing from one root, one of the oldest and biggest in England; the stump of an elm said to have been planted by a Norman king, in which a new elm has seeded itself; and one of the best tulip trees in England, throwing its shadow over a lead statue of the Goddess of Health in front of the house. On a sundial in one of the gardens is this motto:

Ye houres doe flie,
Full soone we die
In age secure
Ye House and Hills
Alone endure!

It was Frances Cromwell, the Protector's youngest daughter, who inherited Chequers and brought to it the Cromwell treasures now here. Little is known of her, yet she is the subject of some remarkable marriage stories, of which we read in the Middlesex volume under Chiswick, where she lies. The first story declares that men sought to bring about a marriage between Frances Cromwell and Charles the Second, who was not unwilling; the second story tells of the efforts of Jeremiah White, her father's chaplain, to marry her; the third story tells of her marriage to the heir of the Earl of Warwick, who died in nine weeks. A fourth story tells of her marriage to Sir John Russell, who died before their son was born and left her a widow for more than 50 years.

The Three Rectors

EMBERTON. Looking over the Ouse, its fine 14th century church, standing amid farms and fields, with two great chestnuts below it, has handsome buttresses with decorated niches; and a cornice round the chancel in which animals sport among flowers and grotesque heads are watching warily.

In a setting 600 years old there is an angel with outspread wings, and an inscription from Kipling beginning, "No easy hopes or lies shall bring us to our goal." It is modern, but for the rest we are with the past. There is an acutely pointed tower arch, beautiful window tracery, stately arcades, rich carving on the piscina and sedilia, and fine tracery on a font at which children were christened in an England mourning the Black Death. Three traceried arches are saved from the 15th century screen, and in the sanctuary are two beautifully carved chairs. In the chancel is a big brass portrait of John Mordon, a rector under Henry the Fifth. Three rectors who followed him in three later centuries gave more than half their century each to this pulpit: 52 years in the 17th, 51 in the 18th, and 56 in the 19th century.

The Greatest School in the World

ETON. It is Windsor Castle's old neighbour, but we may call it also its old friend, for even if the Battle of Waterloo was not won on the playing fields of Eton the King of England for 500 years has been able to rely on young and old Etonians. It is one of the great nurseries of the English spirit. Perhaps we may think that Eton's place in history is symbolised by its place in the shadow of Windsor Castle, on the banks of England's noblest river, flowing from the University of Oxford past Parliament and St Paul's.

It began in 1440 in the unhappy reign of Henry the Sixth who, in the midst of a tragic life gave his country two of its noblest possessions, Eton and King's College Chapel. His school was for 10 priests, 4 lay clerks, 6 choristers, 25 poor scholars, and 25 poor men; in our own time we shall find on any day within its walls 80 masters and 1200 boys from our leading English families sitting side by side with sons of Indian potentates and foreign rulers. How many boys have passed through Eton we do not know, but there are 15,000 names on the walls, and 16 Prime Ministers have been Etonians.

Its long and narrow street is joined to Windsor by a 19th century bridge across the Thames, where the College boathouse stretches towards the riverside meadow known as the Brocas, a legacy from a Provost long ago, distinguished by a clump of elms flourishing in

BUCKINGHAMSHIRE

their third century. We pass the boys in the High Street, their formal black suits, white ties, and top hats looking a little odd in a small country town. We may notice that they keep usually to the western pavement, but the traveller will pass across to the other side to see the knucklebone floor of a cockpit at the back of an old timbered shop, or the dignified row of 18th century almshouses tucked away, or Bridge House by the Barnes Pool Stream, with a flood-level mark of 1894 on the walls, a reminder of the time when the weather sent all Eton boys home. A few more steps and we are at the heart of the College, the modern buildings on one side, the old on the other. Under an elaborate canopy looking on to the street from the chapel wall is a small statue of William of Waynflete, the first headmaster of Eton, who brought six boys from his cathedral at Winchester as a nucleus for the new school.

In front of the old buildings is a low wall guarding a row of 18th century limes, behind which rises the dignified Upper School built in the reign of Dutch William; this school and St Mary's Chapel form the frontage to the street. We pass through the archway between them into the great court known as the School Yard, with the founder of Eton standing in the centre, Henry the Sixth, cloaked in bronze and bearing the orb and sceptre. He was but a boy himself when he founded Eton, but his golden deed has made his name immortal, although it is still remembered that one morning Eton woke up to find that the sceptre in the king's hand had been changed for a birch rod.

The Upper School rests on a colonnade of round arches forming one side of this beautiful old Court, and along the wall is a bronze frieze with the names of 1157 Etonians who fell in the Great War; nearly 900 won decorations, and 13 the VC. On the stairs are the names of 6000 boys, and in the Long Room are 8000 more, the names of Shelley and Charles James Fox conspicuous among them. In this long hall most of the teaching was done till the new buildings rose last century, and the classes working together made up a scene of crowded chaos. Now the room is crowded only on the Fourth of June, Eton's annual Speech Day. Round the room are busts of famous Etonians with a few patrons to keep them company. Among them are three rulers, George the Third, William the Fourth, and Queen Victoria with Prince Albert; our first Prime Minister Sir

THE KING'S ENGLAND

Robert Walpole, and the greatest Victorian Prime Minister, Mr Gladstone; two of our poets, Shelley and Thomas Gray; a great admiral and a great soldier, Lord Howe and Wellington; and among the rest Lord Chatham, Lord Grenville, Lord North, Lord Grey, Lord Camden, Lord Denham, Lord Wellesley, Fox and Canning, Richard Porson, Sir John Bayley, and Bishop Pearson. In 1939 an addition was made to the college busts by the presentation of Mrs Leigh Hunt's bust of Shelley, showing him with a mass of curly hair.

At the end of the long room is enclosed the desk of one of Eton's most famous headmasters, Dr Keate; its door still has the holes of the screws which one day fastened him in. By the panelled wall of another room here is the whipping-block, and we understand that there is always a new birch waiting in the cupboard; it is remembered that Dr Keate thrashed 100 boys at once after a rebellion in 1832. "Boys," he would say, "you must be pure in heart, for if not I will thrash you till you are."

Turning the corner from the Upper School is the Lower School, little changed since it was built 500 years ago. The schoolroom is one of the oldest in England, and one of the names on the oak shutters was carved in 1552. The heavy desks are cut and notched by generations of boys, and between them runs for the length of the room a double row of rugged wooden pillars supporting the dormitory; they were put up by Sir Henry Wotton, a Provost here who is remembered far beyond these walls by his poem on The Character of a Happy Life.

In front of us as we enter the School Yard is the Eton Tower familiar to us all, set up by Provost Lupton in the 16th century, and reminding us of the famous gateways of St James's Palace and Hampton Court. It has two turrets rising with the arch between them, and above the arch are two oriel windows. Between these is a canopied niche with a statue of the Madonna, and in one of the towers just above the statue the brickwork has been neatly patterned into a pot of lilies. Above the oriel windows and below the battlements is a clock, and the two towers are crowned with open bell turrets, made of timber and set up in 1765.

Passing through the archway we come into Cloister Court, ages old, and with heavy railing enclosing a little patch of grass. Here are the oldest of all the Eton buildings, some of which we may see. Facing the old cloister pump are the stairs leading to the Hall. The west window of the hall shows the scholars of Henry the Seventh at Eton. The line of nails along the top of the panelling was used for many generations for verses written by the boys on long rolls of paper; Pepys found them hanging here and thought several of the poems very good, "and in rolls longer than the whole hall by much." On the walls hang portraits of old Etonians, among them William of Waynflete, Sir Robert Walpole, Archbishop Sumner, Stratford Canning, with Henry the Sixth and George the Third. The hall contains a little organ built for George the Third, a Jacobean screen, and a long shovelboard table once used by the boys. It was originally the library, but 200 years ago a magnificent new building was set up on the south side of the court, with rooms running into one another and a gallery round the walls. Its roof rests on fluted columns, and there is elaborate plaster work in the ceilings. The floor is covered with its original Turkey carpets.

The library is full of treasures, and set about the rooms are busts of the Founder, one of Pallas Athene, and others of Richard Porson and Lord Wellesley. Most of the treasures are in glass cases, the earliest being deeds of the 11th, 12th, and 13th centuries with fine seals attached. One charter has an impression of the Great Seal of King John, and another deed has the autograph of William Rufus. A deed drawn up 500 years ago has the earliest known picture of Windsor Castle. There are three Caxtons, and books and broadsides printed by Wynkyn de Worde. Perhaps the chief treasure is the copy of the Mazarin Bible printed and illuminated in Germany in the middle of the 15th century. It was the first book printed from movable metal types, and this is one of the six existing copies in the original binding of oak boards, covered with leather. Keeping company with this precious book is Mary Tudor's Book of Hours.

There is a manuscript copy of the first English comedy, Ralph Roister Doister, written by the headmaster Nicholas Udall 400 years ago. Here is Shelley's pocket edition of Euripides with his pencil notes on the margin, a book with an autograph of Thomas Gray, and others with the signatures of Edward Gibbon, George Herbert, Ben Jonson, and Robert Walpole. We noticed also a letter from Nelson begging that his nephew might have a holiday.

At the back of the library is the dining-hall, with a fine oriel window by which is an iron reading-desk fixed to the wall, at which a boy would read aloud while the others ate their meals. Events in college history are shown in a modern window, and over the fireplace is a contemporary picture of William of Waynflete painted on oak. Out of the dining-hall we come to the panelled buttery, with Queen Anne furniture and a 17th century bread bin. Here is kept the college plate, including a coconut cup which has come down from the 15th century. The old square kitchen, with its octagonal roof and lantern, has a 17th century roasting spit worked by elaborate clockwork.

Across the cloisters is the Audit Room, with a collection of portraits (one by Reynolds of his uncle, and one of Provost Warre by George Richmond), and near by is the Provost's Parlour, a fine Jacobean room with portraits of kings and queens. Its quiet and beautiful garden stretches behind it, and at the end of this is an old English garden laid out in our time by a young king who came to Eton, the King of Siam. Standing by a wall in this garden is a bronze figure of Perseus holding aloft the Gorgon's head, and about the garden stand tall earthenware jars found under the school floors. There is another small garden by the Drawing School, a formal space with walls of mellow brick in memory of another eastern ruler, Prince Frederick Duleep Singh. On a stone seat is the prayer, Remember Frederick Duleep Singh. Strange that two eastern rulers should be remembered here by little English gardens.

For the new buildings of Eton we must pass through the Cloister Court through the great School Yard and cross the street to the memorial building built after the South African War; we see from the street the fine dome of the library, capped with a turret and surrounded with carved urns. The dignified pillared vestibule has niches with bronze statuettes representing the four cardinal virtues, and a marble bust of Winthrop Mackworth Praed, who started a library for the boys. The great hall, seating 1200, is lined with 30 groups of twin pillars rising to the curved plaster ceiling. In the apse is a stage on which is an organ with 3372 pipes built round a little old instrument brought from the Duke of Marlborough's English church at Rotterdam. Let into the handsome panelling round the walls are fine portraits, and the hall is decorated with flags and groups of weapons.

BUCKINGHAMSHIRE

In one of the bays is the foundation-stone laid by Princess Alice in memory of the 129 Etonians who fell in the Boer War, and near the stone are busts of Queen Victoria and Lord Salisbury. In front of this bay stands one of the most magnificent Books of Remembrance we have seen, with the names of all Etonians who served, the names of those who fell being in gold. The book was on exhibition in Paris in 1914 when the Great War broke out and narrowly escaped destruction. At the east end of the hall is a richly carved screen on which is Sargent's masterpiece of Miss Jane Evans, the last of the Dames to keep a boarding-house here, and Laszlo's portrait of Alfred Lyttleton. Among the portraits are those of Lord Roberts and Lord Balfour, Edmund Warre (by Sargent), Archibald Philip, Lord Rosebery, Lord Curzon, and E. C. Austen-Leigh (by Charles Furse). In the corridor are books and prints and more portraits, including one of Mr Gladstone and one of Sir Walter Durnford. There is also a bust of Lady Scott, and in the cloister outside is Lady Scott's relief in bronze of Captain Oates, who lies somewhere near Scott's tent in Antarctica.

A step across the corridor brings us to the fine museum, of which perhaps the chief treasure is the manuscript of Gray's Elegy. With it is the manuscript of his Ode on the Prospect of Eton. There are many beautiful and interesting things from Egypt, including a rare collection of vivid funeral masks, many Roman and Byzantine coins, a bust of William Johnson Cory, the poet, and a statue of the Apollo Belvedere.

In this memorial building is the school library, which has been described as one of the most beautiful and stately rooms in the country. The library is octagonal, and its dome is borne on 16 columns. One of its most interesting possessions is the desk of Dr Johnson, on which lies the first edition of his dictionary. Near it is a little black bust of Dr Keate made by a man who was hanged, and close by the bust is the headmaster's cocked hat, which he threw down at the end of his headmastership, saying, "This will not be used again." There is a pocket book with autograph poems by Shelley, a school book belonging to Wellington, a fine model of an Elizabethan ship, and 20,000 books.

Hereabouts are more associated buildings, science school, music rooms, laboratories, drawing school, picture gallery, and so on. In the music school down Southmeadow Lane is the manuscript of

THE KING'S ENGLAND

Sir Charles Parry's famous song, "Oft in the Stilly Night," which he wrote one afternoon at Eton.

We have yet to see the two fine chapels of Eton College, the old and the new. The old chapel fronts the street with the great court side by side with the Upper School. The new chapel belongs to the Lower School, and is among the new buildings, down Keate's Lane.

The old chapel of St Mary rose on a foundation stone laid by Henry the Sixth in 1440, and has been much changed through the centuries. It is raised about 13 feet above the ground, to save it from floods. The chapel has the medieval turrets at the corners, though the pinnacles are new. On the west wall is a statue of William of Waynflete by Sir Arthur Blomfield. Between the buttresses the boys used to play the game of Fives.

The plan of St Mary's is a little unusual, what is usually the nave being known as the ante-chapel, set transeptwise about 60 feet by 30. A statue of Henry the Sixth in white marble looks across to the fine stone screen under which we pass into the choir; the king is sculptured by John Bacon in white marble and wears his crown and ermine robe, his wistful face looking upward and his hands clasping a model of his chapel. The screen through which we pass into the choir was designed by George Edmund Street, architect of the Law Courts, and is the dominating feature of the ante-chapel, with two towers in two stages, open at the ground and with open traceried windows above, crowned with battlements and faced with heraldic carving. Between these towers is a richly carved archway surmounted by a stone screen, on which rests the organ, its pipes neatly disposed. On the western side of the screen are the only medieval statues in the chapel, fine little figures of St George with the dragon and Edmund the Martyr with two arrows. There are four flags in the ante-chapel—a white ensign flown by Admiral Jellicoe at Jutland, two tattered standards carried at Waterloo and in the Crimea, and a French flag of deep interest, because it was recaptured by an Old Etonian under dramatic circumstances in the Great War. It hangs on one side of the organ, facing Admiral Jellicoe's flag, and this is its story. Walter George Fletcher joined the Army with the outbreak of the war, and just before his first leave was due he saw the French flag, which had been captured by the enemy, hung in scorn on a tree.

Eton   The Upper School

Eton   The Lower School

Eton — School Yard and Lupton's Tower

Eton — The Cloister Court

The 15th Century Chapel of Eton College

Eton College Hall

Bletchley
Corbel of Aisle Roof

Castlethorpe
Carved Heads on Font

Lathbury
King's Head by Porch

Haversham   The Monument of Lady Clinton

Clifton Reynes
14th Century Font

Cheddington
Jacobean Pulpit

Great Hampden
13th Century Font

ANCIENT TREASURES OF BUCKINGHAMSHIRE CHURCHES

BUCKINGHAMSHIRE

He brought the flag down to safety and here it hangs in the chapel he loved, serving as his memorial:

> *Swiftly you won your uttermost desire,*
> *Dream lover, lover of Eton, heart of fire,*
> *You served the school and England, and abide*
> *Safe with the flag you saved, and satisfied.*

Looking across the screen from his corner of the ante-chapel sits Joseph Goodall, as if teaching from the book on his knee. The statue was begun by Chantrey and finished by Henry Weekes. Dr Goodall ruled over Eton for the first few years of the 19th century and has been called the ideal headmaster of an English public school. About him are some 300-year-old benches, and on the wall beside him is a range of traceried niches which once held the statues of a vanished reredos. In the corner to which Dr Goodall is looking stands the font, a white marble octagon, on a pavement in which is a portrait of Bishop Abraham, in whose memory the font was given by Eton scholars. It has a fine oak canopy.

An interesting group of brasses has been fixed on the wall by the font and by the Goodall monument, one of the 15th but most of the 16th century. The oldest is a portrait of a master, Thomas Barker, rector of Petworth, shown in his cassock and cap; he is dated 1489. These ten are all 16th century: Henry Bost under a triple canopy; Richard Arden in priest's robes; Thomas Edgecomb in his master's cassock and hooded cape; Richard Lord Grey in armour; Canon Boutrod in cassock and surplice; William Horman; a priest with a chalice; Elizabeth Stokys in Elizabethan dress, wearing a tight dress with fur cuffs and with a tassel on the end of an embroidered girdle; an unknown woman in a fur-trimmed gown; a Fellow kneeling in cap and cloak; an unknown priest in cassock and surplice. In the floor are the gravestones of Sir Henry Wotton and Sir Henry Savile, both Provosts and both with houses named after them, Wotton House being new, Savile House old.

We pass under the screen into the choir, 150 feet by 40, divided by eight bays with clustered shafts on the walls and transomed windows of five lights. Had we come before the war, or even some years after it, we should have been impressed by the long line of canopied stalls on each long wall, but for these today we must go down to the noble school chapel at Lancing in Sussex; here at Eton is the wall above the 70 stalls, the canopies having been removed to reveal a wonderful series of medieval paintings, believed to be the work of one William Baker, paid for by William of Waynflete. It is unfortunate that the paintings, which had been covered up by whitewash, were rediscovered during restorations in the middle of the Victorian Era when taste was at so low a depth that these frescoes were thought poor dull things, and many of them were scraped off the walls while others were covered up. Once more we are in debt to an artist for faithful copying. While the authorities were debating in 1847, and canopies were being set over the stalls to hide the paintings, Mr R. H. Essex made copies of them, and when the stalls were taken away to Lancing in 1923 the remaining paintings were cleaned and restored from the Essex drawings.

Originally there were 32 scenes and 36 figures, but all that now remain are seven saints, five scenes, and a fragment on the south side, and on the north seven saints, four scenes, and two fragments. The scenes on the south side portray the ancient story of the Empress, similar to Chaucer's Man of Lawe's Tale. The figures are St Catherine with book and sword, St Barbara with tower and palm, St Apollonia with pincers, St Ursula with an arrow, St Dorothy with flowers and fruit, St Lucy with palm and book, and St Juliana leading a chained demon. The scenes on the north show miracles performed by the Madonna, and the recognisable figures are St Sidwell with a scythe, St Martha leading a dragon, St Etheldreda with a pastoral staff, St Elizabeth with three loaves of bread, St Radegund in nun's clothing, and St Margaret coming forth from a dragon.

Opening off the choir are two chapels, the memorial chapel to the Etonian heroes of the Great War, the Lupton Chapel in memory of Provost Lupton, who built the tower in the great court and was buried here with much pomp 400 years ago. The chapel is entered through a beautiful stone screen in which is the letter R for Roger and the letters LUP on a tun, the rebus of the founder. At the top of the screen are two small figures of Victory, one reproducing a Greek figure from Naples (given by a mother in memory of her only child who died for England), the other cast from Victory in the hand of Canova's colossal statue of Napoleon. On the floor of this chapel is the brass of Roger Lupton, who is wearing the mantle of the Garter with the cross of St George on the shoulder, which he wore as a canon of Windsor. From his brass Provost Lupton looks up to a great boss hanging from the rich fan-vaulting of the roof. On the east wall of his chapel is Benjamin West's picture of the Presentation in the Temple, and on the west wall is a brass with the names of the 129 Etonians who lost their lives in the Boer War.

The memorial shrine, a small chapel only 16 feet by 12 but 20 feet high, has east windows looking into the Lupton Chapel and a pierced stone screen with three lights looking into the choir. The chapel was designed by Mr Walter Godfrey, and its most impressive feature, the north window, was designed by the Provost of the day, Dr Montague James. It is this window which gives the keynote to this chapel of remembrance. A great red cross covers the width of the window, and is filled with figures of Our Lord, saints, and heroes, illumined by the rosy glow. The cross is encircled by a rainbow, with small scenes from the Bible in the spandrels. In the tracery is King Henry the Sixth kneeling before Christ, presenting two Eton boys. At the four corners of the chapel are four archangels carved in oak: Gabriel, Michael, Raphael, and Uriel, all the figures being painted in ivory and gold. The altar rails are 17th century and on the top rail are cut the names of some of the boys who used to sit beside them when they were in the choir. The two altar candle-sticks came from the chapel of Catesby House, of Gunpowder Plot ill-fame. The roof of this small shrine is panelled in oak elaborately carved with bosses in medieval style. The east window is filled with glass inscribed with the names of the Fallen, decorated with a cross and the Lilies of Eton. The design of the roof is by Gordon Godfrey, the oak carvings are by Burns Brown, the east window is by Jessie M. Jacob, and most of the stone work is by C. F. Bridgman.

The reredos and the brass lectern are both of much interest, the reredos being part of the South African Memorial. It is of harmoniously coloured tapestries, the centrepiece being Burne-Jones's Adoration, carved out by William Morris, with the side panels of angels worked from Burne-Jones designs for Salisbury Cathedral. Over one of the tapestries are the names of the weavers who wove the tapestries at Merton. The lectern is one of the oldest possessions of the chapel, coming from the 15th century. It is said that it was much damaged during the Civil War, and it is recorded that the college then paid sixpence for its removal. At the corners are the emblems of the Evangelists, and there are four lions on the stem.

There is little to say of the windows here, but one or two monuments remain to be seen. With the altar rails is the Jacobean memorial to Provost Murray, who was tutor to Charles Stuart and is here in his coloured robes, smiling across the sanctuary, with his oak skeleton tucked away below. Facing him on a canopied tomb is the marble figure of Provost Hawtrey, the last man buried in the chapel. His kindly face is full of sympathy, and near him lies Headmaster Balston, a 19th century Provost smiling in his sleep. Between these monuments hangs G. F. Watts's Galahad, given by the artist.

These are the 13 Etonians who won the VC in the Great War and are remembered with their fellows in this memorial shrine. Captain A. H. Batten-Pooll had his hand shattered immediately he entered the enemy's lines, but continued to direct and cheer his men and to rescue the wounded. Colonel A. D. Borton, in a dark and unknown country, captured a position with fearless leadership which was "an inspiring example to the whole brigade." General J. V. Campbell captured objects of the highest importance and rallied his men with wonderful gallantry at a critical time. Major La Touche Congreve showed most conspicuous bravery for 14 days before his death, his constant gallantry inspiring all. Lieutenant G. H. Drummond was in charge of a vessel following the Vindictive to Ostend, and remained on the bridge severely wounded; "It was due to the indomitable courage of this very gallant officer that the majority of the crew of the Vindictive were rescued." Lieutenant Dunville remained at his post severely wounded and directed a successful raid. Colonel Elliott-Cooper rushed out of his dug-out unarmed and directed his men so that they forced the enemy back 600 yards. Colonel L. P. Evans forced a garrison to surrender by rushing at a machine-gun emplacement and firing his revolver through the loophole. Captain J. R. N. Graham stayed a heavy counter-attack and averted a critical situation. Captain Francis Grenfell won the first VC of the war for gallantry in action against unbroken infantry and in saving guns; his story is told under Beaconsfield. Captain J. R. Gribble, whose fate is unknown, was last seen fighting with his company surrounded at close range; he prevented for some hours the enemy obtaining mastery of a ridge, and enabled his brigade, another garrison, and three batteries to be withdrawn. Major P. H. Hansen rushed forward under heavy fire over 300 yards of open ground to reach the scrub which had been set on fire, so saving six wounded men from burning to death. Lieutenant Boyd-Rochfort, scorning a chance to save himself, seized a bomb and flung it over a parapet to save his men.

The modern chapel of the Lower School is apparently modelled on the medieval chapel, with its fine range of windows, though here the glass is a splendid feature. The architect was Sir Arthur Blomfield, and the decorative plan was part of the memorial for the Great War. The exterior is a good example of modern Tudor architecture, with a turret at one end and pinnacles along the parapet. The lofty roof is of chestnut. The altar frontal of old brocade, the massive silver and blue enamel cross of Christ in Glory, and the six silver candlesticks are given by a sister in memory of her brother, an Etonian drowned on his holidays. The processional cross was given by Arthur Christopher Benson. Four tapestries on the wall, designed by Lady Chilston, represent the boyhood of St George, the appeal of a woman for help (typifying Belgium calling to England), St George responding, the martyrdom, and the patron saint as protector.

The nave windows, all in memory of Etonians, are by Kempe, and represent the Virtues, each with an ideal figure centred between men and women of the Bible typical of the Virtues, and small scenes illustrating events in their lives. The Virtues represented are Reverence, Wisdom, Justice, Hope, Faith, Charity, Humility, Fortitude, Prudence, and Learning. In the sanctuary are more windows with the Annunciation and the Salutation, the angels appearing to the Shepherds, and the Presentation and the Doctors in the Temple. In the gallery are two-light windows with figures of Arthur and Galahad, St Alban and St George, Mary and Martha of Bethany, King Wenceslaus and St Pancras.

All about Eton is something to draw the eye, to impress the mind, or to touch the heart. We may see the famous playing fields, the Poet's Walk beloved by Thomas Gray, the Fellows' Pond, the Fellows' Eyot from which they watch the fireworks on Romney Island on the Fourth of June, Romney Lock where the King's boats are saluted on swan-upping days, or Black Potts, where Izaak Walton used to fish. Out in the playing-fields the youth of Eton is not permitted to forget that it plays for England, for here we came upon a stone to an Eton boy, an only son, who was 20 when the Great War broke out and was shot down while flying in Mesopotamia in the year it ended. He was John Henry Campbell, of the Cameron Highlanders, and, being captured by the Turks, he escaped, and travelled 60 miles on foot in the desert, but died of exposure 15 miles from the British Lines. Nor are they permitted to forget their Founder, for every year on May 21, the day Henry the Sixth died a prisoner in the Tower, three white lilies are laid on the spot where the king was struck down at prayer by the bloodstained Richard. The lilies are provided from the interest on £10 of War Loan, and are removed the next day and buried. Every year also on Founder's Day three lilies are laid on the king's grave in St George's, the choir singing the King's Prayer.

It is a pretty remembrance, the purity of the Lily for the king who strove to make peace between the quarrelling Houses of the Rose, and we may hope it will long continue as a symbol of the interest of Etonians in the past and their faith in the future. Floreat Etona!

Wolsey's Clerk of Works

FARNHAM ROYAL. The Farnham of the Saxons became royal when the manor was granted to a Norman with the hereditary duty of supporting the right arm of the king as he held the sceptre at his coronation.

The Elizabethan rectory, a timber-framed house with gabled wings, has its original dormer windows and quaint chimneys. The fine elms in the churchyard look older than most of the church, which was largely remade last century. But the chancel is Norman, as is one of the windows; the piscina was carved when Normans and Saxons were blending, and a doorway through which we no longer pass was built 600 years ago. On a wall is a modern painting of the Adoration of the Wise Men. There is a 15th century font and an Elizabethan chalice.

A tragic chapter of history comes to life as we read the brass inscription to Eustace Mascall, for he was associated with the fall of Wolsey. He was clerk of the works when Wolsey was the foremost figure in Europe, building his college at Oxford. Mascall knew that he was building the finest college ever planned, a college intended to be a little world of civil and ecclesiastical learning, to dominate the University, and to be the centre of a new intellectual movement. His master fell with the work unfinished and the college was involved in his forfeiture, saved at the eleventh hour, and continued on a smaller scale under the name of Christ Church, with Wolsey forgotten. But Mascall was remembered, and for the last 17 years of his life he was Henry the Eighth's Chief Clerk of Accounts for the royal buildings within 20 miles of London.

A sword hangs in an aisle above a tablet to Surgeon-General Henry Bellew, who, born in India, was not only a gifted surgeon but was deeply versed in native languages, habits, and beliefs. He won the confidence of rulers and their subjects, and by teaching simple hygiene he contributed largely to the health and happiness of vast numbers of Indians.

Fearless Father and Fearless Son

FAWLEY. It lies on a hilltop overlooking the splendour of the Thames, and we reach the riverside through woods leading down to Fawley Court, which had a heronry of over 70 nests when the last census was taken. It was refashioned by Sir Christopher Wren and occupied for 200 years by the Freemans, whose mausoleum is in the churchyard.

The impressive church tower, 16th century at the top and 14th century at the base, still serves as a porch. The nave is late 12th century; the chancel has been made new.

The magnificent carving on the pulpit, with cherubs at six corners, and on the reading desk, with acanthus leaves, is attributed to Grinling Gibbons. There is 17th century carving of fruit and flowers on the panelling of the chancel, and many seats have Jacobean enrichment. On a fine 17th century tomb, with painted heraldry and figures of Mercy and Justice, lie Sir James Whitelock and his wife. A fearless judge, he was the father of Bulstrode Whitelock, who refused to sit in judgment on Charles Stuart.

For two generations the Whitelocks were conspicuous in national affairs. Sir James, the father, was twin brother of a Whitelocke who died at sea fighting under Drake. A distinguished lawyer, he sternly resisted the pretensions of James to rule by prerogative, and was imprisoned by a gross breach of privilege. He prospered under

Charles, and filled various judicial offices. He once drove at high speed from here to Westminster to adjourn the law sittings owing to plague, not daring to stay anywhere going or returning for fear of infection. He boldly contested the legality of forced loans, but, growing more compliant, was one of the judges who consented to the proceedings against Sir John Eliot and his associates in the fight for Parliament, and concurred in the judgment.

Bulstrode Whitelocke, his eldest son, musician, scholar, and lawyer, loved this countryside, but was called to great affairs, and as a member of the Long Parliament voted against the arbitrary measures of Charles, and was chairman of the committee for the impeachment of Strafford. During the Civil War his house was pillaged and garrisoned by Prince Rupert, but Whitelocke, although serving with the Commonwealth forces, repeatedly attempted mediation, and was a member of commissions sent by Parliament to negotiate with Charles. Appointed one of the committee to formulate charges against the king, he condemned the trial, but after the execution urged Cromwell to accept the crown.

He held many posts under the Protectorate, being Keeper of the Great Seal, and for a time Speaker. He was the constant adviser of Cromwell on foreign affairs. Through his eyes we see Cromwell without his armour, at home, merry with music. "He commonly called for tobacco, pipes, and candle, and would now and then take tobacco himself; then he would fall again to his serious and great business."

A member of Cromwell's House of Lords, and Lord President of the Council, he was loyal to Richard, but with the fall of the second Protectorate he was one of the first to open negotiations with Charles the Second and to send him money, his plan (defeated by Monk) being to recall the exile, not unconditionally, but on terms.

The Rich Man Who Became Poor

FENNY STRATFORD. It is on the Watling Street of the Romans. The 18th century brick church, replacing one destroyed by fire, sprang from the devotion of Browne Willis to his grandfather, one of Charles Stuart's surgeons, who made important advances in our knowledge of the structure and functions of the brain, and probed the age-old mystery of diabetes. Here is his

East Claydon   The Way to Church

Fingest　　　　　　　　　　The Rare Norman Church

memorial; he rests in Westminster Abbey. Here lies Browne Willis himself, the antiquary. His tombstone, upright beside an altar, has a Latin inscription telling of his act of homage to the great surgeon, but omitting to mention that because his grandfather lived in St Martin's Lane, London, this church was dedicated to St Martin, and a fund was established by Browne Willis for a yearly service, a dinner, and the firing of cannon on St Martin's day.

But no longer is the popgun cannon fired at the festival of the saint and the surgeon, for both days fall on November 11, and are therefore merged in a greater solemnity shared by all Christian peoples. One memorial of the grandfather is in the vestry, and an engraving of his portrait in the Bodleian library.

Browne Willis, brought to rest here in 1760, was a rich scholar reduced to penury but not to despair, a man whose benefactions outran his resources. Additions have been made to his building, but his roof is here with the arms of those who helped him boldly painted on its 40 divisions. An aisle window has 17th century glass, with the heads of a woman and a Roman soldier and two shields of the Fortescues; and there are more shields in 18th century glass, among them those of Oxford and Cambridge, Oxford's held by a woman in a yellow cloak, and that of Cambridge by a woman in Oxford blue.

In the nave hangs a modern picture entitled Humanity, by Frank King, in which are grouped men, women, and children, with the shadowy figure of Christ in the background, His yearning arms outstretched towards them. But the real touch of humanity here seemed to us to centre about the pathetic figure of the old scholar who built this church as what he considered a small tribute to his hero and, by a succession of such acts of beneficence, brought himself to poverty. Here his great days are remembered, and his name and fame shine bright.

The Norman Tower

FINGEST. Overhung by a sharp, wooded bluff, with the Hambledon valley winding away at its feet, it lies in a deep hollow of the Chilterns, remote and lovely. Its old name, of Danish origin, means a meeting place. Near the shady church a wall still stands of the palace they built here 800 years ago, when the church was bigger than it is.

The tower and nave of the church are both Norman, the nave being slender in comparison with the strong tall tower, which has a secretive look, as if it were meant for defence. It is a striking spectacle. Tradition says that the nave was once the chancel, and the lowest stage of the tower was the beginning of the nave. In that case the superb Norman arch which spans the whole width of the tower would have been the chancel arch. The present chancel was built in the 13th century, the east window in the 15th.

The tower rises in three stages and is capped by a rare double saddleback roof added in the 18th or 19th century. Small double Norman windows built in each face give a perfect and finished look to the top stage; in the lowest stage is a 13th century window, a splendid example of its kind, marked by beautiful detail in the carving of the shafts and capitals; and there are very small windows looking odd in the great mass of the wall.

The church has another Norman window deeply splayed in the thick walls, and two slender lancets in the chancel.

Few churches have retained so much of their original structure. The beams and brackets of medieval days are still to be seen in the high pitched roof. In the 15th century font are the staples to which the cover was locked to prevent the holy water being stolen by witches and there is a 17th century chest of deal and the churchyard has two 17th century gateways.

The Farmer and His Sheep

FLEET MARSTON. On a little hill overhanging the Aylesbury Plain lie the few cottages, the farm, and the church which make up this solitary place. The ancient church, set in an oval churchyard, was built in the 12th century and restored in the 14th and 15th. The splendid old roof of the nave has five handsome queenposts 500 years old, which, as we see from the traces that remain, must have been glorious in colour in the 15th century. There are also traces of painting on the sides of a window and on the doorway of the nave, and more colour in a few fragments of 14th century glass in the chancel. The 600-year-old chancel arch is decorated with half-open buds on the capitals. The oldest possession of the church is the plain font, crudely made in the 13th century; the newest is the oak lectern carved with the names of the three men who went out from this small place to the Great War and did not come home.

BUCKINGHAMSHIRE

Near by is the hamlet of Quarrendon, now little more than a farm, which has been here for 300 years. In one of its fields are the ruins of a 13th century chapel which Queen Elizabeth would see when she stayed in the neighbourhood with Sir Henry Lee, her staunch friend and one of England's best farmers. His thousands of sheep roamed over Aylesbury Plain, and he lost 3000 in a great storm of 1570. A manuscript in the British Museum tells of the grandeur of his funeral at Quarrendon. His house has vanished with all signs of his grave; only the farm and traces of Civil War entrenchments remain to tell of the past of this small place.

The Roman Lady

FOSCOTT. Sixteen hundred years ago a Roman lady kept house within hail of the spot where a small medieval church now stands. Some of the money she counted, and some of the leaden pipes which carried water then, were dug up last century, together with a perfect square of tessellated pavement on which her sandalled feet would walk; it is now part of the floor of a temple of music at Stowe School.

Encircling the church and the cottages is the park of a 17th century manor house from the slopes of which we look out on the valley of the Ouse. The workmen who in later centuries restored the Norman church have left us its sturdy walls, so thick that the church bell, set inside one of them, never swings beyond the face of it. To this severe structure were added details which delight us today. We pass through a plain Norman doorway and see in the roof fantastic corbels of the 14th century, among them a man with a pig's ears and his friend with a lion's mane. Over the chancel's 14th century doorway is the face of a woman in a wimple and of a man in a hood, and at the ends of the chancel arch are pleasant little shapes of opening buds carved 600 years ago when the chancel was new. Another woman's face looks sorrowfully down from a chancel window, all that remains of the ancient glass which once filled them. The fragments are 16th century. The stairs and both doorways of the roodloft remain from the days before the Reformation, there are traces of texts on the walls from the 16th century, a medieval piscina, 17th century panelling in the pulpit and 17th century altar rails, and the village is summoned to worship by a 14th century bell.

THE KING'S ENGLAND
Napoleon's Debts

FULMER. It is Arcadia, dreaming in a vale amid noble woods, with memories of great names and great days. Its church, much refashioned, has still its 15th century doorway, through which its builder, Sir Marmaduke Dayrell, must often have passed. Lord of the manor, he rebuilt the church in 1610, and he lies within it, his inscription telling us that he served Elizabeth in her wars by land and sea, and after in her household, was treasurer to two Stuart sovereigns, and was "favoured by all these renowned princes, and employed in matters of great trust for the space of 50 years."

Here he is in armour on a canopied monument of great splendour, his wife in black with two bearded sons, each son kneeling face to face with his wife and their children. On the canopy are mystic figures and cherubs.

Four faded old lights in a nave window show us pictures of an elephant trampling a woman, a Cupid on a winged horse riding over two crowned figures, a queen on horseback with a Cupid at her feet, and Death astride a horse which is stamping a woman underfoot—all symbolism as strange and unlovely as any we remember to have seen in our English windows.

Fulmer Place is an 18th century house with a strange history, built on the site of the old manor by Richard Eskrigge, high sheriff of the county, whose grandson Richard Owen lived here, a merchant prince with great contracts from Napoleon for the supply of the French troops at St Dominique. During the war with England Napoleon repudiated his English debts, and Owen was beggared, being driven from Fulmer Place to die heartbroken and to leave a sorely embarrassed family. Fifty years afterwards his son Sir Richard Owen, world-famous as our greatest anatomist, but very poor, came to visit his ancestral home; and in his letters we read that he saw his father's fishponds, plucked a leaf for his sister from an old apple tree, and suddenly came face to face with the owner, who welcomed him most kindly as the great-grandson of the founder of the house.

Sir Richard longed for this home of his ancestors to the end of his days, but he never saw it again. It seems odd to reflect that had Napoleon paid his debts our famous scientist might have been born

BUCKINGHAMSHIRE

in the home of Sir Marmaduke Dayrell, which Richard Eskrigge rebuilt two centuries ago.

A Man and 500 Churches

GAWCOTT. Beautiful lace was made by hand in its old cottages long before machinery came to make it. The old cottages are older than the church, which was made new during the great religious revival last century at the time of the Oxford Movement. In the churchyard is a granite memorial in memory of the men who fell in France, and in the church is a brass to one of them, Andrew Melless, the vicar's young son. There is a tablet to a vicar who was the father of one of our famous church architects; he was Thomas Scott, who lies here. He was a famous Biblical commentator in his day and his father was a great friend of the poet Cowper. His son was Sir Gilbert Scott who was born here in 1811 and inherited from his father a love of old buildings. He became an architect, and his first notable work was the martyrs' memorial at Oxford, an adaptation of the 13th century Eleanor crosses.

This at one bound established the young architect's fame, and he became the chief architect of the age, his work extending to the Continent, where he built a great Lutheran church at Hamburg. At home he built the fine town hall at Preston and St Pancras Station, and from the time of his appointment as architect to Ely Cathedral and Westminster Abbey he practically presided over the architecture of the country.

Reluctantly abandoning Gothic for Renaissance, he designed Government offices for Whitehall, but returned to his favourite manner with the Albert Memorial, modelled on a 13th century reliquary, and, like so much of his work, absurdly out of place. His prodigious record included the building or restoration of 38 home and colonial cathedrals, abbeys, and priories, 474 churches, 26 schools, 23 parsonages, 58 monuments, 42 houses, 27 public buildings, 16 colleges, and 10 college chapels. He became professor of architecture at the Royal Academy, and lectured brilliantly. He wrote a story of his life with a diverting picture of Gawcott as it was in his father's early days, when the road was made impassable by a pit dug in a badger hunt. He died in 1878 and sleeps in Westminster Abbey, having done much fine work in his long career and much that most of us would like to see undone.

A mile away, at Lenborough, is the 17th century farmhouse, with gabled dormer windows and its original chimneys, which was for long the home of a branch of the Lincolnshire family of Ingoldsby. Here was born Sir Richard Ingoldsby, who entered the Civil War under John Hampden, signed the death-warrant of Charles Stuart, secured royal favour at the Restoration, sat in four Parliaments, and sleeps in Hartwell church.

Drake House and Wren Church

GAYHURST. It has distinction indeed, for it has a house sold by Francis Drake and a church built by Christopher Wren. The house is the most magnificent home in the north of Buckinghamshire, built in Queen Elizabeth's reign and given by her to Drake as a reward for his voyage round the world. Drake did not want it and sold it the next day to William Mulsho, who refashioned it into the beautiful place we see. In one of its rooms are two legal documents concerning the house, both with the portrait of the queen and one with the signature of Francis Drake. The doorway of the gabled porch is flanked by fluted columns rising to the second storey, and over the doorway is a dragon's head. One of the walls is three feet thick. Across the lawn in front are two medieval fishponds now resplendent as a water garden.

The house came quickly into history, for Mary Mulsho the heiress married Everard Digby, and here he involved himself in Gunpowder Plot. Here his famous son Kenelm was born, and from here the plotting father was taken to the Tower. After the discovery of the famous plot the conspirators rode to a fixed meeting-place at desperate speed, 80 miles in a night, and with death before them Digby deserted his companions. He spent two miserable months in the Tower and was sentenced to death, being drawn on a hurdle to St Paul's churchyard and there hanged with ghastly barbarity. The two sons he left behind did much to redeem his ill fame, for one became a General on the king's side in the Civil War, and the other made a considerable reputation as a writer, a diplomatist, and a naval commander.

By the house stands the church, designed by Wren for George Wrighte, who bought the house in due course and enlarged it in the reign of Queen Anne. The low square tower has a cupola, and the beautiful interior has carved wooden coping in the chancel. It has a three-decker pulpit with a beautiful canopy, and a monument with a dragon's head crest in memory of Sir Nathan Wrighte, who lies here with his son George, There is a statue of Sir Nathan by Roubillac showing him in his legal robes, for Sir Nathan was one of the King's Counsel at the trial of the Seven Bishops.

Dutch William Dying

GERRARD'S CROSS. Except for its Saxon camp, it has little that is old; the church has yet to complete its century. A Byzantine building with an Italian campanile, looking strangely foreign in this lovely English setting, it has dignity, and the fine light interior, with massive pillars supporting the painted dome, is stately and impressive. The church was the gift of two sisters in memory of George Alexander Reid, an army officer who sat in Parliament for Windsor.

Facing the common is Bulstrode Park, which we found menaced by hard times and up for sale. Here history has been made from which the village derives reflected glory. In the park is a great defensive earthwork. It was from here, the story runs, that Saxons, bestriding bulls instead of horses, made a night attack on the Normans, who fled in panic before enemies so strangely mounted. The Conqueror forgave the assailants, whereupon the doughty Saxon chief assumed the name of Bulstrode, and the park shared his title. The estate passed to the infamous Judge Jeffreys, who rebuilt the house, and to this house afterwards came Hans William Bentinck, who began as page to William of Orange and had a romantic career. He risked his life to nurse him through a disfiguring disease (by which he himself was afterwards stricken), sailed with him to England when he came to take the throne and served him as soldier, ambassador, and adviser with only one clouded interval till the end, when he was Earl of Portland.

As Dutch William lay dying he called for Bentinck, whose name was the last audible word he uttered. Bentinck bent over him, and the king whispered words unheard. Taking the hand of his earliest and best-loved friend, William pressed it tenderly to his heart and died still holding it. Bentinck died here in 1709, and was buried in Westminster Abbey.

Bulstrode was long the home of the Dukes of Portland. In the second duke's time it received the famous Portland Vase, now one of the borrowed treasures of the British Museum. The third duke, after having been twice Prime Minister, made the house a centre of political influence. For a century it was one of the most famous homes in the country, but its glory and its ancient sway can return no more.

Two Discoveries

GRANBOROUGH. It has a few thatched cottages and a church of great surprise. Twenty generations have passed through its doorway and more than 20 have been christened at this plain font. The roof of the chancel is older than the ships of Columbus.

The church has strangely and happily discovered two rare treasures. One is an alabaster panel 15 inches high carved with the Crucifixion, probably as part of a medieval reredos. It was found built into the gable of a farm in the village, and is now preserved under glass near the chancel arch. The second discovery was made in the church itself towards the end of last century when there was found built into a niche of the wall what is called a chrismatory, a vessel which held the holy oil in the days before the Reformation. The vessel found here, six inches long, is of pewter, and fitted with three inner cups, two with lids to which are attached hooks for the tow used in anointing. As these vessels played a vital part in church ritual they were eagerly sought and destroyed at the Reformation, and this one, hidden by a priest who hoped for better days, must have lain in concealment for three centuries.

Many a child of medieval days was christened with this pewter relic, after which a piece of linen, called a chrism, was applied to its head to prevent removal of the oil. If such an infant died within a month it was called a chrisom child, or a christom child, so that for once Dame Quickly used good English in Shakespeare when, in her immortal description of the death of Falstaff, she declares that he "made a finer end and went away an it had been any Christom child, between twelve and one, even at the turning o' the tide."

Through the 600-year-old chancel arch we have a delightful peep of the east window, with the Crucifixion and the two Marys. The sanctuary walls round the windows are painted with angels. There is a brightly coloured roll of honour, done by a vicar of the war years, with altar rails and lamps in memory of another vicar, and a carved reading desk in memory of one who fell in Gallipoli.

GREAT BRICKHILL. It is on the rolling sandhills looking into Bedfordshire, standing high with pine woods about it. Its church is mostly 13th century and has a central tower with beautiful moulding in its arches. The nave arcades are 15th century. There is a small oak chest with two locks, carved with circles and ovals, three centuries of tablets to the Duncombes (some adorned with skulls, golden cherubs, and weeping children), and an oil painting of Joseph and Mary watching over the cradle in Bethlehem.

The Fight with the King

GREAT HAMPDEN. Here lived and died John Hampden, who defied the king and gave his life for the people. Here he lies with his ancestors, and on our way to his sleeping-place we pass, near Honor End Farm, three fine sycamores where the road falls steeply to Hampden Bottom. In the shade of the trees is a cross set up last century with this inscription:

For these lands in Stoke Mandeville John Hampden was assessed in 20s ship money levied by command of the king without authority of law on the 4th of August 1635. By resisting this claim of the king in legal strife he upheld the right of the people under the law and became entitled to grateful remembrance.

John Hampden's home was built in the 14th century, and is today part of the great house of his descendant the Earl of Buckinghamshire. Fashioned as we see it in the 18th century, it is enriched with Adam ceilings and fireplaces, but its staircase is a rich example of 17th century craftsmanship. The house has still the 600-year-old doorway through which John Hampden passed, a fireplace at which he would sit thinking, the old hall in which he would receive his friends, and a room (called the Brick Parlour) in which he received the Commissioners sent to arrest him. Here is his helmet, worn by him on many a battlefield and carried on his coffin to this church. Here is the cup from which he took communion in this church, and here is his family Bible, containing the signature of his mother, a daughter of Sir Henry Cromwell and aunt of Oliver.

Hanging on the walls are paintings by Peter Lely and Vandyck, and portraits of Queen Elizabeth and her host Griffith Hampden, who was so impressed by the visit of the great queen that he levelled Grim's Dyke to give her easier approach to the house. The dyke runs across Hampden's fields for miles, with a rampart 6 feet high and a ditch 36 feet wide.

Hampden's house and Hampden's church have stood in the park for six or seven centuries. We come into the church by a 13th century doorway, the nave and aisles were raised in the 14th century, and the tower was fashioned in the 15th. Here is still the font at which John Hampden and his ancestors were all baptised, a band of flowers round its rim 700 years old. There are brass portraits of two early John Hampdens, one of 1496 in armour with his wife and ten children, one of 1553 with two wives and three daughters; and on a stone are brass portraits of seven children who have lost their parents. They may have seen their grandfather entertaining Elizabeth. There is an 18th century medallion portrait of Anne Hampden with her husband on the sanctuary wall, and above them has been unveiled a modern east window in memory of her famous ancestor.

The great hero was laid to rest without a monument, but on a wall is a curious sculpture set up by a descendant a hundred years after his death. It has two cherubs sitting on the edge of a sarcophagus, one resting wearily, and one oddly carrying his hat on a stick; and above them is an oval of a family tree with a relief of Hampden falling wounded from his horse on Chalgrove Field, the village shown in the background. Much more thrilling is a marble tablet set here to his wife by John Hampden himself, with these beautiful words he wrote for her:

In her pilgrimage
The stay and comfort of her neighbours,
The love and glory of a well-ordered family,
The delight and happiness of tender parents,
But a crown of blessings to a husband.

It was from Chalgrove Field that they brought John Hampden to his manor house, and then to this church he knew so well; very dramatic is the description of his burial in a paper of July 1643:

All the troops that could be spared from the quarters round joined to escort the honoured corpse to its last resting place, once his beloved abode, among the hills and woods of the Chilterns. They followed him to his grave in the parish church close adjoining his mansion, their arms reversed, their drums and ensigns muffled, and their heads uncovered. Thus they marched, singing the 90th Psalm as they proceeded to the funeral, and the 43rd as they returned.

The church has 14 Jacobean seats in the nave, and a Jacobean panel in the modern pulpit, the work of men who may have known John Hampden. The roof of the nave is 15th century, set on angels carved in stone, and the same craftsmen may have carved the eagles of the Hampden arms and the Tudor roses in the porch. There are still traces of medieval painting on the walls—Gluttony, Sloth, Anger, and Pride with a demon perched on her shoulder, representing some of the Seven Deadly Sins. In a cupboard are kept some coloured carvings of long ago.

It is over a hundred years since a strange and gruesome drama was enacted in this church, in an attempt to solve one of the mysteries of history. John Hampden died at his home from a wound sustained at Chalgrove. Clarendon the historian wrote that the great Puritan was shot in the shoulder by two bullets which broke the bone and lodged in his body, so that he rode from the field with his head drooping and his hands resting on his horse's neck.

But Sir Robert Pye, Hampden's son-in-law, was said to have stated that the fatal wound resulted, not from Royalist bullets, but from an over-charged pistol exploding in Hampden's hand and shattering his forearm, and, this version finding its way into books, protracted controversy arose, which led Lord Nugent, when writing his Memorials of Hampden, to put the matter to proof. Having obtained authority he came here with the rector, a representative of the Earl of Buckinghamshire, six friends, 12 gravediggers, a plumber, and the parish clerk, took up part of the church floor, and excavated until they reached a coffin lying at the feet of Hampden's first wife. The coffin plate was corroded, and crumbled. The coffin was opened and two inner lids of wood removed. Within was the body of a man of the size of Hampden, with one hand missing and bones loose in the coffin. The left arm showed a dislocation. At first, in spite of the major injury, Lord Nugent was disposed to accept the theory of the exploding pistol, although obviously the loss of the hand might have been due to natural decay long after death. The body was restored to the grave, and in his book Lord Nugent refrained from reference to this unpleasant quest.

John Hampden, the Pure Englishman

JOHN HAMPDEN has a unique distinction. He is the one great Puritan leader who has received fair treatment from posterity.

Pym has been neglected. Cromwell has been steadily traduced by those who support the Divine Right of Stuart kings to override Parliament and fleece their subjects. But Hampden has everyone's good word. No one casts a stone at him.

The reason for Hampden's fair fame is that he deserved it. He upheld a great cause in a noble way. Well balanced, firm, with an instinctive sense of right, "he nothing common did or mean." Though modest, he was a central man to whom everyone looked up. His opponent Clarendon said of him that he was a supreme governor of all his passions and affections, and had thereby a great power over other men's; and Richard Baxter said he had "the most universal praise of any gentleman of that age." He was precisely the man needed to keep the Parliamentary cause worthy when it was triumphant, but when that testing time came Cromwell had no Hampden or Pym by his side.

Hampden was a Buckinghamshire man, born of a family that had lived in the county since before the Conquest. His mother was Oliver Cromwell's aunt. He was educated at Thame Grammar School and Inner Temple, and had "a great knowledge both in scholarship and the law." He served in Parliament from his 26th year till his death at 48. The key to his public life is his profound belief in the legality of Parliamentary control of taxation and the need for preserving the privileges of Parliament and the freedom of its members. Parliament also claimed the right to impeach Ministers of the Crown who were a danger to the country. To Hampden these rights of Parliament were fundamental.

It was on the question of the right of the King to levy loans and taxes directly without Parliamentary assent that the chief clash came. The most obnoxious forms of illegal exaction were forced loans and inland ship money. Hampden, like many others, refused to pay a forced loan, and was confined in Hampshire for his resistance. When the sheriff was ordered to collect £4500 in Buckinghamshire for Ship Money Hampden challenged the legal right of the imposition, and though he lost the case it was this stand that made him a national figure.

Before that time Hampden had been a quiet influential worker behind the scenes in Parliament. Committees welcomed him in shaping their business. His judgment was valued highly. In the Commons he seldom spoke, and never for long. He was quite content that others should take the lead—the impetuous Sir John Eliot, the solid John Pym, the over-cautious Essex. But all relied on him, and with the rank and file he was the most popular man in the House. He held no extreme views, but saw clearly the principles of government that were involved in the deadlock between the Stuart kings and the British people; he read aright the characters of the men chiefly concerned; he foresaw that neither side would give way, and that the settlement would come by force of arms, and he steadily faced and understood the facts, as Charles Stuart never did.

He had opportunities of knowing Charles well, for he was one of the Commissioners appointed by Parliament to attend him when he went to Scotland, and there he gained an insight into the intrigues on which Charles constantly relied, and which led to his doom. It was Hampden's level head that restrained Parliament from making war on the Scots, and preserved that unity of action between the Lords and Commons which kept the national character of the Parliamentary protest against the King's methods.

Hampden was one of the Five Members whom the King attempted to arrest in the House by force, the action which precipitated the Civil War. When the war began Hampden and Cromwell agreed on the necessity of training a force composed of men who had the fear of God before them—the inauguration of the corps of invincible Ironsides that won the war. Hampden, who had the rank of Colonel, was never a great military leader. His influence went into the scale for a vigorous offensive, and he was uneasy about the timid dilatoriness of the Earl of Essex. He favoured striking at once at the King's headquarters in Oxford, and so shortening the war.

It was when this step was being tardily prepared for that Hampden rode to his death. Essex was gathering his troops to the south-east of Oxford when Prince Rupert raided towards them with a thousand troopers. Hampden boldly charged him from the rear on Chalgrove Field with some hastily gathered troops, to cut him off from the city, but he was shot through the shoulder. He rode on to the town of Thame and there died six days later.

The newspaper that announced his death said; "The loss of Colonel Hampden goeth near the heart of every man—his memory is such that in every age to come it will more and more be had in honour and esteem"; and Clarendon admitted that his reputation for honesty was universal, and his affections seemed so publicly guided that no corrupt or private ends could bias them. He was one of our purest great Englishmen.

Famous Rectors

GREAT HORWOOD. It has charming Jacobean cottages, and preserves in its records the names of two distinguished men who made it their home. The church, with a stately turreted tower from which gargoyles have been looking out 600 years, is light and lofty, though not a window is higher than the piers of the 15th century arcade. Twenty stone men hold up the medieval roofs of the aisles and nave, and keeping them company we noticed a grotesque and a lone monkey. The wide chancel arch frames the richly traceried sanctuary window, lighting a modern roof supported by angels. Here are stone seats carved for priests before the Tudor dynasty. The 14th century font is carved with shields, and there is glass in the windows through which light was streaming for its first baptism. A little brass is engraved with the portrait of Henry Upnore, who was rector here while Richard the Third was wading through blood to the throne; and in a carved recess we found the remains of an oak figure of a man who must have been among his contemporaries, one of only about a hundred oak figures in our churches. Most of the screen was here in their day, with beautiful 15th century carving to which has been added a fine roodloft, with two angels which seem to float below the cusps of the doorway.

The striking peace memorial is a canopied painting of St George, on whose shield in letters of gold are the names of those who came not home again, the list ending with that of the John Chevallier, rector from 1898 to 1914, who was killed in a road accident when on war service as mathematical master at Giggleswick School. The most famous rector here was William Warham, who left this pulpit to become Chancellor to Henry the Seventh and to marry Henry the

Eighth to Catherine of Aragon. A later rector was the benevolent and learned Joseph Spence, an 18th century professor of poetry at Oxford, whose fame rests, not on his learned writings as he hoped, but on the stories he jotted down from conversations with Pope and other immortals. He gave us his Literary Anecdotes 52 years after his death, when two publishers issued rival editions on the same day. The parish saw little of him, but he had £900 a year and a generous heart, and both were at the service of the poor of Great Horwood.

John Hampden Protests

GREAT KIMBLE. It must for ever have a place in history as the opening scene in the struggle between the King and Parliament, for it was here that John Hampden made his dramatic protest against Ship Money. The roots of Great Kimble reach deeper into the past than this, however, for if local tradition is to be trusted one of its great earthworks was a camp of Shakespeare's Cymbeline.

What is supposed to be the site of Cymbeline's fortress is a stronghold in Chequers Park, known as Contour Camp and comprising four acres. It lies 800 feet up on Pulpit Hill, and, in spite of a plantation rising thick above them, we can still trace the outer and inner ramparts and defensive ditches. A tumulus in the churchyard, opened last century, contained Roman and older relics, but Contour Camp was old when the Romans ruled in Britain. Those who believe that this was Cymbeline's camp declare that Kimble comes from Cymbeline.

Great Kimble's church stands on a little knoll. It has a tower from which masks and faces have been looking out 600 years, and a handsome stone head in the porch facing a 700-year-old doorway. The nave has a lofty 16th century roof, the chancel arch is 14th century, and there is a massive oak chest bound with 13th century ironwork. Across the tower arch is a beautiful oak screen in memory of Robert Hampden, who left this vicarage to serve in a South African cathedral, but older than all these is the magnificent font which was made by a Norman craftsman; it has a fluted bowl with traces of colour and there is a wide band of foliage round the top, the stem and the base being richly carved.

Hanging on the wall is a fine copy of Raphael's Madonna of the Chair, the gift of two Americans, and on a pedestal is a graceful terracotta statue group of the Madonna and Child. But it is a simple little thing that stirs us most here, a copy of the report of the parish overseers setting out the names of those who one January morning in 1635 refused the demand of King Charles for Ship Money. At the head of the list of names is John Hampden.

The Petition of Right had then been law seven years, and its first provision was that "No freeman shall be obliged to give any gift, loan, benevolence, or tax, without common consent by Act of Parliament." Ship Money was levied by Charles in violation of his word. To raise money to enable him to defy Parliament he imposed taxes regardless of law, and this tax, as Clarendon, the Royalist historian, wrote, was meant not merely for the Navy but "for a spring and magazine that should have no bottom, and for an everlasting supply of all occasions."

From Buckinghamshire a ship of 450 tons, manned and equipped for six months, was demanded, and Hampden's tax for the manor here was 20 shillings. He confronted the assessors, made his protest and refused to pay. A law-abiding patriot, and himself a barrister, he had taken the highest legal advice and awaited with confidence the trial he knew to be inevitable. He was sued for the tax, and the paltriness of the sum was commented on at the trial, but as Edmund Burke said in a later age:

> Would 20 shillings have ruined Mr Hampden's fortunes? No. But the payment of half 20 shillings, on the principle it was demanded, would have made him a slave.

The case was argued from November 6 to December 18 before servile judges, one of whom, Chief Justice Finch, shocked the country by declaring that they are "void Acts of Parliament that bind the king not to command their subjects, their persons, and their goods—and I say money, too, for no Acts of Parliament make any difference." Eventually, by seven to five, the judges decided against Hampden. In 1640 both Houses of Parliament declared the judgment against the laws of the realm and ordered it to be cancelled.

A Lord Mayor and a Crisis

GREAT LINFORD. In this scene of dreaming peace it is a surprise to be reminded of historic events finally bringing great men to shame and death. Here are these memories, with a 14th

Great Linford — 17th Century Almshouses

Great Hampden — John Hampden's House

Great Kimble   Medieval Tower   **Hambleden**   Modern Tower

Grendon Underwood   Village Church

century church, an Elizabethan rectory, a barn of Tudor days with a dovecot housing 400 pairs of nesting birds, walnut trees about the church, and, startling picture, canal barges floating above our heads!

The 13th century tower crowns a church a century younger, with many fine windows, a beautiful arcade, and richly carved capitals. A jaunty winged figure, carved before the Tudors, rises above a modern porch, and a second porch has a vaulted roof with a fine carved boss. Roger Hunt paved the church while the Wars of the Roses were at their height, and here is his brass, telling us what he did and showing him with his wife. In an aisle is the 16th century brass of Thomas Malyn in his fur-trimmed cloak and square-toed shoes, with his wife and their child, and in the chancel are the 17th century brass portraits of John Uvedall, his wife, and eight children.

The chief monument is that of Sir William Pritchard, who, having bought the manor, enjoyed it for an exciting quarter of a century, and then was brought in great state from his London home (in 1705) to sleep in his church. He left his estate to two nephews, and when we called one of the most recent monuments was to one of his descendants, on whose memorial an otter is carved in oak because he was the master of the otter hounds. Pritchard, a London merchant, became Lord Mayor in 1682 and helped to bring to a head a political crisis as grave as that which led to the Civil War. Charles the Second, secretly Roman Catholic, had menaced the rights of the nation, and the Lord Mayor resisted the taking of office by two sheriffs elected by the people to defend the Constitution. The result was that two sheriffs of the Court party, by appointing packed juries, obtained power to dispose of the life and liberty of every man who opposed the king. The wronged sheriffs retorted on Pritchard by causing him to be arrested and detained for some hours in custody. His election, acclaimed a signal triumph for the Court, was made the subject of royalist poems and ballads, one of them set to music by Purcell. On his release Pritchard brought an action against the sheriffs, one of whom fled, while the other was fined £10,000 by the infamous Judge Jeffreys.

Their overthrow in London drove the popular party to despair, from which sprang two plots, the Rye House Plot for the murder of Charles and James, and the Insurrection Plot which aimed at dethroning Charles and banishing James. The one plot engaged obscure extremists, the second attracted great men.

So it came about that Pritchard, himself a nobody, became a lever of events which shook the nation. Personally he was a generous man, and built the charming red-roofed almshouses here.

Friend of the Slaves

GREAT MISSENDEN. It is a gift of the River Misbourne, which carved the valley in the Chilterns where it lies among hills ennobled by countless beeches. Little remains of the old abbey with its immense range of buildings, but there are sculptured fragments, a 13th century arch in a summer-house in the park, and in the house itself is reconstructed the 15th century roof of the dormitory in which the monks slept 700 years ago. Some of the abbots live in history. One was hanged for clipping the coinage of Edward the Third, and a better abbot compiled a famous book which, in addition to recording the grants, properties, and privileges of the monks, set down such heartening discoveries as infallible cures by oil of black snails and marrow from horse-bones.

Part of the Norman abbey, the 14th century church is a memorial of days and doings which ended at the Dissolution. Some of the timbered houses existed when the crash came and the last abbot was transformed into the first vicar; others are of Queen Elizabeth's days. The Gables has on its 17th century walls oak panelling and a mantelpiece carved while she reigned. The church stands on a plateau in open country amid yews and sycamores, the modern abbey on one hand, the village on the other, with the fields sloping steeply where the monks raised their crops. Aggressive gargoyles seem ready to leap from the tower and the roof. The spacious interior, with its stately columns, is flooded with light from windows added 500 years ago, when the high roofs now grey with age were built. A mellow fancy directed the carving of delightfully quaint heads on the arcade mouldings, but the stone angels with shields supporting the nave roof have a touch of solemnity. The chancel wall has a beautiful 14th century arcade of seven bays, with finials and pinnacles ending in jovial little figures. The east window is flanked by canopied niches, whose carved capitals have still traces of the colour given them by an artist 600 years ago.

BUCKINGHAMSHIRE

The Norman font at which the monks baptised the children is one of a group known as the Aylesbury type. Its sides were recut in the 15th century, but its stem has chevrons, and its base is finely carved with foliage.

Another link with the past is a number of tiles from the ruined abbey, one with a shield and three crescents, others adorned with foliage. In the transept pews are over a score of traceried panels which were here for a century before Nemesis came to the abbey door.

There is one brass, a 16th century portrait of a kneeling woman in flowing robes. A remarkable monument over the south doorway is to William Blois, a Cambridge scholar who lived into Stuart days. Below a figure representing Mortality is reared a marble arch of books, some with clasps showing, all with their edges coloured. A recess in a transept has the remains of ancient painting.

The last abbot compromised with his conscience and changed his status; but Christopher Shoemaker of Great Missenden did not compromise; he died a martyr half a century before the Dissolution banished the monks.

Nearer our own time the village was the home of James Stephen, a lawyer who suggested a blockade in response to Napoleon's attempt to prevent our trading with Europe. His early experiences in the West Indies made him an ardent friend of the slaves. He married a sister of Wilberforce, who was a frequent visitor here while the struggle for emancipation went on, Wilberforce Walk commemorating the jaunts and fruitful labours of these two.

Did Shakespeare Sleep Here?

GRENDON UNDERWOOD. We do not know, but it is thought possible that Shakespeare here received his inspiration for Midsummer Night's Dream, for he is said to have slept at what is now called Shakespeare's Farm and was then the village inn. It is not impossible, for this timbered house is old enough for Shakespeare to have been in it, to have sat by its open fireplace, and to have mounted the four flights of its old staircase with the acorn on its newel posts. The story of Shakespeare's visit here was told by no mean authority, old John Aubrey, one of our forerunners in touring England, who must have heard the story from people living in Shakespeare's day.

Here are many old cottages and farms John Aubrey would have seen, some of them a little askew owing to the sinking of their clay foundations. Lawn Farm has a doorway and three oak mullioned windows three centuries old. Grendon Underwood could never have had any anxiety about time: has any place more mass dials? We found four on a single buttress. The battlemented tower is 15th century, but the thick walls of the nave are witness to their Norman builders, and we come in through a doorway with deep mouldings carved by men who learned their building from the Normans. Here are the flowers they carved. The chancel arch, sweeping up to the roof without a break, is 14th century, the font is 15th, and the pulpit is Jacobean. Two 18th century wall monuments face across the altar, a weeping woman in memory of Lord Saye and Sele and a winged cupid in memory of his widow. Sitting with one hand on his knee is John Pigott, who must have known them. His monument is in the chancel, an altar tomb with a cherub holding a medallion with his wife's portrait. It is all by Peter Scheemakers, the Dutchman who put so many fashionable sculptures into our churches.

Lord Chesterfield's Village

GROVE. The Normans loved it and built its little church. Lord Chesterfield owned it, and its revenues were a mite in his princely expenditure at the Hague and in the cost of the lordly pleasure house he built himself in London; but we find no mention of it in his famous Letters to his son. All told, it consists of half a dozen cottages, a farm, a hospital, a quaint, steeply-arched bridge spanning the Grand Junction Canal, a little church above ground, and evidences of a greater church beneath the turf. The Norman font remains in a 14th century nave with a bellcot above it. On each side of the altar is a niche with trefoiled head. One contains a modern figure of St Michael in gilt armour, over which a red cloak is draped, a charming addition to the little church, very happily housed.

Saints and Dragons

HADDENHAM. In its miles of village are dozens of old houses, several ponds for boys to catch tiddlers in, and a great green for them to play on. One of the ponds has walls topped with overhanging thatch "to keep the ducks dry," as the children say. A timbered wing of the farm touching the churchyard wall is 500 years old, but the imposing church is 700. Dozens of queer heads look over the lovely arcade round the belfry. There is a new statue in the 14th century niche over a door dated 1637; the inner door is older still. Two dragons have been fighting round the huge font for nearly 800 years, their tails entangled with the foliage round the top. There are dragons in the screens, curvetting among the exquisite Tudor tracery across the tower arch (perhaps the old rood screen cut smaller), and in the Tudor screen between the chancel and the vestry. Tracery of a 15th century screen separates an aisle from a chapel, and 16th century bench-ends with faces on the poppyheads complete the heritage of rich woodwork. The art of the medieval stone-carver is in the piscinas and the weird heads supporting the roof of the chapel, where a helmet still gleaming with gilt hangs over a skull and three saints shine in 15th century glass. Two priests of 500 years ago have left their portraits in brass.

The Outlaw and the King

HALTON. The home of ancient Britons is up above it on Boddington Hill, 800 feet high, where farm buildings enjoy an unrivalled picture of spreading beauty. Here was their primitive city, 18 acres in extent, and here are the ditch and rampart inside which they withdrew their sheep and cattle when threatened in the plains. The modern village lies lower, by a beautiful park which is now a Royal Air Force training ground. In a charming churchyard stands the 19th century church. Its oldest possessions are the fine Tudor portrait brasses on a chancel wall showing Henry Bradschawe in his robes as Chief Baron of the Exchequer, with his wife and their four sons and four daughters, all kneeling. The bowl of the handsome font, supported by a twisted stem, is inlaid with a mosaic border, and guarded by winged monsters.

In the woods here in 1266, tradition says, occurred the encounter between Edward the First and the redoubtable Sir Adam de Gurdon. Dispossessed of his estates, Sir Adam wandered as an outlaw ravaging Buckinghamshire. Edward advanced against him, met him hand to hand, and overthrew him, but, moved by the martial skill and valour of his enemy, he pardoned him, restored his lands, admitted him to his friendship, and found him faithful all his life.

The Royal Air Force Station at Halton has its own church, in which is a tablet in memory of men of the station who lost their lives in the earthquake at Quetta in 1935. The lectern is like a globe, and crowned by an aeroplane, the Bible resting on the wings.

History and Beauty

HAMBLEDEN. We are captivated by its stern beauty as we come upon it in one of the most delightful valleys in the Chilterns. It is sheltered by beeches for its whole length from the hills at Fingest to the Thames a mile away. In the heart of the village stands the old pump under two great chestnut trees, and standing by it in the big square, with gabled houses and timbered cottages about us, we have a fine peep of the old church and its magnificent modern tower. It is a place of history and beauty too.

Here were the Romans, whose tiles, mosaic floors, pottery and writing implements found here with other remains of a villa are now in the splendid little museum of local archaeology built by Lord Hambleden in 1913. Here was born and baptised the last Englishman to be canonised until our own day, Thomas of Cantelupe, friend of Simon de Montfort. He was brought to the Norman font in the church in the days when the Clares were lords of the manor here, the Clares of that family whose name is first on Magna Carta. Today the manor house stands on the site of Cantelupe's birthplace, a splendid Jacobean building with gabled windows and a huge copper beech and a chestnut at its gate. In Hambleden also was born that Earl of Cardigan who led the Charge of the Light Brigade.

We come into the churchyard by the grave of a man whose name is known to everyone in England, W. H. Smith. He was the remarkable man who founded the firm which will deliver any paper in the world at our doors. The churchyard has three great cedars and a remarkable mausoleum with eight arches on classical columns, the monument of the Kenricks. The 14th century church has what is left of a Norman doorway on an outside wall, with the carving of a lion's head on it, and in the nave is the Norman font at which Cantelupe was christened. On its rim are the marks of the staples when it was locked against witches. There is beautiful carving in the chancel, with heads and twisted monsters on the piscina and the sedilia, and the church has three splendid monuments and interesting brasses. On a fine altar tomb with painted Tudor shields lies Henry Sandys;

BUCKINGHAMSHIRE

and Ralph Scrope his neighbour has a carved and painted monument on the walls of the tower. The third monument has on it the alabaster figure of Sir Cope Doyley, who is here with his ten children and their mother, she having been a sister of Francis Quarles, King James's poet laureate.

On her tomb are figures of Charity and Faith and these lines, the sort of poetry poets laureate wrote in those days:

> *Rebecca in grace, in heart an Abigail:*
> *In works a Dorcas: to the Church a Hanna:*
> *And to her spouse Susanna:*
> *Prudently simple, providently wary:*
> *To the world a Martha, and to Heaven a Mary.*

There are three brasses of the 15th century, one of John Shipwash of 1457 with his four children on their knees, one of John White and his wife, and one of Catherine Scrope in a handsome mantle which has lost its enamel inlay. On a Stuart brass is John Saunders with two wives.

One surprising possession stands in the tower, a piece of magnificent carving believed to be the end of a bed which belonged to Cardinal Wolsey. It has carved panels separated by pilasters, on which stand canopied figures, and on the panels are figures of men and angels. There are two medallions with men riding on beasts, and queer scaly monsters glaring at each other, and over this strange piece of craftsmanship are carved the arms of Wolsey and his cardinal's hat.

There lies in Hambleden churchyard one of the bravest men of the Great War, and one of the most effective benefactors of the men who were disabled by it. He was Major George Howson, who organised the poppy factory run by the British Legion at Richmond. Nowhere is there a happier family than these 360 men who live in a delightful row of flats by their factory, and they owe their happiness to the inspiration of Major Howson, a soldier of the noblest type.

Himself disabled in the war, where he won the Military Cross, he was eager to help when it was over, and he founded the Disabled Society, out of which grew the idea that the men might be set to work making things. He set them to work making flowers, and the first beginnings of poppy-making were in a room he hired off the Old Kent Road. Now this factory at Richmond, the House of Remembrance that never forgets the men who won the war, produces over forty million poppies in a year. The major is no longer among his men, for at Armistice time in 1936 he lay dying on a bed of pain and would be not denied his longing to see once again the Field of Remembrance at the Abbey. The inspiration for it had come to him in a dream, and they laid him in the ambulance and drove him there, and, as he lay watching the pilgrimage to this little garden of crosses and poppies, the King came to the ambulance and talked to him. It was his last sight of the Garden of Remembrance. He went back to Richmond, and his last words at the factory spoken to one of the original five members of the staff were: "Remember, if I peg out I go in the factory van." As the ambulance left he led the singing of Are we Downhearted? and that is how his men remember him.

The Village Boy Who Became a Saint

THOMAS DE CANTELUPE, the Hambleden boy now in the calendar of saints, was one of four brothers, two of whom became famous knights, while three of four sisters married into noble houses. He lived with his brother in Paris, where they kept two poor scholars daily and had always a number of paupers feeding daily from their table. His uncle was a close friend of Simon de Montfort and Thomas was drawn in on his side. He became Chancellor after the Battle of Lewes had made the barons master of the king, but his post was unsafe after the death of Montfort and he returned to Paris and was abroad for years. Then he came back to England, a man of great wealth and liberal hospitality. He built churches and bestowed alms, and was a great friend of the poor. No man more rigorously defended the rights of the Church. He was made Bishop of Hereford even while he declared himself all unworthy, and became an intimate adviser of Edward the First. He was in all his councils and Parliaments, though once with tears in his eyes he begged the king to set him free rather than give a Jew the right to bear witness against Christians in court. He was always against Jews and refused the gifts they offered him. He hated corruption and expelled all loose monks from his diocese. He turned all women out of his household. He became involved in controversy over an excommunication issued by the Primate, and was finally excommunicated himself, on which he declared he would appeal to Rome in person. But he was wearied by the journey, worn out with anxiety, and died and was buried in Italy before his case could come before the Vatican. He lies in Hereford Cathedral, and was made a saint, the last Englishman to be canonised before our own time.

The Spire Seen From Three Counties

HANSLOPE. The spire of this rare old village on a hill is seen for miles by travellers in three counties; it rises 186 feet on a high embattled 15th century tower springing from pinnacles with flying buttresses. The village is delightful with gabled cottages of the 17th century, a thatched post office which we found almost lost in wistaria, and a farm with an Elizabethan dovecot.

Great gargoyles peer from the walls of the church, round which run grotesque faces carved by medieval artists, who also sculptured curious animals on a turret over the chancel. In this outdoor sculpture gallery are strange birds, the bear and staff of the Warwicks and a man wearing a turban, and with all these animals are a score of heads of animals carved by Norman masons. Some of them are over three tiny Norman windows and a priest's doorway, richly carved with zigzag and horseshoe ornament.

Into this fine church opens a door which has been opened by the congregations of 500 years; it hangs in one of the two 15th century porches in a doorway cut through a 700-year-old wall. The eye is instantly drawn as we come in to the bold chancel arch which must have attracted travellers for 800 years, for it is an impressive structure with four depths of carving and with capitals of which no two are alike. Within the thick wall to the right of this great arch a 15th century doorway with its old door leads us up a spiral staircase which emerges in the little turret, the walls of the stairway having traces of medieval painting; we noticed the Warwick bear gripping a ragged staff. The chancel has a piscina and three stone seats for the priests with shafts and arches carved 600 years ago, and facing them is a Norman window deeply splayed, looking into a 13th century vestry. All the roofs are modern, but above the clerestory of the nave are three medieval stone angels with musical instruments. There are two stone coffins with lids which have been here 700 years, and a band of ornament round the resting-place of the man who turned the Norman church into the great building it is today. There is a small brass near the font with a portrait of little Mary Birchmore, aged six, looking very charming in Elizabethan dress.

Long afterwards they brought to this churchyard an old lady of 101 who left behind 174 living descendants to mourn her, and long after that they laid here under a chestnut tree a prize fighter named Alexander McKay, of whom we are told that, alas, he fought with Simon Burn but lived not to return, his epitaph winding up:

> *If you have ever fought before,*
> *Determine now to fight no more.*

We found hanging in the tower two of those great hooks kept in thatched villages for dragging the thatch from burning roofs.

Dramatic Memories

HARDMEAD. In this quiet place, remote on high ground near Bedfordshire, with church and rectory standing among splendid pines and sycamores, we are linked with a great conspiracy and reminded of a bitter Arctic tragedy.

The Normans began the tower, and their font, replaced by another 600 years ago, lay in fragments by the 15th century doorway when we called. Over the priest's doorway are the heads of a bishop and a civilian, carved before our serfs were freed. Set in the modern roof are bosses with flowers chiselled in Tudor times. In these pews sat the men who heard the thrilling news from Bosworth Field.

Here lived the Catesbys, whose house gave Richard the Third a minister, Shakespeare a character, Parliament a Speaker, and in a later century produced the author of Gunpowder Plot. On the wall is a brass portrait of Francis Catesby, in a fur-trimmed robe such as he wore in Mary Tudor's reign. Another long-gowned Francis Catesby, who lived while his kinsman was preparing his plot, kneels on the wall with a man and two women behind him; they are in a niche which seems to be built of books, apparently symbolising his love of literature.

Another wall monument has a thrilling scene of a schooner in full sail. It is the Nancy Dawson, which Robert Shedden fitted out at his own cost to sail in search of Sir John Franklin, lost with all his men in the frigid silence of the Arctic. Shedden was in the Far East when he heard that the expedition was lost, but he crossed the world and passed through the fierce heat of the Tropics to urge the little

Nancy Dawson as far north as ship could sail. His was one of the first of the 15 attempts made during six years of suspense to reach the unhappy men who had already starved to death. Exposure, storms, and privation exhausted the brave searcher, and he returned baffled and discouraged, to rest, re-fit, and sail away never to return from the wide Pacific, in which he found his grave in 1849, a year before the first news of Franklin came.

The church has been much cared for, and still it has a heavy bier on which the old folk of the village have been carried to their rest for 250 years, a Bible of 1772, and a Prayer Book of 1760, both looking as fresh as when they came from the printers.

The Circle of Friends

HARDWICK. Built on a low hill in the Vale of Aylesbury, of which we have a fine view from the churchyard, it has under it a charnel house of our ancient past, from which have been dug great numbers of giants which roamed the land in the Age of Reptiles, in addition to an almost incredible multitude of ammonites and other extinct creatures.

Cheerful cottages cluster about the churchyard, in which a peace memorial cross keeps watch, and in which lies a group of men who fought in the Civil War. In 1818 the remains of Cavaliers and Roundheads who fought the desperate battle of Aylesbury in 1642 were found in a field near the site of their last engagement; and Lord Nugent had them brought here, 247 of them, and buried in a common grave, friend and foe united in the soil which bred them.

The church was old when the battle was fought; it was old when the Conqueror came. The nave is Saxon, and very impressive. Over the north doorway is a deeply splayed narrow lancet, with a bright picture of the Madonna. In a doorway, carved with bold foliage, swings a door on hinges which have supported it 600 years; and in the tower is another door, almost as old, with its original ironwork. An arcade and a piscina remain from the 14th century, and the newest windows were put in nearly a century before Columbus crossed the Atlantic; the oldest windows, with the exception of the lancet, are 14th century, one with elaborate tracery and one with fragments of the original glass, in which is the head of Our Lord. The vestry has an 18th century chest, but its chief treasure is a

Crusader's jug. The most interesting monument is to Sir Robert Lee, an ancestor of the Confederate leader in the American Civil War. Sir Robert, who died in the same year as Shakespeare, is here in armour, kneeling beside his wife, with their eight sons and six daughters. The fine reredos in white and gold, in memory of a rector for 29 years, has saints in its six panels.

At Weedon, a hamlet close by, is the 19th century house called Lilies, with trees encircling stone seats on which are carved the names of friends of Lord Nugent, who lived here for a generation industriously working on the history of the county. His Memorials of Hampden formed the subject of one of Macaulay's essays. Called the Circle of Friends, the stones have a Latin inscription expressing the hope that the friends would often meet there.

Here Lived a King of France

HARTWELL. It is one of the much-visited villages round Aylesbury, famous for its beauty. Its great house, on whose roof flew the royal flag of France, stands in a park of formal grandeur, with the homes of the villagers set in the shelter of its walls. Here, in the exciting years of Napoleon's march to triumph and defeat, came King Louis the Eighteenth with his Court, crowding the house to the attics with his 140 followers; and here he stayed till the spring of 1814 brought the daffodils to the gardens of Hartwell House and sent Napoleon into exile. Here in those troubled years died the Queen of France, to be carried hence for a service in Westminster Abbey, from where the coffin was taken to Sardinia. The finest feature on the outside of the house is the entrance porch, flanked by carved pilasters supporting a handsome frieze, with a round oriel over it resting on beautiful corbels. The rarest delight inside is the staircase, a magnificent spectacle with 24 newel posts, each supporting a historical or mythological figure, all with swords or lances. The balusters are carved with small double figures.

The fantastic beauty of the house and park runs over into the village lane. To reach some of Hartwell's delightful cottages we walk by hundreds of prehistoric ammonites, some as big as cartwheels, built into the park wall, near a shelter carved with figures of animals drinking. The bailiff's house, with a peaked red roof and a charming porch, stands near the great gates through which we pass into the park, which is crossed by a double avenue of noble chestnuts. The green sward is broken by a long ornamental water spanned by an arch which has been seen by generations of London folk, for it belonged to old Kew Bridge.

Set here and there in the swelling grassland, with great trees in the background, are 18th century statues. George the Third, dressed like a Roman in the fashion of those days, stands on a tall pedestal. At the end of a long avenue of elms are two more statues and an obelisk. Frederick Prince of Wales is set on horseback, a magnificent figure in a more enclosed part of the grounds. The wanderer in the park will find a forester's cottage, thatched and timbered, tucked away in the shelter of a wood, which must have set the French hearts aching for Fontainebleau.

By three tall cedars in another corner of the park is the village church, built in the 18th century by Sir William Lee, Chancellor of the Exchequer. It is interesting as a curious little copy of the octagonal chapter house of York Minster, with the addition of two pinnacled towers, one built over the entrance porch and one over the chancel. The roof has graceful fan-vaulting. The reading desk and the pulpit were designed by George Street, architect of the Law Courts. The memory of the church which this one replaced is treasured in the worn figure stones from old tombs set in the floor. On the walls are the names of people buried here.

We noticed the name of Sir Richard Ingoldsby, a kinsman of Cromwell and Hampden and a curiously interesting character of the Civil War. He fought in many battles and sieges, and was appointed one of the judges of the king, though he did not attend the trial. He signed the death-warrant, however, and was tried for his share in the execution. He always declared that he did not wish to sign the sentence, but that his kinsmen Oliver compelled him. He sat in Parliament and was called to Cromwell's House of Lords, and after Oliver's death he remained faithful to Richard Cromwell, who said of him "Here is Dick Ingoldsby, who can neither pray nor preach and yet I will trust him before ye all." When Richard resigned Ingoldsby was appointed one of the Committee of Safety, and at the Restoration, which he helped to bring about, Charles declared that he must earn his pardon. It happened that John Lambert escaped from captivity to rally the Republican forces, and Ingoldsby went out against him and carried him back to the Tower. For this he was spared the penalty inflicted on other judges of the king, and he was knighted at the coronation and sat in four Parliaments.

A little way from the church is the old rectory, a two-storeyed house in which is a richly moulded beam with the date 1552, so that it is older than the Spanish Armada. In the rector's garden is a lead cistern of 1305 embossed with a rose, a lion, and the fleur-de-lys.

Four Times Bride and Widow

HAVERSHAM. It stretches along the quiet wooded valley of the Ouse near the Northants border, and has a red-tiled Jacobean manor with a fine dovecot; it is 17th century and has an oak lantern over its roof. The church has still its Norman tower, stately among limes and chestnuts. On the outside walls we noticed carvings of a cat with a mouse and an animal with a twisted tail. From the interior of the tower we look into the church through a splendidly decorated Norman window, one shaft of which has chevron and the other a capital carved with a bird.

The most remarkable monument is that believed to have been raised for herself in 1390 by Lady Clinton, four times a bride and four times a widow. She lies in alabaster on a magnificent canopied and pinnacled tomb, her rich dress beautifully carved, with angels at her cushioned head and a lion at her feet. In four panels are angels and civilians, the civilians in quaint 15th century headdresses.

There are two brasses, a portrait of Alice Payn in 15th century costume with a horned headdress, and a gruesome skeleton in an open coffin in memory of John Maunsell, who died the year before Shakespeare. A window in the south chapel has fragments of 15th century glass, and a fine window by Christopher Whall has figures of Our Lord, St Peter, and St Paul. In another window we noticed the curious fact that a modern artist has given six toes to a foot of John the Baptist. The nave has many seats with poppyheads crudely carved by Tudor craftsmen; on the tops we found the old iron candlesticks, and on the two-decker pulpit is still the iron frame of its old hour-glass. The organ and the altar table are both Jacobean.

HAWRIDGE. It is a scattering of houses on a delightful wayside common, bright with hawthorn, that lies along a Chiltern ridge, with a tower windmill and a church on the highest ground. The church, built in 1856, stands in place of an earlier building first set up in the 13th century, when the round font was carved with leaves and flowers.

Close by the church is Hawridge Court Farm, on the edge of a historic encampment protected by a rampart 16 feet high and 50 feet wide, which was cut through when the foundations of the house were laid. The barn on the farm, built of timber and brick, is 16th century, and there is a crude chest in the church which is about as old.

The Discoverer

HAZLEMERE. It is on the Chilterns above High Wycombe, with beech woods about it and a giant beech, the village tree, in the churchyard. On the seat round the trunk we can sit and see across the Thames valley into Surrey. The 19th century brick church, built in a simple style, has a comely look inside. The apse is filled with good design of oak stalls, screen, and altar rail, all harmoniously planned. The east windows, where we see the Master in a garden bidding us Consider the lilies how they grow, are in memory of a famous flower lover, Dr Philip Barnes, who lies under a simple stone in the churchyard. Long before he died in 1874, an old man of 82, he had earned the gratitude of flower lovers all over the world, for he founded the Royal Botanic Society, and with his friends started the famous Botanic Garden which for nearly a hundred years made a fragrant zone in the heart of Regent's Park. Not far from his tomb is a simple granite cross. Here was laid to rest in 1916 Sir William Ramsay, KCB, the world-famous discoverer of argon, winner of the Nobel Prize for chemistry. Born in Glasgow in 1852, he became professor of chemistry at Bristol and then for 25 years at University College, London. He was a born scientist; his fingers could work the most delicate instruments. He was a born linguist, lecturing to French, German, and Italian audiences with as much ease as to our own Royal Society. With Lord Rayleigh, another scientist, he discovered argon; with Professor Soddy he proved the transmutation of radium into helium, one of the most important discoveries of the 20th century. He also discovered krypton, neon, and xenon, three gases which occur in minute quantities in the air.

A King's Cloak?

HEDGERLEY. It lies among gentle hills and gracious meadowland, with a modern church treasuring relics of its ancient predecessor. One of these, silent on a windowsill in the tower, is a bell which rang out first when Englishmen were fighting the Stuarts. The Norman font, with a plain 17th century cover, is carved with heads of a bishop and two other men, a shield, and flowers.

Of the two brasses here, one of the 15th century shows Robert Fulmer, his wife, two sons, and two daughters; the other is one of the most interesting of palimpsests, the brasses used over again. With portraits of Margaret Bulstrode, a Tudor lady, and her ten sons and three daughters, it is a medley of thefts, made up of several portions of stolen brasses. The inscription is hinged so that we may see both sides, and the other side has an inscription to Thomas Totyngton, who was abbot of Bury St Edmunds a generation before the serfs of the abbey rose and murdered his successor, and impaled his head with that of Lord Chief Justice Cavendish in Bury marketplace.

Another storied possession is a fragment of dark red velvet, framed on a wall. The tale told here is that Charles the Second, visiting the old church, noticed that the altar was without a cover, and, removing his cloak, placed it on the bare table. The fragment has been examined at South Kensington, and the experts have pronounced it 17th century work. To the same century belongs a painting on canvas in the tower, quaintly illustrating the Ten Commandments.

Not the least astonishing story in this church of surprises attaches to the satinwood pulpit, reading desk, and two chairs. Until 1843 these formed part of the woodwork of a church at Antigua in the West Indies. Since becoming an English possession in the 17th century the island has suffered from three terrible earthquakes, the second of which destroyed the church of which this wood was part. Nine years after the earthquake the satinwood of a shattered tabernacle across the Atlantic was carved to new use on this side of the ocean, and here it is with its tale of that far-off tragedy unguessed at by most of those who come this way.

The Broken Scholar and the Dying Duchess

HEDSOR. Secluded in a hilly wooded park, it consists simply of Hedsor House and a tiny church, crowning a grassy slope and looking out over as lovely a combination of river and woodland as the county has. Fine trees abound, and among the old yews near

Hanslope — Lofty Medieval Tower and Spire

The Town from the South

Old Church Tower and Quaint Market House
HIGH WYCOMBE

the church are two magnificent veterans, twice as old as the church as we see it. The churchyard, screened by a hedge of yew and holly, is a picture of ordered beauty, in which an appealing element is the simplicity of the graves. Each has its small stone flat on the turf, with merely the name and the date—an unobtrusive practice we should like to see followed in all our churchyards.

The oldest memorial in the rather dark church is a massive 14th century coffin-stone; the newest an attractive little window with Stephen in memory of a soldier who did not come back; the most interesting is a tablet to Nathaniel Hooke, the lifelong friend of Pope. A scholar broken by the South Sea Bubble, he sat by the bedside of the dying Duchess of Marlborough and at her dictation wrote her memoirs, receiving £5000 for his services. It has always been believed that through Hooke the poet Pope received a large sum from the Duchess to suppress in his Moral Essays his picture of her as Atossa, beginning:

> *Full sixty years the world has been her trade,*
> *The wisest fool much time has ever made;*
> *From loveless youth to unrespected age,*
> *No passion gratified except her rage.*

Whatever the truth, Atossa disappeared until after the poet's death, when it took its place among his poems again. Hooke's worthiest title to fame is a Roman History which occupied him over 30 years, only to be banished to oblivion by Gibbon's Decline and Fall.

The church has some carved stalls and a modern stone pulpit. There is a castle-like tower in the park to George the Third, and the house, on the site of an older one, is nobly placed on a hill from which it seems to hail its little church.

The Town that Rejected Disraeli

HIGH WYCOMBE. It is one of the busiest towns in the county, spread along the valley of the Wye and climbing up the hills. On the hills are ancient earthworks and prehistoric dwellings, and Roman villas have been found. High up is the hamlet of Tylers Green with a modern church and the 19th century house of Rayners, built by a friend of Disraeli, who would often come here and look out on seven counties, with a range from the Crystal Palace to the hills of Hampshire.

THE KING'S ENGLAND

Entering the town on the Oxford road from London, we come upon Norman arches of a Knights Templar Hospital with 13th century sculpture round the capitals and ruined lancet windows. From behind these ruins the ancient grammar school has been removed to a height above the town; today the technical school stands in its place. In the High Street, as we pass into the town between charming houses of three centuries, the road widens out towards the Red Lion Inn with the portico from which Disraeli made his first political speech. More than a hundred years have passed since this romantic Jew came into our history by standing for High Wycombe. He failed three times, but it was long before the Wycombites forgot their lively candidate. He yearned so hard to represent them in the House of Commons that he told them he had lived in High Wycombe before the Reform Bill and " was bred there, if not born." He would enter the town in a carriage drawn by four horses, escorted by a band with banners, kissing his hand to ladies in the street and bowing profoundly to his friends. He would stand on the porch of the Red Lion and orate for an hour, castigating the Whigs and delighting the mob with his jokes. After he had been defeated twice he declared that he was ready to try again, for he did not feel like a beaten man: he felt like the famous Italian General who, being asked in his old age why he was always victorious, replied that it was because he had always been beaten in his youth.

At the top of the High Street is the 18th century guildhall, with a wooden cupola on which swings a weathervane of a centaur shooting an arrow into the wind. In the big room is John Mortimer's painting of the Conversion of the Britons. The quaint little market-house, with its sides perched on arches was designed by the famous Adam Brothers. The modern town hall is in a handsome block crowned by a small tower and a cupola, housing not only the civic authority but the public library, the art gallery, and the museum. The town hall has an oak room panelled by local craftsmen and lit by beautiful windows, one with a portrait of Hannah Ball who lived close by and used to teach children at her house on Sunday afternoons. Hers was the very first known Sunday School, an informal gathering years before Robert Raikes had thought of it at Gloucester. Just outside the town today, not far from where Hannah Ball received her scholars, stands one of the finest schools for girls in England,

Wycombe Abbey. It was built by Lord Carrington in 1795, and has a lake in beautiful grounds of 250 acres.

The art gallery has a collection of pictures and other exhibits, bequeathed to the town by John Thomas, and the museum has 17th and 18th century woodwork, with a collection of chairs from James the First to Queen Anne, and on through the Georgian period. There is a fine needlework jewel casket of Charles the Second's time in perfect condition, and a portrait group of Lord Wharton with his wife and their child, who lived at Wooburn House. The museum has also two Adam mantelpieces.

We may roam for hours here admiring old buildings, St Paul's Row behind the Cornmarket has an array of gabled houses, once inns and now shops. Priory Street has the remains of the medieval priory (now shops) and next to them is a group with the gabled Town House, the Chantry, and the Vicarage, all with 16th century work. The Queen Elizabeth almshouses were rebuilt last century.

The 700-year-old church, into which we come through a porch with four modern statues of saints, is the biggest church in the county, about 200 feet long, with the pinnacles of its 16th century tower rising more than 100 feet above the street; in it is a ring of 12 bells. The nave and chancel are 13th century, but the arcades and the clerestory are 15th and 16th. So are the roofs, that in the nave resting on angels holding shields and musical instruments; it was sad to see that the beetle which eats our ancient timbers has compelled the restoration of this fine woodwork. There is fine woodwork, old and new, in screens and stalls, in a great oak chest with six locks, in the painted reredos with figures of our four patron saints, and on a pew enclosure at the east end of the nave with octagonal pillars crowned with wooden statues of Wulfstan, Frideswide, Hugh of Lincoln, and Catherine of Alexandria. The medieval chapel on the south side has a window given by the children, and the south chancel aisle has a screen put up in 1468 by Richard Redehole.

One of the windows is a pathetic memory of three sons of the first Bishop of Buckingham, all of whom fell in the Boer War, but the window of windows at High Wycombe is a magnificent piece of 20th century craftsmanship. It is in memory of famous women, and has portraits of 17 of them, St Margaret with a horseman in the centre, and the four sainted figures, Bridget and Winifred, Hilda and Frideswide. There are three famous Margarets (Margaret Beaufort, Margaret Roper, and Margaret Godolphin), and two Emilys (Emily Davies with a building in her hand and Emily Brontë). The great Elizabeth Fry is with the great Florence Nightingale. Queen Victoria is shown as a girl, and the other women are Grace Darling, Christina Rossetti, Alice Marval with an Indian child, and Mary Slessor with a little black child. The memorial to the men who fell in the Great War is a carved oak reredos dazzling in black, blue, and gold, with painted figures and heraldry. It stretches right across the chancel, and is the work of local craftsmen as an act of homage to their fellow citizens. It is made up of a series of canopied niches filled with figures including the Crucifixion, with Mary and John, and our four patron saints. St David and St Patrick are shown presenting a kneeling soldier to Our Lord on the Cross.

The organ is interesting, having been made in 1783 and played until our own time, when it was dismantled and rebuilt; it has over 2000 pipes.

On a monument as high as the roof, by Peter Scheemakers, rests Henry Petty, Earl of Sherburne, in classical costume with his wife, and on the front of the tomb is a medallion portrait of his father. The wife of the second earl is in marble with her two children. On a sculptured tablet in the wall, in memory of a watchmaker of Holborn who lived in Shakespeare's day, are the tools of his trade; and we read of another watchmaker of a later day that, worn out with repeating time, the wheels of his weary life at last stood still. Hanging on a pillar are the sword and spurs of Lord Wendover who fell in the Great War, and near him hangs the proud banner of his father Lord Lincolnshire, with the staff he carried as Great Chamberlain at the coronation of George the Fifth. Here we come upon two curious facts of much interest to antiquarians. It happened that in 1907 the Red Lion Inn, so familiar to Disraeli, had a new proprietor who was none other than Oliver Cromwell, claiming descent from the Protector; and in the same year there died in this place George Shakespeare Hart, a descendant of Shakespeare's sister.

Love and War

HILLESDEN. Solitary in the meadows, it has only its beautiful church, its parsonage, and a few cottages, for green mounds hide the remains of the great house it has lost, with its story of a famous siege, of the chivalry of Cromwell, and of lovers meeting amid the smoke and din of conflict.

Built by the monks of Notley Abbey, the 15th century church charms the visitor still as it charmed Sir Gilbert Scott, who found in it an exquisite example of its period. Like a gem in a crown, a delightful octagonal turret rises over the battlemented walls, its dainty pinnacles united by tiny flying buttresses to a central column. Faced by the shaft of a medieval preaching cross, the north porch, with an elaborate canopied niche and a fine vaulted roof, has a ring handle of entwined snakes and double doors which, hung here 500 years ago, still show the holes made by bullets of the Civil War.

They bring us into a bright interior with beautiful arcades. Angels guard the east window, and on the walls are 40 more angels painted five centuries ago. The church has ten consecration crosses which have survived the centuries. By the chancel is a vestry with roses round the window and medieval tiles in the floor. Above the vestry is a chamber with open tracery through which the family from the great house could see the altar and remain unseen. A doorway now built up led to a bridge linking the chamber with the house. The spiral stairway of the turret has two oak doors from the time of Columbus. The font, with a Jacobean cover, has served for over 20 generations.

The splendid chancel screen is as old as the church, with double doors in its central arch, a frieze of vine leaves on the canopy, and linenfold on its panels. Tudor craftsmen carved the smaller screen, nine nave seats, and two desks. There is a wealth of 15th century glass, of which that in the sanctuary window shows St John, St George, St Christopher, and a Pope resplendent in colour. A transept window has scenes from the legend of St Nicholas. The rich colouring, the movement, the dramatic situations, and the expressions of the many characters are a triumph of medieval art.

Among the monuments are the tombstone of an unknown Francis Drake who died in 1701; an 18th century tomb, on claw-like feet, with busts of John Denton and his wife; a tablet to William Denton, physician to both Charles Stuarts; and an altar tomb on which lie Thomas Denton and his wife, she in a ruff and an embroidered dress, he in Tudor armour. Their son Thomas married a cousin of John Hampden and was the father of Margaret, wife of the immortal Sir

Edmund Verney. Hillesden House was often the home of Verney and his wife, and here eight of their 12 children were born. It was early in the Civil War that Charles sent a force under Sir William Smith to garrison the house. In the enchanting pages of the Verney Memoirs we have a picture of that time when the fatherless girls daily came over from Claydon, of the raiding of stores and cattle by Royalist troopers, and a Commonwealth attack which failed. The failure prompted sterner measures. Smith summoned a thousand labourers, we are told, ran trenches round the church and the house, built earthworks, made a cannon from a hollowed elm, obtained smaller guns from Oxford, and transformed the church into an arsenal. Cromwell himself leading the attack, the defences were broken and the house compelled to surrender, Smith being prisoner. Coming out bareheaded, Smith angrily complained to Cromwell that a Commonwealth soldier had carried off his hat, and, offering his own hat, Cromwell said, "Sir, if I can discover the man who took your hat he shall be punished. Meantime be pleased to accept this."

While in command of the house Smith had fallen in love with the daughter of Sir Alexander Denton, and married her a few months later in the Tower, where he was a prisoner with her brother. Sir Alexander died in captivity; Smith lived to enjoy years of peace. It happened also that Captain Jaconiah Abercromby, with Cromwell's troops, met Sir Alexander's sister Susan, fell in love, proposed, and was accepted. The house which had been the scene of love and war was burned down and has left no trace.

Here Walked Queen Elizabeth

HITCHAM. It stands on a hilltop overlooking the Thames Valley, with the ancient walls of its lost manor house enclosing a garden. A group of cottages on one side of the garden have built into them four wooden columns on stone bases, and at the other side are two great iron gates. In these gardens walked Queen Elizabeth. In the 600-year-old chancel of the Norman church lies the lord of the manor who entertained Elizabeth here the year before she died. Two soldiers stand on his tomb, holding back curtains to reveal his reposeful figure. Hanging on the wall is his helmet, and in the panel of the tomb kneel his five sons and three daughters.

Light falls into the chancel through much of its original glass, in which is Our Lord with his hand raised in blessing, Evangelists sitting with scrolls, and winged angels standing on wheels. In a recess of the chancel wall are the white figures of an Elizabethan family, Roger Alford, his wife, and two children, and on the facing wall is a peace memorial designed by Sir Banister Fletcher, in which two angels kneel and a little cherub is carved below the names that live for evermore. Here still is much of the work the Normans left behind; the nave itself is Norman and the light still falls into it through some Norman windows. The chancel arch has simple Norman decoration on its capitals; the stone knight on one of the corbels of the arch is perhaps 14th century. There are many old and beautiful tiles, one of a mermaid, one of a hound hunting a stag, and one of a horseman with a falcon. Among the tiles is a great stone in which is set a brass portrait of Nicholas Clarke in Tudor armour, his head on his tilting helmet. On another brass are the portraits of Thomas Ramsey and his wife, he in chain mail and she with ermine cuffs and a long veil, their seven children with them in Tudor dress. The pulpit is Jacobean, with a richly carved canopy.

The Hassock

HOGGESTON. Its Jacobean manor is now a farm, with gables and graceful chimneys, and its Norman church has been made new, delightfully set in a trim churchyard. The 16th century tower, with a 14th century stone head built into a wall, has a modern spire and rests on chestnut piles. The arcades are 13th and 14th century. Two of the doorways are 600 years old, and the newest porch is Tudor. It has an old stone cross built in its wall, and stone seats and medieval timbers. A wall in the chancel has fragments of Norman masonry. The canopied sedilia and piscina have been in use 600 years, and nearly 20 generations of children have been baptised at the font. Under a low arch in the chancel lies a man in a robe, tunic, and hood, holding a model of the church. He is believed to be William de Birmingham, who was living at the manor in 1342. There is a 16th century tomb with shields and traces of colour to Elizabeth Mayne, and a tablet to a rector for 45 years of the 18th century. Three 17th century wood panels have found their way into the umbrella stand—a thing which surprises us as much as the finding here of a hassock of dried grass on which worshippers were kneeling 400 years ago.

THE KING'S ENGLAND

The Grubbs

HORSENDEN. Rich pasture land surrounds its few cottages, the farm with its quaintly designed dovecot, the great house among splendid trees, and the odd-looking little church. Horsenden House replaced, soon after Trafalgar, one which was garrisoned for Charles Stuart by Sir John Denham, a successful dramatist of the days of lewd plays. Denham was captured by General Waller at Farnham Castle, but was restored to favour and prosperity at the Restoration, when he sold Horsenden House to the Grubb family, of whom the church has many memorials.

The church, with an angel projecting from each side, has a little 18th century tower, which makes the building appear out of proportion, as in fact it is. Of the much bigger original building there remains only the 15th century chancel; and the effect is curious, for, as the old chancel is now the whole church, all the seats run lengthwise. Another odd result is that the 16th century chancel screen, its spandrels carved with lions and roses, is at the west instead of the east, while the long slanting peephole to the altar is now part of the west wall. The oldest memorial is a quaint inscription cut on a diamond-shaped stone with a queer head at the top and a skull and crossbones at the bottom; it is to Bathehuel Grubb, who died in 1666 and is absurdly stated to have been 141, so exceeding the figures of a mason elsewhere who, told to put thirty-nine on a tombstone, put it there too literally—309.

A plain tablet records the story of Anne Grubb who died in 1721, daughter of an advocate in the French Parliament at Bordeaux, who fled to England in 1669, one of the victims of the persecution which drove 400,000 Huguenots into exile.

Milton's Paradise

HORTON. It has known John Milton. Here three centuries ago he came as a young man, and loved the beauty of this place. So charmed was he with his first visit that, returning to Cambridge University, he sat down and called on the groves and rivers, and the beloved village elms, under which he had had supreme delight with the Muses, "when he too, among rural scenes and remote forests, seemed as if he could have grown and vegetated through a hidden eternity."

BUCKINGHAMSHIRE

This was Milton's home in his formative years. Here his genius matured. Of the house in which he lived with his parents from his 24th year until the death of his mother not one stone remains, but we may say of him as he said of "the admirable dramatic poet W. Shakespeare,"

Dear son of Memory, great heir of Fame,
What need'st thou such weak witness of thy name?

This countryside, this perfect piece of England, from which he would see the stately towers of Windsor in the distance, and all these little fields laughing with plenty about him, he would remember as a paradise long years afterwards when he was thinking of another Paradise.

The glories of light and life, of sound and scene, amid which he lived like a star apart, thrill us in the poems he wrote here, L'Allegro, Il Penseroso, Comus, and Lycidas. Here he heard the nightingale, "most musical, most melancholy"; here he watched the dappled dawn breaking over these russet lawns and fallows grey, and heard the song of winds whispering into sleep. From time to time he would go up to London to see a play or for instruction in mathematics and music, returning with fresh books to read on a bank "with ivy canopied and interwoven with flaunting honeysuckle," where echoing music "smoothed the raven down of darkness till it smiled."

The wings of his genius having sailed the heights, he too must away. He has stood by the deathbed of his mother; his Lycidas is dead, celebrated in immortal lines, and the poet must be gone:

And now the sun had stretched out all the hills,
And now was dropped into the western bay.
At last he rose, and twitched his mantle blue:
Tomorrow to fresh woods and pastures new.

He found them in Italy, in the company of Galileo and men who were moulding the thought of the world.

Although woods have thinned and some are gone, much is still here as Milton knew it, with something added. The names of those who went out to France and did not come back are on a cross on the green of their little Paradise Lost. In the churchyard are yews which must have been stately trees when Milton shared their shade. The tower and the porch were two centuries old when he came here, and we can imagine with what pleasure he, lover of ancient beauty, would pause before this magnificent Norman doorway, its four orders richly adorned with zigzag, bead, and reel work. The massive piers of the Norman nave, with the 15th century roof, the trefoiled piscina, and the low Norman font, can have seen little change since he came to the grave in the chancel in which his mother was laid. Here she rests beneath a stone with its prosaic inscription sadly worn. The chancel itself has been remade, but its 500-year-old arch has Norman stones in it. On an arcade are traces of painting which must have been bright in the poet's day.

The east window is dedicated to Milton and has the Crucifixion, but a panel in one of its lancets shows him writing Paradise Lost. It is in nightingale time that we picture him vividly here, listening for the bird he loved, and answering it in song:

> *Thee, chauntress, oft the woods among*
> *I woo, to hear thy evensong;*
> *And, missing thee, I walk unseen*
> *On the dry smooth-shaven green.*

All the pictures of nature shining in the poems of his blindness he remembered from those years at Horton when his mind was building up its glowing vision. They were the happiest years of his life; and the thought of what this storied scene meant to him in all his afflictions invests this scene for us with a pathos almost too deep for tears.

Here Lies Benjamin Disraeli

HUGHENDEN. On a ridge of the Chilterns, overlooking a pleasant valley, stands the imposing manor house, with its deep bays, its ornamental balustrade, its terraced garden, renowned as the home of a great English statesman. Here came Disraeli in 1848 to spend his prime within hail of the commons and beechwoods of his boyhood home at Bradenham Manor; here he lived 33 years and here he died.

In the roomy house sheltered in its belt of trees his strange personality made a hiding-place from the storms of a public career and from the griefs of personal loss. At Hughenden in his garden, on the calm hillside, he sunned himself in the incredible triumphs of his old age, found strength to bear increasing maladies, wrote his last novel, and prepared to say farewell to what he had described in a letter to the Queen as a somewhat romantic and imaginative life. He rests now in the little churchyard at the foot of the park among the trees he loved. About sixty acres of the park belong to the people, High Wycombe having bought the ground as a memorial to King George the Fifth; and the house has been given by its owner, Mr W. H. Abbey, to a trust, in the hope that it may become a national monument with a small museum.

It is Jacobean, and stands on the crest of a wooded hill, a white gleaming structure among the trees, with lawns in front and a hollow dividing it from the park. Here Disraeli would entertain his rivals and his friends; and the story is told that when Sir William Harcourt went down to Hughenden for a weekend he was a little awed to realise that Disraeli had thought it necessary to arm all the servants with revolvers as a defence against burglars. They found Lady Beaconsfield delighting in her peacocks, and the grounds now thrown open to the public were stocked with them. One fine bird vanished, whether to adorn a rival park or to be put in a pie was never known, but the loss was deemed so serious that a guardian was appointed to safeguard the rest of the birds. He was a tiny wide-mouthed boy called the peacock-herd. Equipped with a portable wooden seat, it was his duty from sunrise to sunset to parade the park, warding the gay birds. He kept his guard in front of the house, ever on the look-out for intruders.

Four people lie in Disraeli's tomb in the churchyard, and three stones under canopied arches on the wall of the chapel tell of these sleepers: Benjamin Disraeli and his wife, his brother James, and Sarah, widow of James Bridges Williams, who had revered the novelist and at her death left him a fortune and begged that she might share his grave.

The church had been refashioned a few years before Disraeli's death, only the medieval chancel and chapel being allowed to remain, though a bell still rings which was ringing before the Reformation, and the round font with 13th century foliage above the arcading is still at home here, in keeping with the ancient corbels on the chapel windowsill. One of the corbels is the oldest stone in the church, a head with a lolling tongue, carved by a Norman craftsman.

There are two windows in memory of Disraeli. The undergraduates of Oxford having given one of the Resurrection and the Ascension, while Lord Rothschild, Sir Philip Rose, and Lord Rowton (his friend and secretary) gave the east window of Christ in Glory receiving homage from characters in the Bible. Over Disraeli's seat in the chancel hang a banner and the insignia of the Garter, brought from St George's Chapel, Windsor. In the wall is a stone memorial set by Queen Victoria with a portrait in relief by R. C. Belt, and an inscription with a phrase from Proverbs, Kings love him that speaketh right. The pulpit, most elaborately carved, in marble and alabaster, with figures of the four archangels, was put in the church after Disraeli's death.

Separated from the chancel by an arcade with painted shields on the capitals is the de Montfort chapel, which has an appearance as curious as its story. At first sight it seems to be set apart for the memorials of a noble house of medieval origin, but thanks to the scrutiny of our antiquarians, we know now that many of the figures are elaborate frauds due to the vanity of the Wellesbourne family, who lived here in the 16th century, and went to ingenious lengths to prove their connection with the de Montforts, employing craftsmen to combine their coat-of-arms with that of the ancient house.

The figure of a knight in chain mail lying with crossed legs on the floor was long considered to represent a son of Simon de Montfort. It is a vigorous piece of sculpture with queer conceptions. On the coat are the arms of the knight (a griffin with a child in its grasp) and the knight holds a big shield on which is a lion with a child in its mouth. Seven small shields with meaningless heraldry adorn the scabbard of the sword, and more heraldry is on the armour of another figure in a recess. A third knight in mail lies on the windowsill, with outstretched legs and a heart carved on his breast. His feet rest on a lion, his head on two griffins, each with a child in its claws. Like some of the other monuments in the chapel, this is probably a 16th century copy of a 14th century monument. Of the six stone figures here, five are considered to be copies of medieval work done at the order of the Wellesbournes. One alone, which lies in an arched recess, is declared to be genuine, a 16th century sculpture of a corpse in a shroud. In its sunken chest is carved a queer little figure, probably meant for the escaping soul.

Among all these strange memorials is a brass portrait of Robert Thurloe, who died in 1493 and is shown in his priest's robes. In a niche in the chancel wall is the alabaster figure, in Jacobean dress, of Thomas Lane, a boy who died at 14.

One of nature's loveliest memorials stands outside the church, a yew planted in 1690 and cut square. Close by are some gabled almshouses which, like the manor farmhouse some little distance away, were young when the hoary tree was planted.

Precious relics of late 17th century work are treasured in an upper room of the farmhouse—painted panels recently discovered under layers of canvas and paper. The artist was in a merry mood when painting these pictures, which stretch from floor to ceiling. His colours were only black, white, and sepia, but he made of them charming scenes of fishing and hunting. In one picture a gallant in a three-cornered hat has been driven up a tree by a wild boar.

The Romantic Jew

BENJAMIN DISRAELI, Earl of Beaconsfield, is a unique figure in our political history. He was as unlike an Englishman as a man could be, but by sheer strength of will and cleverness he became the head of the Government and personal friend of Queen Victoria. His story is not that of a statesman who achieved great legislative results, but that of a man who played a lone hand in politics and rose to high renown in face of difficulties that seemed insurmountable. The man himself was far more remarkable than anything he did, for his work was of little account.

He was born in London just before Trafalgar, a son of Isaac D'Israeli, a Spanish Jew of good repute. As Jews the family were ineligible for the English Parliament, but when Benjamin was 12 his father escaped that dilemma by having the children baptised into the Church of England. No one can say that Benjamin Disraeli was not faithful to his race. Though he knew that his Jewish origin was a handicap against him he emphasised constantly the glories of the Jewish people, and defied rather than evaded the popular feeling against them. Examples of pride in his race abound in his writings.

His school education was insignificant. He absorbed knowledge from omnivorous reading in his father's library, and from mixing with and studying his fellowmen. After some youthful years in a solicitor's office he determined to trust to his pen to make himself known to the world, and his brilliant and extravagantly imaginative novel Vivian Grey, published when he was 21, at once became a best-seller. Leisurely travel through Spain, Italy, Palestine, and

Egypt followed. Returning to London to fulfil his ambition as a writer, he found the country seething with excitement over the Reform Bill of 1832, and while he continued a series of high-flown romantic novels, in which one character always had a likeness to young Benjamin Disraeli, he plunged into politics.

Twice he fought parliamentary elections as an advanced Liberal. By 1835 he had adjusted himself to the political circumstances of the period, and, changing sides, fought an election as a Tory. A third time he suffered defeat. Before the election which came with the accession of Queen Victoria to the Crown, in 1837, Disraeli had made the acquaintance of a wealthy Tory, Mr Wyndham Lewis, and he and Lewis were returned as members for the two Maidstone seats. Lewis died, and in 1839 Disraeli married his widow. His age was 34 and hers 56. The marriage relieved him of his financial difficulties, which had become acute, and also enabled him to buy Hughenden Manor, which became their country home.

At this time, through his writings, his brilliant conversation, and his unusual personality, he had become a conspicuous figure in fashionable society. His odd appearance, his foppish extravagance in dress, his black hair worn in ringlets, his clothes of many hues, were singularly un-English, and when he made his first speech in Parliament he was laughed at and howled down as a parliamentary misfit; but he finished his speech with the defiant words "a time will come when you will hear me." Already, it was reported, he had admitted that his ambition was to be the Prime Minister of England, and he concentrated his energies on the task.

He began with a change in the tone of the novels he continued to write. They were now political in their aim. Coningsby, Sybil, and Tancred showed him to be a political theorist. He quickly redeemed his failure as a parliamentary debater, and developed ideas distinctly his own as to how the Tory Party could appeal to the wider electorate which he foresaw was bound to come.

When Sir Robert Peel repealed the Corn Laws to cheapen the people's food Disraeli attacked him so fiercely that Peel lost the support of his party, and Disraeli's own position as a powerful critic was established.

It was during this debate that Disraeli reached a depth of dishonour to which few famous men have descended. He savagely

BUCKINGHAMSHIRE

attacked Sir Robert Peel, one of the most honourable men the House of Commons has ever known, as though it were unworthy of an Englishman to serve under such a man; and when Disraeli sat down Peel rose and replied to him with great dignity, not telling the House that he had in his pocket or in his archives an almost whining letter from Disraeli begging for office. It was not until years afterwards, when the revelation could do no harm, that the truth became known.

After this Disraeli set himself the task of educating the Tory Party into the need for accepting popular changes. It was a slow process. Some wished to continue the fight for Protection, but that policy, he said, was "dead and damned." Fifteen years after Disraeli's entry into Parliament Lord Derby formed a Tory Administration and Disraeli became the Chancellor of the Exchequer and leader of the House of Commons. In ten months the Government fell. Six years later he served again as Chancellor under Lord Derby, but only for 18 months. Nine more years passed before, in 1867, Lord Derby formed a third government with Disraeli again as his Chancellor. The conditions were exceptional at that time. A Liberal Government was in a majority and brought in a Bill for an extension of the franchise, but some of the Whigs were afraid the Liberals were going too far, and joined the Tories in defeating the Government. Earl Russell, the Liberal Premier, resigned and Lord Derby succeeded him. This gave Disraeli the first chance he had had in 30 years of making a bold stroke. He took charge and, though his Party was in a minority and his leader said it was "a leap in the dark," he produced a franchise Bill more thorough than the Liberal Bill and "dished the Whigs." Of course the Liberals, and the Tories whom Disraeli had "educated," supported it, and it was carried against the faint-hearted Whigs and the unalterable type of Tories. Next year Lord Derby died, and Disraeli attained his ambition and became Prime Minister.

He began with a mistake. Trusting the new voters, he "went to the country," and the Liberals came back with a majority of 114. Mr Gladstone held the premiership for the next five years, and it was not till 1874, that Disraeli, then in his 70th year, was for the first time Premier with genuine power, and reached the topmost peak of his ambition.

The Liberals, intent on political and social reforms, were accused of handling foreign affairs limply. Here was scope for imagination and self-confidence. Disraeli's first success was the purchase by England for £4,000,000 of a controlling block of shares in the Suez Canal, thereby ensuring the international use of the Canal. It was not his idea: it was urged on him by a journalist, Frederick Greenwood; but he adopted it boldly.

When he retired from his first brief premiership Queen Victoria had become sensitive to the charms of this strange romantic man. His courtliness impressed her, and he always regarded her wishes as paramount and the proposals of premiers and parliaments as *advice offered* and not decisions made. His own views were imperial in scope, and by his advice she assumed the title of Empress of India, and he became Earl of Beaconsfield.

Foreign affairs now became prominent. Russian advances in Asia caused uneasiness. War broke out in the Balkans and Turkey and Russia were involved. The British Government to the edge of war supported Turkey, but Mr Gladstone, with flaming eloquence, denounced the Turkish massacres that had caused the war. Russia halted outside Constantinople, and a Conference at Berlin arranged the terms of peace. Disraeli and Lord Salisbury, the Foreign Minister, were the British representatives at the Conference, and they returned bringing, in the Premier's words, "Peace with Honour." They were received with delirious enthusiasm by those who held that the firm action had checked Russia, and Disraeli was now the favourite of his Sovereign and the idol of society. But he was defeated on going to the country soon afterwards, and died in 1881. His Will precluded his burial in Westminster Abbey and he lies in Hughenden churchyard with his devoted wife.

As a personality he was one of the world's wonders. He overcame difficulties well nigh insuperable and reached the goal of his endeavours. As a statesman he never expressed himself adequately in legislation. The one chance he had he spent in promoting what the Primrose League (founded in his memory) calls "the imperial ascendancy of the British Empire."

Chapter One of a Marvellous Story

HULCOTT. It has a green fringed by cottages, and it keeps part of the old Homestead Moat bordering the churchyard, with its avenue of yews. The church has a bellcot with 16th century

BUCKINGHAMSHIRE

timbers. A 14th century window has stone heads, one with a mail coif; a 16th century doorway has figures of monkeys. A curiosity of the church is that its 16th century aisle is bigger than the nave, which was built 200 years before it. The chancel, made new 600 years ago, has its old priest's doorway, and a marble altar with a fine carving of the Road to Calvary.

The stone pulpit and the font are both carved, and the corbels of the roodloft and the screen survive. In the nave is a beautiful table 300 years old, with a sliding-top and vase-shaped legs. On the list of rectors we found the name of William Morgan, a thrilling one, for it was he who married Patrick Brontë to the little Cornish woman who went to Yorkshire for a holiday and never returned. So he set in being the family which has been a perpetual astonishment to the world and started a marvellous chapter in our literature, for from this union came Charlotte, Anne, and Emily Brontë, with all their wonderful works.

William Morgan was already engaged to Jane Fennell when her cousin Maria Branwell came from Cornwall to Yorkshire to stay with the Fennells, and to fall in love in next to no time with the young curate of Hartshead, Patrick Brontë.

The two cousins discussed their future weddings and decided that they would be married in the same church on the same day, and that Mr Fennell, also a clergyman, should marry them.

When Mr Fennell pointed out that he would be otherwise engaged in giving away first his niece and then his daughter, there were endless conversations as to what would be the best thing to do, and the simple solution was at last arrived at that the two bridegrooms should marry one another and the two brides act as bridesmaids in turn, so leaving Mr Fennell free to give them both away.

Thus it was that, a week before Christmas Day in 1812, Maria and Patrick Brontë stood side by side in Guiseley church while William Morgan pronounced them man and wife, and then the two bridegrooms and the bride and bridesmaid changed places, and Mr Brontë performed the same service for his friend.

Nor was this all that was happening, for down in Cornwall another wedding was taking place, Maria's sister Charlotte having chosen the same day and hour in which to marry her cousin Joseph Branwell. So it came about that two sisters and four cousins had the same wedding day. William Morgan's wife died before he came here (it is his second wife who lies buried in this church), and Patrick Brontë's bride lived only nine years; but all three marriages were happy and one was momentous, for in joining together Maria and Patrick Brontë this Hulcott rector unknowingly turned the first page of one of the most amazing chapters in all our English literature.

Old Yew by the Norman Church

IBSTONE. Its cottages lie scattered about a delightful heather common and open green stretches, on one of which is a row of a dozen lime trees. With beechwood in the background and a clear sight of the Hambleden valley, its church stands on a small green platform sentinelled by a yew with a trunk 16 feet round. Little touched by time, the work of the Norman builders remains. Over their hoary walls rises a small wooden bellcot. We enter through a doorway with diaper carving on the jambs and walk into a Norman nave. There is a low Norman font like a tub. Beyond the tall Norman arch is the chancel as the 13th century builders left it. Striking in its richness amid all this simplicity is the marvellous 15th century oak pulpit. Two arches are carved on each of its four sides, made lovely with the cusps and finials dear to craftsmen of those days.

The churchyard has a big broken stone coffin, and 200 yards away is a 17th century house keeping two of its original chimneystacks.

Nine Men's Morris

ICKFORD. It lies in the meadows with the River Thame streaming past, spanned by a three-arched bridge 250 years old. Here the famous Gilbert Sheldon was rector in the happy days before he was imprisoned as a Royalist. He was to become Archbishop of Canterbury, to build the splendid Sheldonian Theatre, and to help to rebuild St Paul's, but long before all that he sat here by the stone fireplace at which the present rector warms himself. It has still a fireback marked with the CR of Charles Stuart, who was patron of the living.

Of the Norman church there remains only a single arch over the doorway. The saddleback tower, the gabled walls, and the font are all 13th century. There is still a little 14th century glass with bright foliage in the tracery of the sanctuary window. In modern glass are striking figures of Edward the First and Edward the Martyr in memory of Edward Staley, killed in the war. His father, Canon Staley, was a gifted craftsman as well as a biographer, and carved the two beautiful posts supporting the altar curtains.

The oldest monument is a curious Tudor tomb built during his lifetime by Thomas Tipping, who is on it with his wife between black marble columns, their nine children on panels below. On a window-sill we found a curiosity, the markings for Nine Men's Morris, an ancient game played on a table or on a plot of ground; in the Midsummer Night's Dream Titania laments that "The nine men's morris is filled up with mud". In medieval times the villagers must have whiled away at this windowsill many a rainy afternoon. Relics of this ancient pastime are rare; we know of only a few other examples, one at Finchingfield in Essex, and one on a tomb at Dunster in Somerset.

ILMER. Amid little groups of cottages lying in the low meadows of the Thame valley rises a small church. A lane bordered with elms leads us to it, and the slender, oak-shingled spire has a tremulous poplar for company. Over 800 years ago the Norman builders set up these thick nave walls and the round doorway now blocked up. In the nave we see the massive timbers supporting the 16th century bell turret on which the spire rests. There is a plain font over 600 years old, with a cover made in the 17th century in the form of four arches. Through a pleasant screen of wood and stone, set here about 1500, we see the 14th century chancel; the wooden cornice above the old tracery is ornamented with a line of roses.

When the screen was put in place the carvings were new on the chancel windows, where are small figures of the Trinity, two angels, and St Christopher. A window in bright colour tells the story of the Good Samaritan.

Roman, Saxon, Norman, and Tudor

IVER. Here we stand, in this pleasant country of parks and shady lanes, with old houses and what is called Pope's Walk, in the presence of Roman and Saxon, Norman and Tudor. The church has a Saxon nave with Roman bricks visible in its walls, and there are Norman arches, medieval art, and Tudor monuments.

Pope's Walk is in Richings Park, the delightful old houses are gathered about the church, and the Roman bricks are in the eastern corners of the nave. Most of the tower is 700 years old, but its great height is due to the addition of a 15th century bell chamber. In that century, too, they made the new doorway, with flying angels carved at the sides. It is believed that the wooden door has been on its hinges all the time and that all the roofs of the church are 500 years old. A magnificent stone coffin from those far-off days lies in the churchyard.

The clerestory was raised above the Saxon nave, with two aisles, in the 15th century, and the end of the south arcade are the contemporary doorway and stairs which led to the vanished roodloft. On the north side of the nave the Saxon wall has been pierced by two Norman round arches on circular pillars with scalloped capitals. Above one of the arches is part of a round-headed Saxon window in pink stone.

The chancel is 700 years old, its wide pointed arch being richly moulded, and the double piscina and triple sedilia, their slender and graceful round columns fashioned by a 13th century craftsman, form a beautiful composition, the loveliest thing in the church. Strangely enough, they were covered up, and were only found when Sir Gilbert Scott restored the church. Now good modern panelling surrounds the chancel, and there is a fine new reredos with figures of Apostles. On the wall at the end of an aisle is part of the 15th century chancel screen, with delicate tracery in the heads of its oak panels.

The panelled pulpit is 200 years old, carved with cherubs looking out of garlands. The canopy, long used as a table, is now fixed to the vestry wall. The marble font is Norman, the square bowl with ornamental lines being set on round pillars. On the wall near by is a traceried panel from a 15th century altar tomb, found in the stokehole 40 years ago. Opposite are two massive thatch hooks over 300 years old, used for pulling roofs off burning houses in olden days.

On the floor is a brass inscription to Ralph Aubrey, Chief Clerk of the Kitchen to Prince Arthur, whose death changed the face of our history; he was, of course, the first husband of Catherine of Aragon. Forty years ago they found Aubrey's coffin, and on it lay his velvet cap of office and a long kitchen knife, buried in the grave with him 400 years ago. On the sanctuary floor are brass figures of Richard Blount in armour, with his wife Elizabeth in the hooded headdress fashionable in the early years of the 16th century. Standing below are their three sons and three daughters, all in gowns. Above them rises the massive monument of Mary Salter, wife of one of His Majesty's Carvers-in-Ordinary. She died 300 years ago, and there is a figure of her rising from her coffin, with a cherub on each side and an angel in the clouds. Two sons and three daughters kneel below, and a pathetic baby lies on a cushion. Sir William Salter's father is remembered by a black stone on the chancel wall; he died the year before Charles Stuart, having "laboured nigh an hundred year, full forty years a carver to two kings; he and his lady threescore years and three in wedlock spent, a blessing rare to see."

On the wall of an aisle is a little kneeling figure of John King in a black cloak. He died the year after Queen Elizabeth, slain in a drunken fury by his kinsman Roger Parkinson. They had been brought up together, and in a relief are two clasped hands symbolising their warm friendship. Near by is a kneeling figure of an Elizabethan lady in a tall black hat.

On the chancel wall is a stone to Elizabeth Kederminster, granddaughter of Edmund Waller the poet. On the wall near by is a white marble stone to Admiral Lord Gambier, whose ship was the first to break the enemy's line on the Glorious First of June in 1794. Close to this tablet is one to James Whitshed, an 18-year-old midshipman killed in the Mediterranean two years before Waterloo. The inscription tells us that "the last act of his life was saving that of his enemy." He was a pupil of Edward Ward, whose white marble bust by Chantrey is close at hand. It rests on a carved Bible, and shows a kindly-looking man with a firm face full of sympathy. The epitaph says the bust was erected by Ward's pupils as a record of their love, and that he was minister here for 31 years. He died in 1835, and on the opposite wall is a beautiful tablet to his son, William Sparrow Ward, who took over the living and was vicar for 54 years, then resigning owing to blindness, but not before his eyes had seen England transformed during his ministry in this village.

A Gift from Edward the Confessor

IVINGHOE. It is good news that the National Trust has much territory here, and that the old windmill is preserved as a picturesque landmark; for this is a delightful piece of our countryside. Close by the Chilterns, at the forking of the Icknield Way, its

hoary church tower and its Beacon Hill (over 760 feet high) point to
the sky together. The buildings near the church tell of Ivinghoe's old
importance. One, which has a projecting upper storey and original
chimneys, began as a court, became a workshop, and is now a parish
room; one of the inns has a stone fireplace of Queen Elizabeth's
time; a gabled dwelling-house has been here over 400 years, having
the date 1536.

Edward the Confessor gave Ivinghoe to the bishops of Winchester,
who left their mark on the town in the glorious medieval church,
built in the 13th and much altered in the 14th and 15th centuries. It
stands in the form of a cross, a copper spire rising from the central
tower, and its tale of centuries can be read as we go round the grand
sycamore-shaded churchyard. Here we see the noble west porch and
the tall lancet windows of the 13th century blocked up in the chancel,
four of the old clerestory windows left in the transepts when the
15th century builders put in a new roof, and new clerestory windows
to the nave. The roof is a commanding spectacle, rising over the
ranked arches and clustered pillars, with leaf-shaped capitals, of the
nave and tower. The ends of the beams are shaped in the form of
Apostles, and these rest on stone corbels made into grotesque heads
of men and animals, no two alike, those in the chancel very elaborate.
High in the roof angels with outspread wings are looking down.
Near the chancel, where the rood screen was, the roof timbers are
decorated with flowers.

The church has a magnificent Jacobean pulpit of intricate and
rich panelling, set under a sounding-board, supported by a standard
carved with figures in relief, reminding us of Flemish work. Here we
see a group of curious realism only marred by the damaged faces.
Our Lord, holding a Cross from which a banner waves, is stepping
triumphantly out of a coffin, the lid carefully put aside and two
Roman soldiers with halberds standing by it. In the wall by the
pulpit is a cleverly formed iron bracket made to hold the old hour-
glass, which still contains some red sand, a rare reminder of the days
when people loved sermons so much that they cheered when the
preacher turned the glass over to begin again.

There are delightful devices on the poppyhead ends of the 38
benches in which these hearers sat. One has a mermaid with a
looking-glass, strange to find here, so far from the seaboard. They

BUCKINGHAMSHIRE

are all 15th century. Other work of the same century is the base of the simple reading-desk, some open tracery in the altar-rails, and close by them a huge stone figure of a priest in a recess watched over by a crowned head.

The modern builders who put in the new chancel screen, so well made in 14th century style, with five good figures of the Resurrection, also set brass portraits in the transept pavement. They are those of Richard Blackhead and his wife, earliest and smallest of the group; Thomas Duncombe in a fur-trimmed robe with four daughters and six sons; William Duncombe with only 5 of his 13 children left in the picture; and John Duncombe with his wife and their 7 children, all in Elizabethan dress.

An unforgettable reminder of Ivinghoe is Sir Walter Scott's famous novel. Scott visited this place and it is said that he was impressed with its name, probably liking the local jingle he must have heard:

> *Tring, Wing, and Ivanhoe*
> *Hampden of Hampden did forego*
> *For striking of ye Prince a blow*
> *And glad he might escapen so.*

Tokens of the town's past which Scott would have liked to see are on the church wall. One is a great hook which three men together could barely lift, made so that several could share the weight as it was used to pull the thatch off burning cottages. We have come upon several of these throughout the country, but none so big as this. Another odd possession for a church is a mantrap.

The Mayflower in a Country Lane

JORDANS. We are in a little English lane and we may wonder if there is anywhere a place more thrilling to all who speak our mother tongue. We are in the presence of those early builders of our freedom, and at the cradle of our race beyond the seas. Let the cars that hurry by along the road to Oxford turn down towards Milton's cottage at Chalfont and they will pass a timbered barn and a little brick meeting-house, and will know themselves, if they are wise, to be on sacred ground.

The story begins in a little meadow at the foot of the hill, a graveyard in which about 400 people lie; we walk across it to the meetinghouse in which half that number of people can sit on unvarnished deal benches with their feet on a plain brick floor. The leaders sit on a narrow raised platform at one end, and there are panels which can be opened so that those in the upper and lower rooms behind the hall can be brought into the service.

It is the meeting-house built in those days when men were beginning to be free to think the thing they would; it was built immediately after James the Second issued the Declaration of Indulgence. John Penington's mother found £20 to begin it, and John Penington, William Russell, Peter Prince, and Milton's friend Ellwood bought the graveyard in which their friends were sleeping, and set up this small place. Here Thomas Ellwood sleeps, and all the world passes by to see the little cottage he lent to Milton at Chalfont St Giles. The walls of the meeting-house are hung with portraits, autographs, and other reminders of these heroic pioneers.

On a group of simple headstones in the field, set up as a record in the middle of last century, are the names of a few Friends buried here. There is William Penn, the founder of Pennsylvania, with his two wives. There are Mary and Isaac Penington. There is Joseph Rule, who is known as the White Quaker because he dressed in undyed clothing; he was a Thames waterman who joined these early Friends.

We come up the hill from this secluded spot and find ourselves at Old Jordans Farm, now a hostel which bids us welcome. Here lived a yeoman in the days of Charles the Second, and here he welcomed the Friends. We may be sure they would meet in the barn, the great wooden barn 90 feet long and 20 wide, set on walls of brick which have never been moved.

What is there in this great black barn that brings the world to see it? We do not think there is a doubt that these are the timbers of a ship, for we see the holes in which the bolts were set. They are impregnated with salt, and one of the beams which came from the stern of a ship has still a few letters on it: R HAR I which are believed to stand for all that is left of the words Mayflower, Harwich. Dr Rendel Harris studied it all for years, and there is little doubt that he established the truth that these are among the most historic timbers in the world.

The Mayflower was owned partly by Christopher Jones of Harwich, partly by Robert Child of Amersham, partly by a Buckingham-

Jordans — The Mayflower Barn

Jordans — The Meeting-House

Hughenden — Disraeli's Home

Hughenden — Where Disraeli Sleeps

Ivinghoe's Grand Medieval Church

Water Stratford — Carving over South Doorway

Twyford — South Doorway Hanslope — Priest's Doorway

NORMAN HERITAGE

shire man named Moore, and one other. The owner of Jordans Farm in 1625 was a man named Gardiner, and there was a Richard Gardiner among the pilgrims on the Mayflower. Gardiner of Jordans Farm was a kinsman of the man who valued the Mayflower when she was broken up in 1625, and the payment would be due to the four owners. What more likely than that the fourth owner was Farmer Gardiner whose kinsman was among the pilgrims? He could do with the timbers and would buy them from the other three and build his barn with them. It sounds convincing, but there is another witness still, for on one of the doors in the kitchen, the oldest part of the house, is a carving of a mayflower.

Here stands the old barn which we may well believe carried a handful of pilgrims to be the founders of America, and to carry our English spirit across the sea and spread it everywhere. One fragment of its timbering has gone, cut out and presented to Americans who have set it in a place of honour on the Gate of Peace which marks the unfortified boundary of the United States and Canada. It is a thrilling symbol of that peace and freedom which must move us all as we stand here in this great barn in this small country lane.

The Quaker Friend of a Stuart King

WILLIAM PENN, who lies in this small field, whose name gives distinction to a State of the American Republic, was a familiar associate of kings, and at other times an inmate of various prisons as a persistent outdoor preacher of Quaker beliefs. His father was an Admiral of the Stuart period and his mother a Dutchwoman. William was born in London, in 1644, a Civil War child. He grew up susceptible to religious impressions, and when he was sent to Oxford he heard a Quaker's sermon which largely determined the course of his life. Oxford, according to his own account, "banished" him, and his father sent him abroad to forget Quakerism. He returned before he was of age, with manners that struck Pepys as affected, but Quaker seriousness soon resumed its sway. He was then taken to sea by his father, and later was sent to Ireland, where the admiral had property, but there he met again the preacher who had first impressed him, and presently he found himself in prison, making his demand for absolute freedom of conscience which he was to repeat consistently throughout his life.

He now had a period of preaching, public discussion, and writing of tracts and books on the Quaker faith, derived from the Christianity of the first century, and a defence of the lawfulness and right of everyone to preach what he believed. When a jury brought in a verdict of "not guilty" for Penn it was the *jury* that was fined and imprisoned, so determined were magistrates to suppress free speech. This imprisonment of the jury, however, was appealed against and a dozen judges unanimously declared it to be unlawful. In 1670 Penn's father, the admiral, died and left his son a fortune of £1500 a year, and a debt of £16,000 owed by Charles the Second for money lent to him. Penn, because of the religious persecution in England and the greater freedom in the American Colonies, began to take a personal interest in colonial settlement and speculations, and this eventually led to his receiving a grant of an area roughly corresponding with the State of Pennsylvania, in discharge of the debt of £16,000. His purpose was to form a State governed according to principles accepted by Quakers.

Of course the plan did not work. There were infinite complications, with boundaries of other holdings and lands already occupied. Penn was associated with Pennsylvania for 36 years, but he was only in the country for four years. During his first visit he founded the "city of brotherly love," Philadelphia, and won the cordial cooperation and admiration of the Red Indians. The spirit of his work was admirable, and no doubt cast a valuable moral glamour over the region. But actually, in practical matters, visionary views held in England did not apply to actual circumstances in a foreign land. The colony could not be built like a house. It grew like a living organism and as it grew the ready-made plans did not fit. Penn's schemes had to change like a kaleidoscope. His agents cheated him, and the harassment broke his strength. Penn's fame does not really rest on what he did in Pennsylvania.

At home in England Penn was also in a difficult position. He was a friend (a real friend) of James the Second. But James was greatly disliked by the people who sympathised with Penn. James was a Roman Catholic bent on securing religious freedom for his sect, and that was what a majority in England then refused to allow. But such freedom had always been Penn's ideal. Quaker as he was, he believed in freedom for *all*, and said so. The result was that he was accused of being a Roman Catholic and a supporter of the exiled Stuarts. The fact was that he was an honest man. During the reign of James no man was fawned on for favour more than Penn, because it was thought he could influence the king. No doubt he did so sometimes, as when 1200 Quakers were released from the prisons. The friendship with James continued after the king left the country.

Penn continued his religious work as long as his health allowed him, both in England and abroad, and was recognised as the leader of the Society of Friends. His later years were made unhappy by ungenerous treatment by the people of Pennsylvania, the dishonesty of a steward who involved him in debts he disowned. As a consequence he spent nine months in the Fleet prison. He has been sharply criticised because he could not keep the colony he founded on the high lines of his own ideals, but fair judgment by posterity has established his historic standing as that of an honest man, sincere in his piety, with a remarkable influence wherever his personality came directly into play. Penn was a copious writer; about forty pamphlets and books deal with questions current in his day. Two of his works, No Cross No Crown and Some Fruits of Solitude, may still be read with advantage.

Thomas Ellwood and John Milton

THOMAS ELLWOOD, who sleeps here at Jordans with William Penn, was the son of a Puritan landowner, was born in 1639 at Crowell in Oxfordshire, and spend his early years in London, where, drawn by a footman, he would ride in a little coach with Gulielma Springett, who grew up to marry Penn. At school he was a lively youth, and when his father cried, "Disarm them, Tom!" he sprang with his rapier on two ruffians who were about to waylay them.

Turning Quaker, Tom startled his father by refusing to remove his hat, even at meals, lest he should be guilty of a deference to his father which he thought due only to God. Even though Tom was 20, his father beat him and took away all the hats he could find. So the two drifted apart, Tom to imprisonment for his faith, his father to London.

On one of his visits to London a friend introduced Tom to Milton, whom he describes as "a gentleman of great note for learning throughout the learned world, for the accurate pieces he had written on various subjects and occasions." Milton was then blind, and living in retirement. Milton liked the young Quaker, and admitted him six afternoons a week to read to him. Tom had forgotten his Latin, but it was Latin he had to read, the poet patiently correcting. Illness drove Ellwood back to the country, after which he was confined with other Quakers at Bridewell and Newgate, where the prisoners had to sleep in hammocks three tiers deep.

In 1665 Ellwood secured the cottage at Chalfont as a retreat for Milton from the plague, but he was in Aylesbury gaol when Milton arrived. On his release he came to the cottage to welcome the poet, who put a manuscript in his hands, bidding him take it home to read. It was Paradise Lost, and on returning it Ellwood lightly remarked, "Thou hast said much here of Paradise Lost, but what hast thou to say of Paradise Found?" Milton made no answer, but "sat some time in a muse; then brake off that discourse and fell upon another subject"; but when Ellwood next visited him in London the poet showed him a second poem, Paradise Regained, and in a pleasant one said, "This is owing to you, for you put it into my head by the question you put to me at Chalfont, which before I had not thought of." His autobiography, full of piety, of persecution cheerfully born, introduces us to all the great Quakers of the period, including George Fox, whose journal it was the proud task of Ellwood to edit.

The Library and the Pew

LANGLEY MARISH. It grows apace, but it has two beautiful parks, and all unspoiled is the delightful corner where the white-walled Tudor inn, the Jacobean almshouses, and the 800-year-old church cluster together near a hollow yew.

The church has three remarkable features: a wooden arcade, of which we have only a few examples in this country; an extraordinary manor pew; and a library unique in our experience. The nave and one aisle, with herringbone work in their walls, are 12th century. The chancel was remade when Bannockburn was still fresh in the memory of men, and here are the stone seats in which the priests then sat, and the piscina they used, beautiful 14th century work with clustered columns and trefoil arches. The font, which was here in time for the baptism of the first Protestant children, is richly decorated with flowers and the heads of kings, a bishop, and a layman. In the tracery of the sanctuary the north chapel windows glow red, blue, and gold in 14th century glass.

On a chancel wall is a striking monument to the Kederminsters, a family whose record is writ large in the church. They owned the manor, lived at Langley Park, built one group of the almshouses, and left for themselves an astounding memorial. This monument, with the original colours still fresh on its marble figures, has on it 22 members of the family grouped in four panels, with columns, shields, and Cupids. It was erected during his lifetime by Edmund Kederminster, who kneels with his wife, both in Tudor ruffs and gowns, with their 13 children below them. To the right are his parents with their five children below, all named except for four infants in cradles. One of them is Sir John Kederminster, of the famous pew and the remarkable library.

Early in the 17th century (when the tower was built) he pulled down part of the south aisle wall and took in the whole of the south porch, and here is the result of his three years of work, a wonderful example of Jacobean craftsmanship. His library, an extension of the porch, has a fireplace with a magnificently carved mantelpiece, and admirable 17th century table and chairs. The walls and the ceiling are elaborately panelled, and decorated with painting of saints and landscapes, in which we noticed Windsor Castle and Eton College, arabesques and figures, and portraits of Sir John and his wife. Many of the panels form doors, with their inner sides painted like open books; and behind the doors are the books themselves, mainly Latin theological works, but including Bunyan, Holinshead, Purchas, and recipes warranted to "comfort and strengthen the heart."

The books, intended for the use of the clergy, were not chained as in other churches, but Sir John had his doubts, and it was the custom for at least one person from the almshouses to attend at the library and not depart so long as anyone was reading there.

A door leads from the library into the family pew, which, taking the full width of an aisle, is eight feet high, and in design suggests the dark secrecy of an Eastern palace rather than an English church. It is completely enclosed by painted panels, the upper ones latticed, so that the occupants can see into the church while they themselves are invisible.

The panels are continued inside the pew, covering the sides and ceiling, and masking the doorway through the wall into the churchyard. Some are painted like marble walls, some with dark oval centres, others as backgrounds for heraldry, while on some of the ceiling panels is a great eye, with the warning in Latin, *God sees*. This piece of lordly exclusiveness was effected by Sir John on the pretext of seeing better the place "where godly sermons are preached," and for their preaching he gave this oak pulpit, with his arms on one of its panels. After this the Gothic pillars and arches of the north aisle were removed and in their place were set up four pairs of oak pillars, hewn from trees grown in the park. Probably the west door came from the same park; although its outer panelling is 18th century, the door itself has been swinging on its hinges for 500 years, and the screen is of the same age. There is a portrait brass of John Bowser in a long gown and ruff, the inscription saying that he died in the 50th year of the Peace of the Gospel in England, 1608. A brass to Julian Higgins is inscribed:

> *A most kind child, a wife most mild*
> *A spouse and daughter deere.*

In the visitors' book we found an odd and rather moving entry, recalling Anatole France's story of the little juggler who, stopping to pray at a wayside church, and, having no money to leave, gave of what he had, his skill, piously juggling before the altar, in the hope that his offering might be acceptable. The visitor whose entry we came upon here was one as poor in pocket but as rich in spirit, and his scrawl is the most eloquent and touching in the volume: *Tramp. Lovely House of God.*

The great house in Langley Park (500 acres rich in oaks and cedars) was built by the second Duke of Marlborough 200 years ago. Black Park, so called from its many Scots firs, is another delightful place of 500 acres, and, many of its trees being self-sown, it has a romantic suggestion of beautiful and ordered wilderness. A mile away at Horsemoor Green are the playing fields opened as the memorial of the men who did not come back from the war.

The Proud Duke and Margaret Andrewes

LATHBURY. We come through a field with elms and chestnuts and a giant ash from the rectory to the Norman and medieval

BUCKINGHAMSHIRE

church. Its 15th century tower rests on Norman foundations, and has among its gargoyles a striking demon-ape stretching out from a corner carrying a load of mischief, a second ape on its shoulders. The Norman doorway has fine foliage on its capitals, but its tympanum has been brought indoors. It is a remarkable carving about three feet long, showing a fantastic tree with a lion on one side and a browsing horse on the other. Above the distorted tower arch there used to be a thrilling representation of Cain striding solitary through the wilderness, his side pierced by an arrow, and a drawing shows us what it was like. Wonderfully clear and fresh are the carved leaves and fleur-de-lys on the capitals of the Norman arcade, and on the capital of one strong pier are long-tailed dragons feeding.

A 14th century rebuilding gave the church its present chancel with the sedilia and piscina; but an older piscina in one of the aisles is remarkable for a finely carved corbel under the basin. An aisle window has a little ancient glass, and the north aisle roof is 600 years old, as are the angels supporting the roof of the nave.

The chancel floor has a story which might have come from a medieval ballad. The old family of Andrewes lived at Lathbury House, in the beautiful grounds by the church, and there in 1680, the pride and delight of her house, was Margaret, a girl of the same age as Juliet: "A fortnight and odd days; come Lammas Eve at night she shall be 14"; and, like Juliet, she was to be married. The suitor was in the saddle on the way to woo her, a youth of 18 who was to become known to history as the proud Duke of Somerset—so proud that he reduced by £20,000 the dowry of a daughter who dared to sit in his presence. It was he who came riding to woo; but little Margaret lay dying, and instead of studying marriage vows she was pledging her parents to divide her money between the poor and church (the church's share to be the black and white marble pavement of this chancel). She died and her bridegroom-elect became the husband of the most-married child in England, Elizabeth Percy, who, holding in her own right six of the oldest baronies in the kingdom, was wife and widow at 12, was then married to Thomas Thynne of Longleat, the magnificent house in Somerset, and was Duchess of Somerset at 15. Margaret sleeps here, a long inscription telling her sad story.

A brass to Richard Davies tells that in 1661 he died at the house of his son, the rector, and that the brass was placed here by his other son Thomas, "Agent-General for the English nation on the West Coast of Africa," who, having erected a cenotaph at his father's birthplace, added this small memorial for "such Cambria-Brittaines as shall this way travaile."

A still older sanctuary memorial is that to Alice Chandflower, who died a year after Queen Elizabeth and is shown on an engraved stone kneeling at a desk, with a son behind her, and twin baby boys in swaddling clothes.

But the most important possessions of the church are perhaps the impressive 15th century paintings on the wall. They are fading, but we may reconstruct them for ourselves from photographs. The paintings extend from the walls to the arches. In a Doom picture over the chancel arch the head of Our Lord is so clear that we recognise the Byzantine style of the drawing; on His right are the mansions of the heavenly kingdom, on the left the last home of the impenitent. Other pictures show a dying woman receiving extreme unction; a burial scene with three mourners; and the weighing of souls, which has a crowned Madonna in the background.

Thomas Fuller's Lost Wager

LATIMER. Overlooking a secluded valley through which runs the River Chess (and in which the Romans lived, for one of their villas is on Dell Farm close by), the clustering cottages with old timbers and bow windows make a picture of delight. Their proud neighbour, Latimer House, a red-brick mansion, stands high with its back to the woods, facing the vale; it was to the house before it that Charles Stuart was brought a prisoner two years before he died; here, in the course of his flight to France, Charles the Second took refuge.

The small brick church built by Sir Gilbert Scott, which stands in a corner of the grounds, has some memorials taken from an earlier church. One is nameless: a square tomb with four charmingly carved cherub heads on the top and a cupid about 24 inches high standing on the floor beside it. Anne, wife of Sir George Morton, has the oldest memorial in the church, a neat wall monument made of two black columns flanking her inscription. She died in 1632, while Hester Sandys was alive. Hester was born at Latimer and married

Little Missenden — By the River Misbourne

Latimer — In the Valley of the Chess

Ivinghoe Beacon

A Scene near Chequers
IN THE CHILTERN HILLS

Sir Thomas Temple of Stowe. Her real memorial is a paragraph written by Thomas Fuller, telling us that she had four sons and nine daughters who lived to be married and so exceedingly multiplied that this lady saw 700 descended from her. "Reader (he says) I speak within compass and have left myself a reserve, having bought the truth hereof by a wager I lost."

There are two angels on the memorial of the nine men of Latimer who fell in the Great War, and the arch of the apse is bright with angels painted gold, yellow, and blue in memory of Charles Cavendish, a youth who fell in the South African War. On a red granite obelisk in the middle of the village green, rising from a pavement made with Roman tiles, are written the names of 100 men of the district who served in that campaign. At their head is Lord Chesham, who is also remembered in a wall tablet in the church. Lord Chesham brought back from South Africa a famous horse, Villebois, who had been wounded when his master was killed in battle. The horse has a tomb to himself near the obelisk.

Sir Isaac Newton's Kinsman

LAVENDON. It is the county's Farthest North, and its ancient monuments were here before the Conqueror came. It has traces of an ancient castle with a farmhouse on its mount, it has a house built on the site of a Norman abbey with part of its moat still visible, and it has a Saxon tower. One of its houses, rebuilt in 1625 from old materials, is Lavendon Grange, the home of a kinsman of Sir Isaac Newton; a sundial is inscribed, They perish, and are reckoned.

The church has seen the castle and the abbey wax and wane, for its builders were Saxons, and their work still rises above the nave in the fortress-like tower. Its lowest openings in Saxon days were 16 feet from the ground, and no man could be squeezed into them though arrows could be shot out of them. The Saxon tower arch remains with an opening high above it, and there are three 11th century windows one above the other, with arches of rough stone. The window at the top of the tower is 15th century. The Saxon walls project a little way into the west of the nave and are seen again in the west of the chancel, though the chancel arch is modern. It was the successors of the Normans who gave the sanctuary its deeply splayed lancets, and built the doorway with the massive piers and capitals of grim heads which has been reset in the south aisle. The 15th century gave the church its porches, the high clerestory, and the font, which has tracery and foliage on a coloured background. There is a rich Jacobean pulpit with arches and a frieze of foliage, and a 17th century chair with heads of mastiffs projecting from its arms.

The kinsman of Sir Isaac Newton who lived at Lavendon Grange is remembered in a draped urn memorial on the wall. He was Richard Newton who died here in 1753, having founded Hertford College at Oxford. He was for over 20 years rector of a Northamptonshire parish, and at 34 was appointed principal of Hart Hall, Oxford, which had given him its degree of Doctor of Divinity. Here he was accompanied by two of his pupils, the Duke of Newcastle and his brother Henry Pelham, the future Prime Minister, for whom Richard Newton is said to have written the King's speech.

For nearly 30 years Newton struggled to get Hart Hall incorporated as Hertford College, spending what would be £10,000 of our money in building, and at last did get his college established, with himself as its first head. We read that in fixing the dietary he appointed small beer and apple dumplings for one day's dinner, and peas and bacon for another. He would not allow his students to write poetry unless they showed a genius for it; but he did make them write English, an innovation in an age which loved the classics exceedingly, and where little else mattered—except divinity. Newton was the butt of fierce satires among the rich classicists, lost his luxury-loving pupils and was involved in disputes with other colleges. Only one petty preferment came his way, his Prime Minister friend explaining that the fine old man never asked for any!

The Medieval Craftsman in the Norman Church

LECKHAMPSTEAD. It is hidden away from the world, church and cottages set in a little remote valley, shaded by elms, and watered by the River Leck, a tributary of the Ouse. We feel that time has stood still by the flowing stream as we enter the church by a doorway which has been in use for 800 years. It is one of three distinguished doorways here, and was treated by the Norman sculptors with special grace. In addition to its zigzag ornament there are winged heads carved on the capitals, and on the tympanum winged dragons seem to be fighting desperately over the head of an indifferent little man whose fingers are not afraid of their claws. By this doorway is an ancient mass dial, and two others are scratched in the south wall of the nave and a buttress of the tower. In the north doorway, which was built a little later, three bold heads adorn the hood moulding. Another doorway was made when the tower was built in the 13th century. Two hundred years later the repairers added a stringcourse, set two huge gargoyles for ornament, and built the porch to protect the rare south door. On the dragon tympanum are traces of colour made by medieval workmen, and much clearer reminders on the stout square Norman piers of the nave. We see Ave Maria and a Cross in red on one, and on another Latin words meaning Here sits Isabella. The friends of the 13th century painter who made this unknown Isabella immortal rebuilt the round Norman arches, carved their mouldings, and set heads over them.

After another hundred years more chisels could be heard in the valley, craftsmen turning the font into a little sculpture gallery. It had first been a Norman tub font patterned with strap work and leaf design. The newcomers made it octagonal and carved figure groups, allegorical scenes and flowers in the panels. We see the Crucifixion, St Catherine and her wheel, Mary and the Child under a rich canopy, a mitred bishop with a staff, and a curious picture of a boar uprooting a small tree which Bible scholars will recognise as an illustration of a verse in the 80th Psalm. The altar tomb which stands near the font was made in the 14th century. On it lies a knight wearing the armour of Bannockburn, his head on two flat cushions, his spurred feet (his spurs are strapped to them) resting on a lion. The sculptor was particular about armour details. We are surprised to see the long thin sword still intact, and the elbow and knee protectors perfect though the plates on the legs and the feet are worn smooth.

There are two brass portraits, one of a lady in a Tudor headdress and one of Reginald Tylney in a fur-trimmed gown, with his three daughters. A modern brass in the chancel reminds the village of the soldier and sailor sons of Robert Gore-Browne, the sailor falling at Jutland and the soldier at Namacurra. Vivid colour of ruby, green, and gold shines in the reredos, where we see the adoration of the Wise Men, a picture composed of coloured tiles set here in memory of Heneage Drummond, rector for 46 years.

THE KING'S ENGLAND
Three Men in a Window

LEE. Secluded in Bray's Wood a mile away are remains of British and Roman settlements, but it is another prehistoric fort that has become the centre of the village, for the old church and the new church, and what is called Church Farm, are all within an enclosure of seven acres shaped like a pear surrounded by a rampart and traces of a ditch.

A path bordered with roses brings us to the mother church, entered by a small porch in which hangs the door that was hung when the church was new 700 years ago. It is plain, with strap hinges, and may be as old as Magna Carta. The font is of the same age, and has in it two staple holes made so that it could be locked against witches lest they should steal the holy water. There is a beautifully carved piscina of the 14th century, but the stone seat for the priest which was once in range with it has been moved to the new church. Projecting from the chancel walls are carved fragments which were once part of a stone screen, and on another wall are traces of medieval painting. In the east window is a little glass 700 years old with heads of saints, and below this are three stately figures of champions of freedom, each with his hand on his sword: Cromwell, Hampden, and Sir Miles Hobart. It was Hobart who locked the door of the House of Commons and put the key in his pocket to keep the military out and the members in while the Speaker was held in his chair so that resolutions could be put and carried; he was thrown into prison with Eliot—Eliot to lie there till he died, Hobart to languish for two years till plague drove him to submit, and he was set free only to be killed by the overturning of his coach soon afterwards.

The story of this window is curiously interesting, for it was offered by Sir Arthur Liberty to the church of Great Hampden in memory of John Hampden who lies there; but the window was refused because it contained a portrait of Cromwell (a surprising case of intolerance in the 20th century), and so it is that these three courageous figures look down on this old church now used by the Sunday school scholars of Lee.

The path bordered with roses brings us at the other end to the new church, to which the village is summoned by a bell made about the year 1300 by Michael de Wymbish, who put his name on it. In the churchyard, shaded by oak and beech and surrounded by a holly hedge, a high granite cross marks the grave of Sir Arthur Liberty, to whom those who love beautiful things owe so much, for he gave London its most beautiful shop. In his memory the church has been made attractive with a baptistry enclosing a simple font, and delightful fittings in metal, wood, and stone. A window with a figure of St Catherine is in memory of Dame Emma Liberty, who also lies here.

The Church by the Lily Pond

LILLINGSTONE DAYRELL. The house of the Dayrells, Old Tile House, has fallen from its high estate but still bears over the porch the arms of the family who lived in this place for 500 years and watched over the little church set down in the fields near a lily pond. The park of Stowe school now runs close to the boundary.

The church was already old when the first Paul Dayrell and his wife were laid to rest here in 1491, in an altar tomb with their brass portraits on the top, Paul in elaborate plate armour with his feet on a lion and Margaret in a fur-trimmed gown. A grand tomb in the middle of the chancel reminds us of another Paul and his wife who died 75 years later, when it was the fashion to build gorgeous memorials with Italian columns and ornate designs. Small figures of their nine sons and six daughters are shown on the sides of the tomb, kneeling. On the top lie Paul and Dorothy, imposing figures, he in armour, Dorothy very grand in an embroidered robe, fur tippet, and puffed sleeves. Hanging from the wall is a faded red velvet curtain embroidered in gold and white, bearing the Dayrell motto Do Well, and the date 1659. Near it are two helmets with little goats in wood, the Dayrell crest. The last Dayrell remembered in the church served as vicar for 51 years. A wall tablet tells that he was buried here in 1832.

Time has dealt gently with the church. Its walls, built soon after the landing of the Conqueror, still stand, and we see the alterations made when the early Gothic builders repaired the Norman work. The tower and chancel arch are untouched. In the tower the 13th century men cut a long lancet window, and we can stand today on the floor of the church looking through it to the little window that lighted the priest's room, where he sat with a look-out on the altar. The engraved headless figure in brass of one of these priests, who was rector in 1493, is set in the middle of a huge black stone under a broad arch in the chancel wall, opposite the stalls (divided by round columns with beaded capitals) in which he sat with his choir men.

We cross the chancel reverently, for here are tiles laid by workmen to whom great beauty was an everyday sight. They are very rare, some with crowned heads at the corners. A few were made in the 14th century, others earlier, baked in the time of Magna Carta, when an aisle was added to the nave and the chancel was rebuilt. The chancel has a steep-pitched roof, a 13th century Easter sepulchre, and stone seats for the priests.

The Forgotten Francis Drake

LILLINGSTONE LOVELL. It lies in the sloping fields close to the Northamptonshire border. At a point where the road bends toward a row of thatched cottages the saddleback roof of a church tower with faces at the corner stands out above the rectory trees.

We enter the church by a porch with a sundial built in 1635 over a beautiful doorway, richly moulded and with flowered capitals which, with the narrow nave and the lower part of the tower, was built in the 13th century. A hundred years later the slender aisles and the chantry chapel with its double piscina was added. As we go round the church we find another double piscina and the sedilia, with carved heads on the moulding; and there are many little treasures of the past, such as the top of an old font and its cover, a medieval key, a pair of crow's foot spurs, an ancient fastening now set in a shutter in a low chancel window. There is a beloved Bible here, a metal bound copy of the original edition of the Authorised Version which is about the same age as the richly carved pulpit.

As we go into the chancel to look at the brass portraits we are struck by the beautiful lettering on the panels on either side of the altar, where the Lord's Prayer and the Creed are painted on a gold ground. On the oldest brass, in memory of John Merstun, a rector who died in 1446, are hands holding a heart. A little later the portraits of Thomas Clarell, his wife, and three children, were engraved each with a dove at the foot of the plate. Thomas is shown in a fur robe with a collar of suns and roses, the only example of this order in Buckinghamshire. The son wears a priest's dress. Two brass portraits, to William Rysley and his wife, in Tudor dress, are on the floor of the nave. An inscription tells of William Lloyd, an 18th century rector who died here in his 90th year after serving the church for 63 years.

There is a tablet in memory of some forgotten Francis Drake, Captain of the Invalids and a major in the army, who died in 1738 "after hard services in the most distant and opposite parts of the world," rather in the manner of his famous namesake, apparently. Another soldier of last century has a memorial sculpture of the Angel of the Resurrection.

The Dragons on the Font

LINSLADE. Old and new have drifted asunder; the new Linslade is like an expansion of Leighton Buzzard, just across the Ouzel. In the tower of its 19th century church chime five bells taken to it from St Mary's of the old Linslade up the valley.

St Mary's, a wonderful picture as rosy dawn comes up from Bedfordshire, has only a cottage and an old manor house to bear it company, and stands solitary in its lovely churchyard.

The tower is 15th century and the chancel 16th, but the chancel arch is Norman, and the font was here when King John sealed Magna Carta in a rage. A lovely piece of work it is, possibly the work of an artist who made the famous font at Studham, a few miles away. Round the top of the bowl is a deeply cut frieze of foliage, in which lurk four nightmare dragons, browsing. In the chancel one of the windows comes down to form a stone seat for a priest, fashioned in the 13th century, when the curious round recess in the west wall was made. The timbers of the chancel roof are Elizabethan; the screen with its delicate tracery is 15th century. A painted wooden memorial in the chancel, set up before Waterloo by Sir Andrew Corbet, is to another Sir Andrew of this old family who outlived Shakespeare, and to nine other members of the house. A 15th century brass has a civilian family showing a man with three wives dressed alike and two rows of children, six in a row. The west window, a fine picture framed by the splendid tower arch, has ancient glass with figures strongly outlined on a gold background, showing a king with his sceptre, accompanied by a stately queen. In another window are tiny foreign panes, one showing St John, with a cup from which a snake is issuing; the other the pathetic figures of Hagar and Ishmael. The east window shows in brilliant colours the Adoration of the Kings, the Madonna serene behind the manger, and Joseph in strangely rich garments as resplendent as the kings themselves.

In the Ouzel Valley

LITTLE BRICKHILL. It lies on Roman Watling Street, and has a church which has grown from one the Normans built. From the embattled 15th century tower there opens out a fine prospect embracing the rich valley of the Ouzel to the west, and to the north the splendour of the pine-clad hills of Woburn. The 700-year-old church doorway has been reset in an aisle built while Shakespeare was writing his plays. The cup-shaped font has served for 20 generations of baptisms. There is a dainty trefoiled canopy to a little piscina in the 14th century chancel, and two stone heads at the end of the nave have been here since the Wars of the Roses. In a chapel is an alms-shovel dated 1664. In a table-tomb sleeps Edward Jones, vicar for half of last century, and there is a painted coat-of-arms in wood which has been here since 1658. In memory of the heroes of this village is a stone cross with a bronze figure of Christ and the two Marys, dedicated to "those who left, all to face, some to meet, death."

The Pictures on the Wall

LITTLE HAMPDEN. Lying at the end of a winding lane on a slope of a valley in the Chilterns, it has, in a churchyard with four giant pines, a tiny church with white walls and a red roof enclosing a Norman nave. Its 15th century porch has two storeys and a striking doorway made from two great rough weathered oak trunks, whose natural curve has been utilised to form a pointed arch. In the chamber above hangs a bell whose sound issues from small shuttered openings in triangles formed by the beams. The inner doorway was inserted in the Norman wall when the people here were talking of the death of John of Gaunt. Moulded Norman stones are reset in the arch of a chancel 700 years old, with a lancet in which remain the original hooks and bolt used for a shutter. In the wall of the sanctuary stands a little bishop in stone. The great altar stone, with its original consecration crosses, lies under a communion table made in Cromwell's time. Beside it is an ancient piscina with a band of foliage under its moulded canopy. The roof has echoed to the praise and prayer of 15 generations.

BUCKINGHAMSHIRE

But the chief possessions of this church are its wall paintings, lost for centuries and found again in our own time. St Christopher is the hero of much of the work. He appears on a nave wall, a tall figure with fish swimming in the water at his feet, in a painting over 700 years old. In another, of the 15th century, less well preserved, he is in company with Paul, who has a sword, and Peter who has a key. Five hundred years have elapsed since the Judgment scene was painted, showing the Madonna pressing down one end of the scales against the opposition of a demon on the other side. Another picture, a little obscure, shows a singular figure of a man holding a staff horizontally, possibly the torturer in a scene from the martyrdom of St Catherine. Before the chancel arch was remade in the 15th century there were 13th century paintings on either side, of which we now see, cut into by the arch, a bishop in a niche under a trefoiled canopy, with banded scrollwork above and below.

The St Christopher tradition lives on in a lovely lancet in the chancel. Here he wears a blue robe, and on his shoulder is a delightful Child, the window being in memory of "one ever ready to bear another's burdens." Altogether an astonishing little treasury to find by a crooked lane in the heart of quiet country.

The Curious Paintings

LITTLE HORWOOD. Amid its group of cottages, some with thatched roofs, stands the church, its pale stones gleaming against the churchyard sycamores. Close by we see the 17th century gables and original timber-framed walls of the vicarage. There remain delightful traces of the medieval church. In the nave are three round arches, a wall bracket shaped to a cheerful head in the 14th century, and remains of curious paintings, which are particularly interesting because we see that a 16th century craftsman painted on the top of a 13th century picture, and bits of both work are now visible. The earlier one shows St Nicholas with two of the three children he rescued from the cooking-pot. Close by we see parts of the bodies of standing knights. The 16th century picture is part of an allegory of the seven deadly sins. Its chief figure is symbolical of Pride, a bearded man with scrolls about him which end in monsters carrying a demon and a man in their mouths. The proud tail of a peacock sweeps in front of this grotesque image. Another painting adorns the church, a huge landscape picture of the Good Shepherd and his sheep painted by Don Alonzo Pobar, an 18th century Spaniard who was so clever in copying Murillo that many of his canvases passed for Murillo's work. One of his pictures, Our Lady of Consolation, is in Seville Cathedral.

An odd brass panel, dated 1641, is set in the wall by the wide chancel arch, inscribed with the first words of each commandment, and below is a verse beginning

> Both old and young these laws befit
> Which God himself in Sinai writ.

The panels of the pulpit are 17th century; the piscinas are 14th century.

Tiny Church in the Chilterns

LITTLE KIMBLE. It nestles in the Chilterns, great elms guarding its tiny old church, with a quaint little bridge in the fields behind. The traceried head of one window of the church was cut from a single stone six centuries ago. From another window a knight has kept watch since those days. Within is a harvest of interest, a Norman font, a pretty little piscina carved in the 13th century, a 14th century carving of a queen's crowned head, and in the chancel floor six 13th century tiles. Thought to represent passages from the story of Tristram and Iseult, they show two bold figures of enthroned kings, a knight on a gallant horse, and a stately queen.

The greatest treasure of the church is the painting on the walls of the nave, 600 years old. The best picture shows St George with lance in hand, the red cross bright on his white coat and on his shield, the details of his armour affording a faithful picture of that in which princes and knights warred against Robert Bruce in Scotland and with the Black Prince in France. Another fresco shows a saint lying on a bier, two angels with outspread wings hovering over him. There are faint traces of a painting of St Francis preaching to the birds, a very rare example of the subject on an English church wall.

In the windows is a little 14th century glass, two shields with the arms of England and France still gleaming as brightly as when Englishmen in armour made the two kingdoms one.

The roof is modern, but has in it some medieval work, with flowers carved on the spandrels, and there is good Jacobean carving on the panels and friezes of the pulpit and the reading desk.

BUCKINGHAMSHIRE

LITTLE LINFORD. In the grounds of the 17th century Linford Hall is the little 13th century church, with the old gabled bellcot in which swing two medieval bells. The church, only 18 yards long, a pretty picture within, has one arcade of two bays and one of three, six and seven centuries old, and there is an altar table made by a carpenter 500 years ago.

Hard to Find

LITTLE MARLOW. It still has the flint wall of a convent guarded by a moat fed by the Thames in medieval days. In the walls of Abbey Farm are stones from the same house. In the centre of the village is a gabled Jacobean manor with its fine original staircase. Joining it is the church, which, with a little green looking on to a churchyard gay with roses when we called, has an ancient lychgate with a pulley on the post which once opened the gate.

The church the Normans built has a bold 14th century tower and a Norman arch dividing the chancel from a chapel. The round chancel arch was pointed by our first English builders, as the Norman style was passing away. The font is Norman and on a windowsill we found a Norman piscina. The nave and aisles were rebuilt 500 years ago, mainly by Nicholas Ledewich, whose altar tomb is in the chancel. His brass has gone, but his wife's is here. The roofs of the chancel and chapel are 15th century, and there are fragments of 15th century glass in which are two angels. A modern window shows St Christopher with the Child and St Nicholas with golden fruit at his feet; the window is in memory of Edward Finch, one of the 800 men killed when the battleship Bulwark blew up in the Medway in 1914. There is a wall tablet to a sailor who must have known Nelson, Sir Charles Nugent, who entered the navy in 1771 and was made Admiral of the Fleet 62 years later, probably a record in long waiting for a great reward.

Midway between Little Marlow and High Wycombe is a gabled barn of the 17th century on what is called Hard-to-Find Farm.

To many who come this way Little Marlow will be a place of pilgrimage for the grave of one of the astounding men of our time, journalist, poet, novelist, inventor of mysteries, Edgar Wallace.

Edgar Wallace

BORN in London in 1875, Edgar Wallace began his career as a newsboy and later joined the Army as a private, serving for six years.

During the South African War he became a war correspondent, later breaking into poetry in imitation of Kipling's barrack-room manner. While in South Africa he founded a newspaper, and for the rest of his life his abounding energies were devoted to all forms of writing. He served various newspapers, editorially, as special writer, Parliamentary correspondent, and even as dramatic critic. His career as a novelist, after an uncertain and unsuccessful opening, was marked by almost unexampled activity.

Novels poured from his pen, punctuated by sheaves of short stories, and articles on a host of subjects. He turned playwright, and proved as prolific here as in all other avenues of production. At times he had four plays running in London. His dramas, like his novels, were mainly highly coloured thrillers, rich in plot and invention, enlivened by the racy dialogue of which he had a rare mastery. He wrote scenarios for films, American and English, and established his own company for the production of those planned for home consumption.

In industry he excelled the elder Dumas, and he enjoyed life as much as any man. Yet with all his success his expenditure exceeded his great income. He must have lost a fortune over horse-racing. During the last few months of his life he was in America, writing film stories for Hollywood, yet was glad to send home weekly articles for English papers. He could not help it; from the days when he would come to the writer begging him to use a manuscript for the sake of thirty shillings he wanted, to the days when he had more money than was good for him, he loved writing and must be at it. He was fair and square and generous, a good companion and a ready friend. When he died, in 1932, it was found that he was over £70,000 in debt, yet such was the value of his copyrights that this heavy sum was paid within two years. There has been no parallel in Fleet Street to the career of the dazzling and romantic Edgar Wallace.

The Pictures Lost and Found

LITTLE MISSENDEN. It is flanked by the Chiltern hills, with the River Misbourne gliding past under the trees. Its cottages centre round an Elizabethan manor house and a church with an astonishing gallery of medieval paintings on the walls. Between the church and the house a yew tree rises as high as the tower, in which hang two medieval bells, one 15th century and one older still, for it rang out the news of the Black Prince's victories and the sorrowful news of his death.

The church was built by the Normans, and on their foundations rises the medieval tower, with its turrets and battlements, and buttresses resting on high sarsen stones reminding us of Stonehenge. On the porch, which has a 15th century wooden arch and medieval window tracery, we find the signatures of men who plastered its walls two centuries ago.

Four interesting discoveries have been made in the church in our own time. The Normans built the arcades, with their graceful shafts and moulded capitals, added the north aisle, and raised the clerestory of which one open window and two blocked ones are left; and above the chancel arch they pierced a doorway through the wall leading to a chamber over the sanctuary. The door remained until the 15th century, when the chamber was embodied in a new chancel roof. The doorway was plastered over, and an artist painted a picture on it. It was not till our own century that the lost doorway was found. In panelling the chancel in memory of the men who fell in the Great War another discovery was made under the sanctuary floor, where lay the massive old altar stone, six feet long, buried with a number of tiles made 600 years ago. On the tiles are catherine wheels, shields, and mounted men. The ancient altar is now back in its place in the 13th century chancel. The peace memorial panelling has standards carved with the Madonna and other figures in elegant niches. The third discovery made in our own time is of a remarkable series of paintings on the walls, begun by Norman artists and continued through the centuries, a gallery of Bible scenes and legends which must have been a wonderful sight in medieval days, was lost to sight for centuries, and has been brought back to light in our own time. The fourth discovery was made during the restoration of the baptistry window when the vicar came upon four ancient scratch dials, three inside and one outside the church, the inside ones having clearly been moved.

Round the nave run traces of a yellow scroll from which spring red buds and trefoils. On an arch is part of a Crucifixion of about 1250, showing Our Lord against a dark red ground. Above the chancel a Doom picture is fading, in company with an unusual 16th century painting of the arms of Queen Elizabeth. The north wall of the nave has a very early St Christopher, with details wonderfully preserved after seven centuries. The saint is ten feet high, and the Child, in a brilliant tunic, holds in one hand the orb of the universe while the other is raised in blessing. We noticed in the water about his feet an eel and a pike. Also of the 13th century is a remarkable series of nine panels telling the story of St Catherine, three of them admirably clear. The first shows Catherine in a red robe and white mantle facing the persecuting Emperor Maximinus, who is seated on a red throne. In the next she confronts five pagan scholars summoned in vain to dispute with her before the emperor, who here wears gloves and carries a sword. The seventh scene shows the miraculous breaking of the torturer's wheel at Catherine's touch, its shattered fragments descending on the heads of those who gaze with upturned faces at the wonder. The wrath and amazement of the emperor are vividly suggested; his tongue protrudes, his red beard bristles with rage and fear.

In the chapel an angel is faintly seen appearing to the shepherds; but the best painting is framed in the red and yellow mouldings of a recessed tomb. Against a greenish-blue background Our Lord, in a red mantle and with a white cross, raises both hands to show the wounds as He sits in majesty on a white throne.

The church has still its Norman font, and there is a small brass portrait of John Style in a ruff and cloak of Shakespeare's time. The old key is 15 inches long and massive enough for a fortress.

Dora Pattison

LITTLE WOOLSTONE. A hollow oak on a mound points the way to the lane in which, between a 17th century farm and a 17th century mill house, stands the little church. It has a round Norman font handsomely carved, a 13th century chancel arch, and lofty timbering on which the bellcot was set up when the nave was rebuilt 600 years ago. The feet of nearly 20 generations have worn the tiles under the bellcot, but the beams of the roof seem as sound as when they were set up in the days of Richard the Second. In the tracery of two windows are fragments of glass that were admitting light when the villagers came to return thanks for the victories of the Black Prince; and we noticed in it a golden lion and a black and white dragon.

On a wall is a tablet to Dora Pattison, describing her as "loving and beloved" in this village. The sister of Mark Pattison, she lived at her father's Yorkshire rectory at Hauxswell till she was 29, when, feeling called to work for children, she came here, and, in a little place the modern school has superseded, taught from 1861 to 1864. From here she went to Coatham, to deserve the fame she won as a nurse and philanthropist at Walsall. This Staffordshire town has a fine statue of her, the immortal Sister Dora.

Queen Catherine's House

LONG CRENDON. It is rich in old cottages and great houses; there are about 60 cottages of the 16th and 17th centuries. At their doors we may still see old ladies making beautiful lace under the thatched eaves. It is believed that it was this lace-making that Shakespeare had in mind in Twelfth Night, when he makes the Duke say of the song the Clown was about to sing:

> *The spinsters and the knitters in the sun*
> *And the free maids that weave their thread with bones,*
> *Do use to chant it.*

It was one of three great houses here that Henry gave to his Catherine after Agincourt, fulfilling his promise that if she would say *Harry of England I am thine*, he would tell her that "England is thine, Ireland is thine, France is thine, and Henry Plantagenet is thine." Catherine's Court House is the rare possession of the village and was one of the first houses to come under the National Trust. It has a long overhanging front of brick and timber with five bays, four of which form one big room with queen posts and magnificent curved beams in the roof. The lower storey is washed white. The house has been many things in its time, once a hall for the wool merchants, and again a meeting-place for the warden and scholars of All Souls College, which was founded as a chantry for singing masses for Henry the Fifth, the revenues of this village being allotted to the college. Of the other two fine old houses here, the manor house has a Jacobean roof and a 16th century door, and Long Crendon Manor, a gabled house of the 15th century, has a Jacobean chimneystack, and a big domed hall which is now the kitchen, open from floor to roof.

There is Norman masonry in the walls of the 13th century church, with weird gargoyles peeping down from the battlements of its beautiful tower. There are three porches of three centuries. Of the massive nave piers which support the central tower one is so huge that in it is a spiral staircase. The chancel is 700 years old; and the font is guarded by lions 600 years old and by angels with outstretched wings.

The oldest memorial is the 15th century brass portrait of John Canon in civilian attire, with his wife and their 11 children. The finest monument is the magnificent tomb (protected by railings of blue, green, and gold) on which lie Sir John Dormer and his wife, he in armour, her head on cushions, with tassels of white and blue. In the niched recesses of the tomb are figures holding hourglasses, and the monument has richly coloured heraldry.

There is fine Jacobean carving in a transept screen, in the altar rails, in the lectern, and on the lid of a chest. A rose window over the altar has angels with trumpets in memory of a nineteenth century lady of the manor.

He Saw Sir John Moore at Corunna

LOUGHTON. With steep little switchback roads, and Roman Watling Street but half a mile away, it has a 14th century church, with a fine timbered farmhouse for a neighbour. A tombstone in the churchyard tells a thrilling story. It is to Captain David Smith, one of the six officers who, at the end of the great retreat to Corunna, ending in the victory and death of Sir John Moore, stood by the grave on that sad winter night when

> *Not a drum was heard, not a funeral note,*
> *As his corse to the rampart we hurried;*
> *Slowly and sadly we laid him down*
> *From the field of his fame fresh and gory;*
> *We carved not a line and we raised not a stone,*
> *But we left him alone with his glory.*

There is a scratch sundial on a buttress near the 15th century porch, which has its original roof. Amid much restoration corbels 500 years old have survived on the fine tower arch, with carved spandrels over the little doorway of the turret stairs, carved heads on two 15th century brackets in the chapel, oak bosses carved before the Wars of the Roses, and two oak panels with grotesque figures

Long Crendon — Old Court House and Church

Quainton — The 600-Year-Old Church

Medmenham The Abbey by the Thames

Marsh Gibbon The Gabled Manor House

carved in Shakespeare's day. The chancel has a portrait brass of Hugo Parke, a rector of the days when Catherine of Aragon was Queen of England; and among many monuments to the Crane family is one to John Crane, chief clerk of the Board of the Green Cloth at the Restoration. Over the altar is a fine 18th century picture by Gonzales, Court painter at Madrid, of the two disciples at Emmaus, and in the chancel are two beautifully carved chairs. In memory of a rector of our time the south chapel has a window showing Christ in red, St John in green, and the Madonna in blue.

Lettice Knollys and Her Husbands

LOWER WINCHENDON. A church with an uneven cobbled floor and a red-tiled roof, some twisted chimneys built in Elizabeth's day, and a group of pretty thatched cottages here tell their own life story and paint a picture of peace. The chimneys rise from a manor house outside the village, known as the Priory. Near the west door of the church is the manor farm. When these old houses were young a tiny girl destined to become a great lady was born in Winchendon. She was Lettice Knollys, daughter of Sir Robert Knollys, the famous Puritan statesman to Elizabeth. Lettice became Queen Elizabeth's friend, and her long life is bound up in the glittering pattern of that reign. She married three courtiers. The first husband was the Earl of Essex, and she therefore became mother of the Splendid Earl, the gallant of Elizabeth's old age, who died a miserable death for all her friendship and the ring she so romantically gave him. Then she married Lord Leicester, Elizabeth's dear Robin; and last she married Sir Christopher Blount, died at 94, and was laid beside Leicester in the famous and beautiful Beauchamp chapel at Warwick.

The little 14th century nave and chancel and the 15th century tower have some inviting features. The flower capitals in the tower doorway are unspoiled by time, and on the face of the tower is a single-handed clock, set there in 1772 by Jane Beresford, who hoped that it would remind people that life should be soberly and honestly lived. Jane said her prayers in one of the 18th century box pews built round the canopied three-decker pulpit, which has arches on its sides and the date 1630. Under the gallery are ten seats of the 16th century. A low font, brought to the church a hundred years earlier, stands near them.

In one of the nave windows is a 15th century picture of Peter with a very big key, and another (made by foreign craftsmen) of the baptism in Jordan. Four brass portraits of old Winchendon are treasured in the chancel: Margaret Barton, very grand in a butterfly headdress, and her husband John, who died in 1487; an unknown soldier in 15th century armour with a lion at his feet; and an unknown woman beautifully engraved, kneeling at prayer in the full gown the ladies wore at the time of Agincourt.

The Immortal Rector

LUDGERSHALL. Here is the wide common where serfs were herding pigs and cattle on that day when a great scholar came riding across to preach. He was John Wycliffe, the new rector, who arrived in 1386 to sow here the first seeds of the Reformation. Unless he travelled regularly to and from Oxford, which is thought unlikely, he lived where the rectory now stands among the great elms facing the church.

Like the pinnacled bellcot over the chancel roof, the tower was built in the century after Wycliffe. The Norman font at which he christened the children is still here, with its acanthus leaves and bead ornament; here is the carved piscina in which he washed the holy vessels, the ancient tiles he trod on, a figure of Christ in golden glass which he would see in an aisle window, and a wooden chest he may have used to keep his papers in.

There is wonderful carving on the capitals of the piers, stiff 13th century foliage with figures in hooded capes and caps, some with linked arms, some with arms akimbo, all the faces with character and individuality. An internal buttress of the tower has five capped heads, each distinct from its fellows. Two peepholes, one with a charming canopy, pierce the chancel arch. The 15th century chancel roof is splendid with moulded pendants to its hammerbeams, and grapes and flowers on the spandrel-brackets; the 16th century roof spanning the nave is borne on oak angels. The altar table and the carved rails are Jacobean, and there is a chair of that time. On an altar tomb in the chancel is a Tudor brass with portraits of a grandmother, a mother, and a daughter, all in Tudor costume, the child of four dressed like her grandmother, a remarkable woman (wife of Mihil Englishe) who lived in nine reigns. During her lifetime America was discovered, the last battles of the Wars of the Roses were fought, Henry the Sixth was murdered, Richard the Third died like a dog, and Lady Jane Grey was sent to the scaffold. This venerable lady saw the Reformation, and heard of the fall of Wolsey, of the executions of Sir Thomas More and Thomas Cromwell, and of the burning alive of Latimer, Ridley, and Cranmer. She was born before the first English book was printed, and when she died Edmund Spenser was at school and Shakespeare was born.

There is no visible memorial of Wycliffe's six years here, only the proud knowledge of his ministry. Here reform first stirred his spirit; he had barely left for Lutterworth before he flung the thunderbolt forged in this place, which brought on him the ban of the Pope. Another notable rector the church has had, Henry Martyn, who was for 63 years professor of botany at Cambridge University and was the first Englishman to grasp and expound the system of Linnaeus. He left here in 1784 with nearly half a century of service before him.

Church Magnificent

MAIDS MORETON. It has one of the most astonishing churches in the county, a 15th century legacy from two sisters. Twelfth century stones in a porch, and a beautifully traceried font suggest that they pulled down a Norman church; but superbly they justified themselves.

Rising when architecture in the county had reached the zenith of perfection, the church is a blend of massive strength and rich imaginative beauty, Gothic poetry in stone. The tower, which roused the enthusiastic admiration of Sir Gilbert Scott, is a magnificent structure, with moulded battlements and bell turret, its upper stages pierced by deeply recessed windows. Above them the stringcourse links huge bird gargoyles at the corners. The west front, which would grace a small cathedral, has a lovely window above a doorway of three orders, and a porch with fan-vaulting springing from cherub corbels. The north porch, with embattled parapet, gargoyles, and fan-vaulted roof, has doors with carved panels below a lintel of 1637, but the elaborate inner door and the immense lock were placed here by the original builders 500 years ago. The south porch has a traceried roof still perfect.

The splendour without is matched by splendour within, by the great transomed nave windows, the lofty tower arch, and the fine chancel arch, whose lovely screen is crowned at each end by an angel bearing a shield with the hammer and nails of the Crucifixion. Beyond this is a wonderful east window, its fine stonework carried down to the altar and the reredos. In the side walls are similar but smaller windows, their splays continued to meet the stone benches.

The old glass has suffered violence, but some 15th century fragments remain in the upper lights of the east window, showing saints with halos, and two faces, one of an angel, the other of a demon. Below these treasured remnants is a 19th century addition, a charming group of scenes from the life of Our Lord.

Exquisite tracery adorns the high projecting canopies of the sedilia, each seat with clustered columns at the sides. At the back of the seats is a painting of the Last Supper which, like a Crucifixion opposite, we found to be fading after its long exposure; but six consecration crosses on the walls are still clear after all the centuries. From the chancel a doorway leads to the vestry, which has a fan-vaulted roof, with a carved central boss, still as it was when Columbus was a boy.

The roofs, all original, are adorned by bosses with angels and shields and in the centre of the nave roof is Christ with a hand raised in blessing. A treasure dated 1623 is the altar table, with prodigious urn-shaped legs, its sides carved with grotesques, with dragons so gentle that they breathe not fire but foliage, and with heads recalling Van Dyck portraits.

Perhaps the most notable memorial is the pair of portrait brasses of the sisters who built the church, shown with flowing hair. These brasses replace earlier ones long lost. In the chancel is a tablet to an Edward Bate whose father, Dr George Bate, member of an old family here, was at first a Puritan but, being at Oxford when the Civil War brought Charles there, turned Cavalier and became physician to the king, at whose death he passed into the service of Cromwell, becoming Court physician once more at the accession of Charles the Second.

There is a pathos and a literary interest in the inscription on an 18th century marble tablet to Penelope Verney, who died at 18, wife of Lord Willoughby de Broke. Seven years before her death Steele, writing in the Spectator, had misquoted from memory Ben Jonson's lovely epitaph on Elizabeth L. H., and the sorrowful widower has perpetuated Steele's mistake—an odd example of an error which has evidently gone too far to recall. This is what the epitaph should be:

> *Underneath this stone doth lie*
> *As much beauty as could die;*
> *Which in life did harbour give*
> *To more virtue than doth live.*

A relic of the Civil War hangs in the tower, one of the original oak doors, pierced by bullets; and beside it an extract from the parish register stating that Commonwealth soldiers damaged and profaned the church by breaking the glass and shooting through this door. A cannon ball has been found in a pond.

Today the village seems a home of peace, its cottages grouped on a hill overlooking the valley of the Ouse, and its churchyard with a view over miles of lovely country; yet grim scenes have been witnessed from here. Here still stands a tree known as Hangman's Oak, which has the iron ring used for the execution of sheep-stealers.

Here Shelley Lived

MARLOW. It is bowered in beauty, its surrounding hills a glory of beeches growing down to the Thames. Here the river is crossed by the fine suspension bridge, with a span of 225 feet, built a hundred years ago by William Clark, the wheelwright genius who constructed the famous bridge over the Danube linking Pest and Buda. The picture of the bridge and the church together is unforgettable, the best view in the town. It was the charm of woods and hills and water which drew Shelley and his wife here, and in West Street is the red-tiled house in which they lived. Sitting in his boat under the beech-groves of Bisham, where

> *Waterfalls leap among islands green*
> *Which framed for my lone boat a lone retreat,*

he wrote The Revolt of Islam, while Mary was at home completing Frankenstein, her eerie masterpiece. The poem finished, Shelley dedicated it to her:

> *So now my summer task is ended, Mary,*
> *And I return to thee, mine own heart's home . . .*
> *The toil which stole from thee so many an hour*
> *Is ended—and the fruit is at thy feet!*

THE KING'S ENGLAND

One of the most charming pictures here is the green with its pines and sycamores, flanked by the church and the people's park. Here is the peace memorial, a handsome cross with 215 names on oak panels, and near it the graceful statue of a seated woman at a drinking fountain by F. S. Merrifield, inscribed

> *For it is not right that in a house*
> *the Muses haunt mourning should dwell;*
> *such things befit it not.*

It is a beautiful tribute to Charles Frohman, the famous American who came to England and produced so many plays. One of the most popular theatre men in this country, he was among the 1200 people drowned in the Lusitania in 1915.

On the green is set up an old prison door with a whipping-post and a set of stocks last used in 1858, and close by is a house with one of its gables almost filled by a sundial. In St Peter's Street is the Old Parsonage, a Jacobean house with a medieval window. The 17th century grammar school, in which Shelley heard the boys saying their lessons, stands near the poet's old home. The town hall in the market square, with a turret and cupola, was built two years after Trafalgar. Harleyford House, with 18th century red bricks in a splendid park, is the centre of a beauty-spot known to all who pass on the river. In a cottage in Oxford Road lived George Payne Rainsford James, a physician's son who wrote 77 novels last century, the best of them in his earlier years, and most of them forgotten. At Widmer Farm is a 13th century chapel converted into a house with a pretty dormer in the roof. Moor and Finnamore Farms both have big 13th century barns. Between Widmer Farm and the town is Seymour Court, set on a hill in splendid grounds and locally believed (though we believe wrongly) to have been the birthplace of Jane Seymour, one of the lucky wives of Henry the Eighth who died in bed.

In the churchyard of the modern church lies John Richardson, born in the workhouse here and famous as a showman. They laid him here in the 18th century with a child from the Caribbean Islands, whom he had shown about the country as the Spotted Boy. By the showman's own desire they lie together, a queer couple, and Richardson has his portrait in the vestry.

The most striking memorial in the spacious church is the monument set up by Parliament in honour of a man of fame who lies here, Sir Miles Hobart. In 1628, during the memorable debate on tonnage and poundage, he locked the door of the House of Commons and kept the key in his pocket until the resolutions were passed. His bust is between curtains drawn back by figures at the sides, and a plaque shows four spirited horses galloping down hill with a coach, one wheel of which is broken; this because he met his death in a coach accident on Holborn Hill after being released from the Tower during the Restoration.

The 16th century monument of William Willoughby shows him in gilded armour with his wife, three sons, and three daughters, all in black and wearing ruffs. Over the monument hangs a helmet. The peace memorial window shows Our Lord and an adoring angel attended by a soldier, a sailor, and an airman. Two bishops from this church are remembered: Robert Milman, Bishop of Calcutta, by a window; and Charles Smythiers, Bishop of Zanzibar, by the panelling of the sanctuary.

In St Peter's Street is a Roman Catholic Church of great charm built last century by the elder Pugin.

Chaucer's Granddaughter

MARSH GIBBON. We can picture Alice Chaucer, granddaughter of the poet, riding as lady of the manor through this wooded village of timbered cottages, perhaps pausing to let her palfrey drink at the roadside pond. She owned the village, with her husband the Duke of Suffolk, who had the experience of being Joan of Arc's prisoner at Orleans, and was afterwards the victim of the terrible crime described in Shakespeare's Henry the Sixth. The duke and duchess conveyed the revenues of this place to Ewelme in Oxfordshire, where she lies in a tomb befitting her immortal name.

Two buildings here go back towards her day. One is the gabled manor house, whose great fireplace blazed before Elizabeth was queen; the other is the grand thatched 15th century tithe-barn in the rectory grounds, facing the 13th century church. The pinnacled tower is 14th century, and on one of the transept buttresses are two mass dials by which its builders may have told the time. Bold arcades grace the clerestoried interior, some of the capitals carved with 13th century foliage. There is a fine stone face over a transept arch. One of the oldest possessions of the church is the 13th century lid of a coffin in which lay one of the first priests here. The wooden cover of the medieval font is worked by a pulley with a balancing weight made of a 17th century gilded serpent round a man's neck. Winged angels support the 15th century roof of the nave, and there are Jacobean pews, with a chair and table of the same time.

Epiphanius Evesham

MARSWORTH. From the low hill crowned by the church with its great treasure, it looks out over a wide sweep of country, with Dunstable Downs on one side, the heights of Tring on the other, and before it the long valley through which runs the Grand Union Canal.

In the massive 15th century tower of the church are traceried stones from the 13th century chancel arch, which has been refashioned and adorned with finely sculptured heads of Hope, Faith, Charity, and Purity. There are two 13th century doorways, and beside an altar are two 13th century coffin lids. In the chapel is the chief glory of the church, a Jacobean altar tomb of great interest because it has been identified as the work of the famous Epiphanius Evesham. Although his signature was always visible, the discovery that this tomb is the work of our first known great sculptor was only made in 1932. Filling a panel at the end of the tomb is a brass portrait of Thomas West of Shakespeare's day, lying on a bier at which kneels his widow, accompanied by their nine children, with Death and his spear in the background. Evesham's name is in a corner of the brass.

Marble panels on the front of the tomb have engravings of a man with an oar, presumably Charon; a figure robed as a mourner; Time with his scythe, and Christ with the banner of the Resurrection. There appears to have been similar decoration on the other side, but two panels are missing, and the rest is hidden. This elaborate tomb, with heraldry and skulls in the conventional fashion of the time, is precious as one of the few works of Epiphanius Evesham known to exist in this country, his chief sculptures being in Kent (at Lynsted and Boughton-under-Blean). Until his time our sculpture, like much of our architecture, was anonymous; as if conscious of his genius,

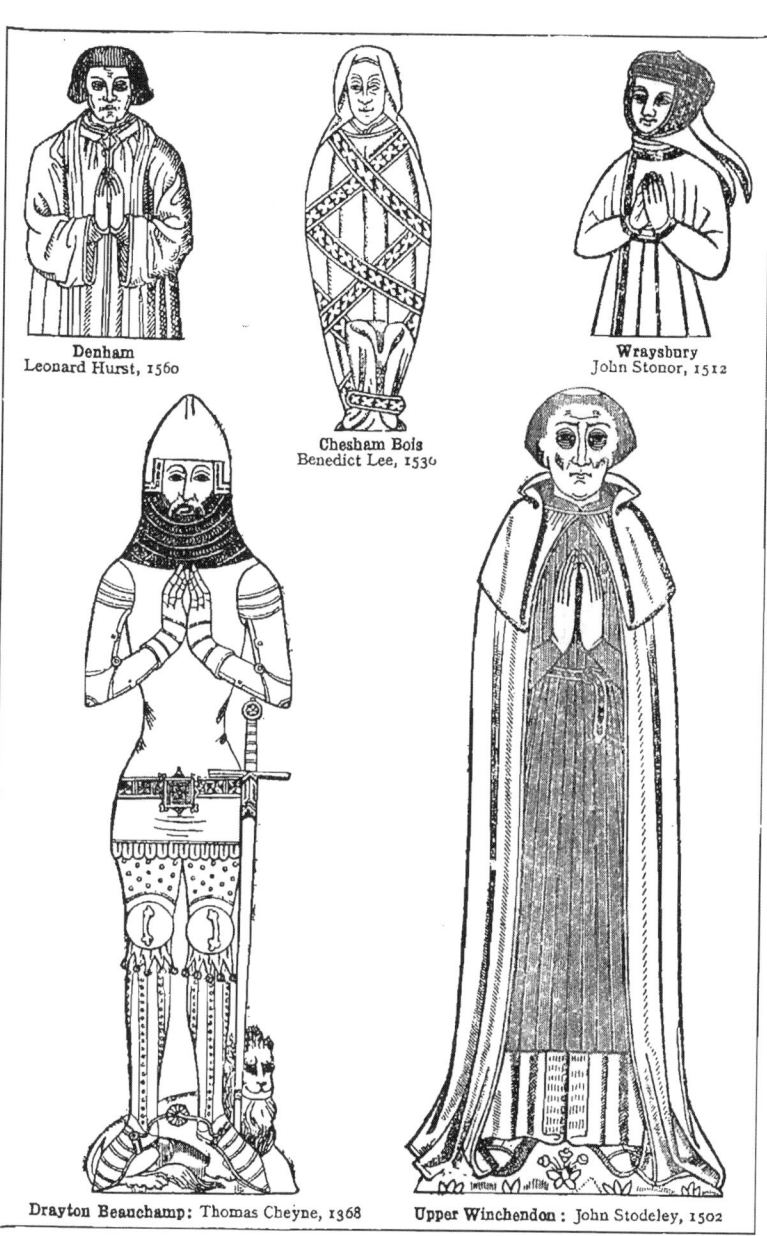

OLD BRASSES OF BUCKINGHAMSHIRE

he signed his works, and it is thrilling to come here and find his name.

Under the chapel seats are brass portraits of two daughters of Nicholas West, trim little ladies in Elizabethan costume; and close by is the brass portrait of Mary West in a delightful Jacobean dress and hat, her child shrouded at her feet.

The modern pulpit here stands on a base fashioned from the huge carved capital of a medieval pier. The charming 15th century font has flowers and little heads. The sanctuary has medieval tiles with fleurs-de-lys. In the impressive east window are figures of Bede, St Aidan, St Augustine, and St Hugh, with scenes below them of Aidan consecrating a priest, Augustine approving the plan of a church, Bede dictating, and Hugh, with a great white swan curving its neck about his robes, carrying stones for his cathedral.

A Set of Wild Fellows

MEDMENHAM. Finding it beautiful as we do today, enshrined in the splendours of the Thames Valley, the Normans built here an abbey which was to fall upon sad times. There are fragments of it in its Jacobean successor, a house with a three-storeyed porch built of chalk blocks. Round the house is a magnificent yew hedge with trimmed openings cut in it like windows. The abbey ruins were restored in the 18th century by Sir Francis Dashwood, one of our Chancellors of the Exchequer. Here, dressed in blue and crimson robes, calling themselves Franciscans, he and a wild set of fellows held their orgies until the discreditable character of the meetings was exposed and the scandal led to their break-up.

Near the church and the river is a charming group of delightful cottages, a timbered 15th century manor house, and the dormered 16th century inn. Flanked by great chestnuts, its churchyard aglow with roses, the church has two Norman doorways and a medieval tower. The 15th century chancel has, instead of the usual stone arch, a timber structure consisting of a kingpost tie-beam with carved braces, a splendid example of medieval carpentry, which also furnished the fine roof still spanning the nave. There is excellent modern carving on the altar table, on the oak cover of the font, and in the decoration of bench-ends.

Four panels of foreign glass show Christ and Simeon in the

Temple, two Crucifixion scenes, and the Ascension, and a striking modern window has a portrait of Colonel Arthur Murray who fell in Palestine in 1917 after winning the DSO. The setting is Jerusalem with its domes and turrets, with an angel bringing the soldier a laurel as he tenders his sword to the Master. The peace memorial is a novel wooden tablet with the names of all the villagers who served in the war, showing how and where they served, at the front and at home. One name is that of Lord Devonport, who was among the villagers in those days; he was our first Food Controller and first Chairman of the Port of London Authority.

A Prime Minister's Son

MENTMORE. From its hillside it looks out on a fair English scene, in which nothing is more beautiful than the park of Mentmore House, one of the most charming homes in England. The house was built by Sir Joseph Paxton (builder of the Crystal Palace) for Baron de Rothschild, who was to become, a quarter of a century after completing it, the father-in-law of Lord Rosebery, for whose heir it was left in trust. Among its treasures is a collection of Limoges enamels and majolica, a chimneypiece from the house of Rubens at Antwerp, and a portrait of Michael Angelo by Moroni.

The clerestoried church occupies the topmost point of the village, its 15th century tower a landmark for many miles. The Norman font is here again after sore misadventures. Removed from the church it found its way to a farm before it came home again.

The most curious feature of the interior is the aspect of the nave pillars. When the nave was made new 400 years ago the builders inverted the piers, so that today we find the stiff 13th century foliage capitals at the base, while the arches rest on battlemented capitals carved by those daring sculptors. It would be the same builders who wrought the little wingless angels and the grotesque heads which spring from the clerestory walls and support the roof. A window of a 14th century aisle has some fragments of 16th century glass.

In the modern chancel is a tablet in memory of one in whom high hopes centred, Captain Neil Primrose, second son of the Lord Rosebery who was Prime Minister; he was killed in Palestine in 1917 and sleeps at Ramleh. His inscription here runs:

THE KING'S ENGLAND

> *Now he is dead*
> *Far hence he lies*
> *In the lorn Syrian town;*
> *And on his grave*
> *With sorrowing eyes*
> *The Syrian stars look down.*

Another memorial of our own time is an alabaster plaque on the wall showing the Madonna and Child, in memory of E.F.C.

The Home of the Verneys

MIDDLE CLAYDON. It has been for centuries the home of a great English family. The house of the Verneys and the church of the Verneys stand side by side amid their cedars and their mighty oaks. In this park played the delicate, serious little Edmund who was to die at Edgehill with Charles Stuart's flag in his hand. Here his son Ralph spent his happy hours making gardens and shubberies, growing trees to send to Richmond Park, carrying visions of greenery to London where he sat in the Long Parliament watching, listening, making those notes which were later of such value to historians. Here in Victorian days walked and rode Sir Harry Verney, facing the difficulty of building up the fallen fortunes of the house. Sometimes Florence Nightingale would walk with him, dreaming of another kind of reform, for she was his sister by marriage and he was her great friend.

Sir Harry was a member of Parliament for 52 years and a fighter for every good cause. He established libraries and schools on the estate, planted trees, and looked carefully after his tenants. The oldest villagers can remember him when he was over 90 and refusing to be old, riding about on his grey pony.

Claydon House, close neighbour of the church, has seen many changes. On the site of the old manor house, already historic when it came into the hands of the first Sir Ralph Verney, Lord Mayor of London in 1465, the Adam Brothers built for the second Earl Verney a great house intended to rival its neighbour Stowe. The earl's successor pulled some of it down, but we look now on a wing of the Adam house, which is remarkable for its superb cornices, fireplaces, and details of ornament. It has an exquisite Chinese room in which everything is in keeping. It has a staircase inlaid with ivory and ebony, with iron balusters of great beauty designed as

BUCKINGHAMSHIRE

cornstalks, delicately sprung, so that they almost seem to rustle as we mount the steps. It has a picture gallery of the Verneys and the Giffards (to whom the first Sir Ralph let the manor on a long lease). Here we see, painted by the immortal Vandyck, Charles Stuart and Sir Edmund Verney who bore his standard, Dame Mary Verney, and Florence Nightingale.

Other memorials of a precious character are in the little church, which, like the house, has been much altered since it was built 600 years ago in the form of a simple nave and chancel. The west tower is 15th century, the chancel 16th, the oak pulpit 17th, and there is a sanctus bell which rang before the Reformation. Four of the windows and the south doorway of the nave have been here 700 years. The hardworking Sir Harry rebuilt and restored the church, saving where he could the fond additions of earlier centuries. We must be particularly grateful to him for saving the 16th century chancel screen, which has a wide doorway with leaves in the spandrels, and panels of delicate tracery. A bronze relief of Sir Harry by Henry Pegram is one of the newest memorials in the church; the rarest and richest is the chancel altar tomb to Margaret Giffard, who died in 1539. Margaret was a great lady, and English and Italian craftsmen vied with each other to make her tomb splendid and unique. It has three shields in cusped tracery on each side and columns at the corners enriched with Italian detail. On it, in alabaster, Margaret lies in her best gown, with slashed and puffed sleeves. Her head rests on a pillow held by angels, and we notice a dog nibbling the folds of her loose gown.

Near a door in the chancel is an important brass group (one of the biggest in the county) of Roger and Mary Giffard and their 20 children. Roger is in fine plate armour and a mail shirt. Over the door is an inscription telling that these two gave the chancel in 1519. Close by are brass portraits of two more Giffards of 400 years ago, Isabella and Alexander holding a chalice, he a priest. High on the wall is a charming little Jacobean monument to Lettice Giffard and her husband Urian Verney, who, with their son behind him, kneels facing Lettice across a prayer-desk. One part of the chancel is filled from floor to ceiling with a huge monument to the 17th century Verneys, two mourning figures crowning the memorial, which is made of marble in many colours; and in round-headed niches are busts of Sir Ralph, who set it up, of his parents, and of his wife. Sir Ralph's father was Sir Edmund, standard-bearer.

The King's Standard-Bearer

SIR EDMUND VERNEY, standard-bearer to Charles Stuart, was the most famous member of a family established in Buckinghamshire in the 13th century. Left fatherless at an early age, he had a brother Francis who sold the property to which he was heir, went on pilgrimage to Holy Land, and died a pirate.

Scholar, soldier, and Puritan, Sir Edmund was first attached to the household of Prince Henry, passing at his death to that of Charles, with whom he was in Madrid when the heir to the throne went wooing the Infanta of Spain. At 22 he married a daughter of Sir Thomas Denton of Hillesden, lying within sight of the Verney home, and it is said that two black trumpeters dressed in red used to sound a reveille, answered by two trumpeters from the other hill. Model landlord though he was, Verney was impoverished all his life by lending money to the Stuarts which they would not pay back.

Eight of his 12 children were born here, but most of his time was spent in London, where he was in charge of the royal palace and 12 miles round it. In Parliament he had the courage to oppose the autocratic procedure of the king, but when the Civil War came he felt that he must fight for him.

In a pathetic interview with Hyde, the Puritan Verney said, "I have eaten the king's bread and served him near 30 years, and will not do so base a thing as to forsake him; and choose rather to lose my life (which I am sure I shall do) to preserve and defend those things which are against my conscience to preserve and defend; for I will deal freely with you—I have no reverence for bishops, for whom this quarrel subsists."

Receiving the royal standard when it was unfurled on Castle Hill at Nottingham in 1642, he bore it to Edgehill to fight against those with whom his sympathies lay, and there he breakfasted for the last time with the king. In the battle, to encourage the wavering, he fought his way with his charge into the ranks of the enemy. They bade him surrender the standard and live; but he answered that his life was his own, while the standard was the king's, and he would not deliver it while he lived, and hoped it would be rescued after he was dead. An eye witness wrote that 16 men perished by his sword before the pikemen slew him, and after the battle his faithful hand was found still grasping the standard.

The Scholar, the Dean, and the Rebel

MILTON KEYNES. It lies among meadows through which wind the Ouzel and its tributary brooks, and has thatched cottages which must have looked for centuries much as they look today. Pines and larches grace the charming 14th century church, with a handsome tower built in a corner. The rich carving outside includes a fox, a dog, a lion, and animals which seem to have escaped from a medieval beast-book. In a buttress is a graceful pinnacled niche, by which is a scratch mass dial.

The south porch, its sides pierced by graceful arches on round shafts, and with its traceried ballflower doorway, is of rare beauty. Remains of an older church are traced in the 13th century carving on the capitals of the tower arch and on the arch of the 14th century chancel, in which are delightful stone seats for the priests and an ancient piscina. There is 600-year-old ballflower decoration on another small piscina in the chapel, where among old tiles are some of the 13th century with fine flower patterns.

The church has a chained Bible printed while Shakespeare was still alive. Here also are the carved and painted arms of the Stuarts, probably the gift of Lewis Atterbury, the stout Jacobite rector who was drowned in 1693 when crossing the flooded Broughton Brook. He sleeps under the altar. His successor was William Wotton, a scholar who translated Hebrew, Greek, and Latin at six, and wrote in this rectory a famous book of Reflections on Ancient and Modern Learning, so entering a European contest of wits in which Sir William Temple extolled the ancients in general and the Essays of Phalaris in particular. These essays the scholarly Wotton proved to be forgeries, and then it was that in came Swift to write his merry masterpiece on the immortal Battle of the Books, supporting Temple against Milton, Bacon, and Dryden. But the world still laughs with Wotton, for he was right and Dean Swift was wrong. A friend of Sir Isaac Newton and other great spirits of the age, Wotton died in 1727.

At the old rectory, now gone, was born the notorious Bishop of Rochester, Francis Atterbury, destined to trouble Church and State for 40 years following the Restoration. During a brilliant career at Oxford he won renown by his defence of Protestantism against the onslaughts of James the Second; as Chaplain to William and Mary he was foremost in controversy, and in the reign of Queen Anne, who made him Bishop of Rochester and Dean of Westminster, he wrote the speech in which the mischievous Dr Sacheverell, enemy of everybody and everything but his own narrow creed, defended himself when impeached before the House of Lords. After the death of Queen Anne the bishop lost his hope of the Primacy, and from now onward engaged in conspiracies to overturn the dynasty and bring back the Stuarts. His treachery led him to the Tower and he was sentenced to banishment.

In France, as "phantom minister of a phantom Court," he acted as chief adviser to the Pretender, and engineered rebellions. Once famous for his Protestantism, he was now prepared to steep his native land in blood to install a Roman Catholic on the throne against the wishes of the English people. He died in Paris in 1732, and his body was brought by stealth to England for burial in the grave he had made in the Abbey when he was dean; but before his body reached the Abbey it was arrested by the Customs officers and searched for smuggled silks and brocades.

Country Charm

MONKS RISBOROUGH. The Chilterns richly clothed in trees rise above it. Looking down on it is the remarkable Whiteleaf Cross, one of two crosses in the county cut in the turf. The one visible from here, occupying a two-acre site, is 80 feet long and 72 feet wide, and has a great triangular base. Believed to have been cut in the 17th century, it is scheduled by Act of Parliament.

Buckinghamshire has few more charming little places than this, with its thatched and timbered cottages and joyous gardens set in a wonderful picture of beauty. Near the church, in a field which has a white stone dovecot with a square lantern, are mysterious entrenchments, whose hollows were used as fishponds in medieval days. The noble church rose six centuries ago, its masterly builders giving it a fortress-like tower, with parapet and turret and gargoyles to keep all safe and seemly. Its chief treasure is a Norman font; it has a fluted bowl, with interlacing bands of foliage exquisitely carved.

Maids Moreton
The Lovely West Doorway

Quainton
The Old Gabled Almshouses

Maids Moreton　　　　　　　　　　The 15th Century Church

Newport Pagnell   A View from the Ouse

Olney   John Newton's Church

Penn   Fine Medieval Church

BUCKINGHAMSHIRE

Here all sorts and conditions of people must have sat for heads to old artists in wood and stone. An angel, surrounded by foliage, projects from the wall behind the pulpit; a winged angel forms the boss of the vault in the tower stair turret; a monk, a nun, and two demons are in a once lovely transept niche; and when we called there was a beautiful head to spare, lying on a windowsill. None of these carvings is later than the 15th century; some, like the corbel heads supporting the grand 15th century roof of the nave, with traceried spandrels, are of Chaucer's generation. The chancel and the porch were built by men who would still be wondering at the news of Joan of Arc. Supporting the aisle roofs, with much 15th century timber, are corbels carved 500 years ago.

Two brasses are notable, one in the children's corner with portraits of two boys and five girls who lived when Henry the Eighth was still the pride and hope of England; the other a magnificent portrait of Robert Blundell, rector here when Joan was burned. He is shown in his vestments, a beautiful example of 15th century engraving. A third brass has portraits of a civilian and his wife who died during the Wars of the Roses, when the medieval tiles in the floor, now pearls of price, were the common product of the trade.

The handsome screen was carved before the Reformation, its panels admirably traceried with foliage; we notice in the spandrels a long-beaked bird, a wild man, and a figure supposed to be Adam. Painted on the panels are pictures of bearded Apostles, with red and green backgrounds. Four splendid poppyheads remain, the best with two wonderful heads of women, each wearing an elaborate headdress. the braiding masterly in its detail. Another has a robed and bearded man whom the villagers identify as Moses; others show a bishop and an armed knight who looks as if he had marched to victory at Agincourt. One window has a patchwork of 14th and 15th century fragments of glass among which stand out a tall Madonna, the eagle of St John, and the winged lion of St Mark. Among cherished pieces in the chancel windows is one showing a 15th century merchant's mark. A 19th century window in memory of Samuel Wilberforce shows him as Bishop of Oxford.

The Rise of a Family

MOULSOE. Serene on its hill, with a frieze of thatched cottages on one hand and open country on the other, its church peers over the border into Bedfordshire, and shades the resting-place of men who link us with far times and distant lands.

It is the shrine of a family of Smiths who rose to high honour, first with a barony and then with a marquisate, the best known of them being the Marquess of Lincolnshire, better remembered as the first Earl Carrington, a colonial Governor and Lord Great Chamberlain, a hereditary office brought into the family by a line tracing back to a Welsh king. The family's wealth came from Abel Smith, a Nottingham banker who grew rich under Queen Anne. The memorials of the house are many and deeply interesting.

The 14th century tower keeps watch over their churchyard tombs, their arms being carved on the pillars of the enclosure in which the old marquess was laid with his kindred in 1928. In the church is a wall tablet to him, with beautiful colour in the heraldic banner hanging over it. The same wall has an elaborate bronze monument to his father, fine scholar and public servant; and beside it, in memory of the Marchioness of Lincolnshire, is a charming monument in red tinted marble, with two golden cherubs. In the south chapel hangs an enormous green Egyptian flag captured by a brother of the Marquess in 1882, a reminder of days forgotten except by the historian. This flag was borne by troops who rose at the bidding of Arabi Pasha against the Sultan of Turkey, before the creation of a British Protectorate over the land of the Pharaohs.

Another striking monument to this family is a series of panels of which a dozen are Jacobean with rose carving, and the rest are skilful imitations; they bear the names of the 37 men of the Royal Horse Guards who died at Ypres in 1915. Among them is that of Edward the Seventh's godson and namesake Lord Wendover, the only son of the marquess. Projecting from the wall are a silver trumpet, two flags, and, framed in glass, the royal arms in rich embroidery. The memorial is the pathetic tribute of the proud father, left sonless in his old age. He was one of the most popular figures in the Liberalism of his day, then at the height of its power.

Almost hidden by the organ is a little coloured marble sculpture showing the two Marys at the empty tomb, placed here in memory of Lady Suffield by her uncle, father of the marquess.

With the exception of the chancel, remade last century, the church has stood almost unchanged for 600 years. Some of the original tiles are still in the floor, the 14th century base supports a modern font, and a new litany desk has in it two brightly painted traceried panels from the medieval screen. There is a medieval chest and a brass in an aisle floor of Richard Ruthall and his wife in Tudor costume.

Cousin of Queen Elizabeth

MURSLEY. Queen Elizabeth must have seen some of the black and white thatched cottages glorifying its wide street, for here she came to visit her cousin Sir John Fortescue. Facing the church is a red-tiled house with Tudor chimneys. The 15th century tower gleams white above the 14th century church, which has original stone brackets of daintily chiselled birds, and a finely carved Jacobean pulpit. Under an arch in the chancel kneels the queen's proud host Sir John, in his costume of red, blue, and gold. His second wife is with him, wearing a richly brocaded gown and a blue cloak, and below them is an altar tomb with the brass portrait of his first wife, richly robed. On a second monument, with a peacock, a bear, and cherubs above it, are his son Sir Francis Fortescue with his wife, and their ten children, the boys in red, the girls in blue.

A mile from the church is a farmhouse with Tudor chimney-stacks, old windows, and oak panelling, all that remains of the magnificent Salden House built by Sir John. The last of the Tudors and the first of the Stuarts came here to visit this scholar-statesman, a cousin of Queen Elizabeth through her mother's family. His father, Sir Adrian Fortescue, lost his head on the block under Henry the Eighth, but his mother was one of the household of Mary Tudor, and Fortescue, famous as a classical scholar, had charge of the education of Elizabeth. He became Chancellor of the Exchequer and received rich rewards in money and grants of land, so that he was able to spend what would be £200,000 of our money in building a lordly pleasure house here, where Elizabeth came to visit him.

A kinsman of Essex, he was the intimate friend of Burghley, Bacon, and Raleigh, and a letter exists in which Essex bespeaks his support for Bacon as Master of the Rolls. One of his duties was to keep in custody prisoners not committed to the Tower, and many illustrious men suffered confinement under his roof, so that he was wont to complain that his house was a State prison.

Oliver's Son Oliver

NEWPORT PAGNELL. It is pleasantly situated on ground rising from the south bank of the Ouse, which, crossed by a fine stone bridge of five arches, receives here the River Lovat after its course through the town. It has memories of the Cromwells, of Bunyan, of a soldier satirized in an immortal poem, and a man dear to the poet Cowper.

During the Civil War the town was a central garrison for Parliament, for whom levies were drawn here from a considerable area. Among them, it is said, came John Bunyan, aged 16, to serve under Sir Samuel Luke, who, Commonwealth commander here for three years, is the derided hero pilloried in Samuel Butler's Hudibras. Bunyan is silent as to the place for which he fought and even as to the side he fought on, but probability makes him a Commonwealth man in Commonwealth Bedfordshire; and this was the depot to which Bedford men were sent.

Cromwell here sustained a crushing blow in the death of his second son, Oliver. His eldest son having died in 1639, Oliver was now the only one of his boys old enough to bear arms, and as a cornet under Essex he won the rank of captain. One of his letters shows him to have been a man of his father's stamp, clear-headed, kindly, but resolute. He died here of smallpox in 1644, when he was only 21, and was serving with the forces. A contemporary writer spoke of him as "a civil young gentleman, and the joy of his father". Oliver, in writing to a friend whose son had fallen in the war, referred to his own bereavement and said he had been greatly sustained by a particular passage in the Bible, and felt that his son had found "the peace we all pant for."

The town has many 17th and 18th century houses, with reminders of days more ancient. By the Ouse near the church Tickford Abbey preserves the name of a priory founded in the days of William Rufus. In the present house are remains of the old building; stones with Norman carving in the garden wall; and in the kitchen a fragment of old glass showing a man, an angel, and a sleeping woman.

St John Street has a house with an inscription stating that the building, rebuilt in 1690, belonged to the hospital of Anne of Denmark, queen of James the First. The hospital itself, founded by Anne on the site of a 13th century charity, has also been rebuilt, but has an original beam with its 17th century appeal:

> *All you good Christians that here do pass by*
> *Give something to these poor people that in St*
> *John's Hospital lie.*

The whole town is dominated by the fine 14th century church with its Jacobean tower (embellished by a modern pinnacled parapet) looking over a big churchyard bounded by the River Lovat. Battlements grace the walls of the aisles and clerestory, and a charming turret rises from a junction of the nave and chancel.

There are two fine porches, one 14th century with a vaulted stone roof and a priest's chamber above: the other with 14th century arcading under a 15th century roof resting on wooden corbels with quaint faces.

The impressive interior has deep moulded and sharply pointed arcades, above which oak figures of the Apostles support the magnificent 15th century roof. In an aisle is a delightful little 14th century piscina, and a sedilia beautiful with ballflower, and medieval wooden heads bearing a modern roof. By the chancel arch is a door with a brass portrait of an unknown civilian in 14th century costume. There are two carved 17th century chests; and writings by Bishop Jewel are attached to the lectern by their original chains.

In an unmarked grave near the chancel sleeps John Gibbs, who, after 12 years' service in the pulpit here was ejected at the Restoration, but risked all to continue his work, the town's first Nonconformist minister. He was a friend of Bunyan, who applied for a licence for Gibbs to preach in William Smyth's barn and in his own house. The initials J. G. which Bunyan put at the end of the Address to the Reader in one of his books are believed to represent Gibbs.

We see a ruined wall of Gibbs's meeting-house beside the Congregational Church in High Street, and in that church is a tablet to his memory. Here are portraits of a dozen immortal reformers, including Wycliffe, Luther, John Huss, and John Knox. The chief treasure of the church is that inserted in the pulpit book-rest, a piece of Bunyan's pulpit at Bedford. It has a brass with Cowper's couplet:

> *Revere the man whose Pilgrim marks the road*
> *And guides the Progress of the soul to God.*

Pleasant memories of a fine character and ripe scholar of the 18th century whom Cowper helped to immortalise, are stirred by the medallion portrait of William Bull, who with his son and his grandson served this church for 105 years. Long a social and religious force in the country, William Bull has a place in literature and history. Son of a Puritan who fell from grace, he taught himself Hebrew from the headings of the 119th psalm and mathematics from an odd volume. By the help of friends he mastered Greek and Latin, and was appointed minister of the Independent Church here. To increase his small income he took pupils, among whom was a future Master of the Rolls. His class developed later into an academy, supported by generous friends who enabled him to send out gifted workers into the ministry. During his ministry here Bull made the acquaintance of Cowper and John Newton, a memorable and fruitful friendship. He took part from time to time in the religious services at Olney for which Cowper wrote the immortal Olney Hymns. Deep affection bound the rigid Calvinist and the poet, and Bull exerted an influence which to some extent counteracted the tyrannous attitude of the old slave-dealer Newton, who was parson at Olney and virtually dictator in the poet's life. Bull lives in Cowper's writings, and is mentioned in one of his poems.

On the Banks of the Ouse

NEWTON BLOSSOMVILLE. A score of swans were sunning themselves on the banks of the Ouse as we passed by to this village whose charm does not belie its flowery name, though of blossom it has no more than most villages. It took its name from a family settled here in the 13th century. The small but lofty church is mainly 14th century, but has a Norman window opening into the porch, Norman herringbone work in the wall close by, and the arch of a Norman doorway in the north wall. A smiling man supports a capital of one of the fine nave arches; a grotesque moustached fellow juts as a corbel from a chapel wall. A 14th century arcade separates the chancel from the chapel lit by a window in which an angel has been vigorously swinging a censer for 600 years. The traceried font is older than the Reformation, and the Gospel has been proclaimed from the plain pulpit since Shakespeare's day. A cherub has kept watch for 200 years on a tablet to the memory of Thomas Sherrington.

The river flows by the church and a group of chestnuts is a lovely sight in due season. A thatched cottage bears on its wall the names of the men who never came back from the war, and on the opposite side of the little patch of green is the village school built by a curate.

St Faith Looks Down

NEWTON LONGVILLE. It has delightful old cottages about its green, but older than all is the manor. With the remains of a Norman priory in its walls it has a medieval doorway and a brick and timber dovecot with a pyramid roof. Close by it rises the 15th century tower of the church, big and impressive. It stands in a raised churchyard in which we are greeted by a statue of St Faith, the patron saint and the martyr of the Roman Emperor Diocletian. She stands on a corbel outside the chancel near a window with a crude carving of a skeleton over it. For 600 years St Faith has looked out on this God's Acre; we may think that perhaps the great Erasmus saw her, for his friend William Grocyn, the Greek scholar, was at this church for 25 years.

St Faith's has a rich interior, in which we are impressed at once by the Norman piers with animals, birds, and foliage on their capitals. There is fine stone carving everywhere, old and new; an angel and five faces in a chapel, three heads by one of the capitals of the chancel arch, five weird heads supporting the massive medieval roof of the nave, crouching figures bearing up the chancel roof, the mail-clad head of a 17th century knight, and delicate carving on three pinnacles of a piscina. The modern carving is on the tapering bowl of the Norman font, which has fine lions and unicorns also in its Jacobean pyramid cover. The church has lost its 14th century screen, but two gems of tracery from it are fixed to the lectern. There is a small chest carved with men with cloaks thrown over their shoulders, and in the aisle is a small cupboard with a medieval door still on its old hinges.

Peter of 700 Years Ago

NORTH CRAWLEY. We reach it by leafy lanes, and picture Cardinal Wolsey paying it a brief visit, and David Boswell paying it a long one. The gabled Grange in the park was owned by both at an interval of over 300 years. Although one wing is modern, the remainder is Tudor, and, with its original chimneystacks and mullioned windows, the house has great beauty. Wolsey was lord of the Grange; David Boswell, a younger brother of James, bought the house on leaving Scotland for a business career in London. Another interesting building here, older than the Grange, is Moat Farm, surrounded by a moat crossed by a brick causeway.

An avenue of yews brings us to the 13th century church, the tower of which is seen far over the countryside. On the porch gable is an 18th century metal group of St George slaying the dragon; over a lancet window is a group of grotesque faces.

The church is one of two in England dedicated to St Firmin, and below a sanctuary window is this finely cut inscription of Peter of Guildford, a 13th century benefactor: "Peter gives to you, Firmin, a new chancel, so that in praising God you shall remember Peter." One arcade is 700 years old, the other 14th century. The font, which has been here six centuries, has a splendid Jacobean cover, carved with pilasters, spandrels, obelisks, and foliage. A brass portrait shows Garbrand, a 16th century rector, kneeling in ruff and gown with a skull, crossbones, and hourglass. The son of a Dutch refugee, he was a friend of Bishop Jewel, who left him his manuscripts.

The roofs, all 15th century, are finely carved. The solid beams of the nave roof are supported by the Twelve Apostles, all whitewashed when we saw them. The nave seats have linenfold carving, and box pews Jacobean panelling. There is a Tudor chest with inlaid work. On the splendid 15th century painted screen, with open tracery and a fan-vaulted canopy, are 16 prophets and saints, primitive drawings, but deeply interesting as the work of medieval artists in a quiet out-of-the-way village.

Queen Victoria and Old Curmudgeon

NORTH MARSTON. It has a 17th century inn, and a church which it owes to the credulity of one age and a miser's bequest in another.

The story begins with a spring impregnated with iron, its rare properties revealed by a 13th century rector, Sir John Schorne. The credulous attributed the virtues of the spring to Sir John himself, who was believed to have gained a victory over Satan; and after seven centuries the rhyme celebrating him is still remembered here: Sir John Schorne, Gentleman born, Kicked the Devil into a boot.

Revered in life, he was made an unofficial saint after his death, and for more than two centuries this church flourished on his reputation. The ailing and the pious flocked to seek health at his spring and sanctity at his shrine, and bestowed on both rich gifts.

There remains today a stately church with battlements and pinnacles, gargoyles, and grotesques, an east window rich with tracery under a pinnacled niche, many scratch dials in the chancel walls, a 500-year-old tower, and a porch and doorway which have defied the ravages of six centuries; the whole a wonderful village picture.

The splendid 15th century chancel, said to have been built from the offerings of the pilgrims, contained the shrine of the reputed saint. Over the vestry is the room, reached from the sanctuary by a little doorway, in which a priest kept watch each night. The Reformation shattering the superstition of those times, a second benefaction came to enrich the church after 400 years. Midway through last century a grim curmudgeon, John Camden Neild, who had inherited property here, left his miser's fortune to Queen Victoria, who testified her gratification by restoring the church, giving it a fine reredos and filling the sanctuary window with glowing glass, showing Christ and the Four Evangelists.

John Camden Neild was born in London about 1780, a son of James Neild who, with a fortune made as a goldsmith, acquired property in Buckinghamshire, and distinguished himself by 40 years of humane service in the reform of prisons. A strain of eccentricity in his character was revealed in his almost insane harshness to his elder son, whom he drove out of England to an unhealthy climate and an early death.

John, the only surviving child, inherited his father's fortune, whereupon he abandoned himself entirely to moneymaking. He lived in mean rooms without a bed, and wore old boots and a shabby suit. As a landlord he was hard and selfish, and would visit his tenants to get free meals. A scholarly Scrooge in real life, he had only two delights—classical literature and making more money to add to the pile he was saving for the queen. He died in 1852, leaving her his entire estate, nearly £250,000 " for her sole use and benefit." Legal objections to the will were filed but withdrawn and the queen accepted the windfall with elation. She awarded £100 a year to a woman who had saved Neild's life, and each of his executors £1000.

It was this miser's money which added a new chapter of splendours to the story of this church already rich in 15th century work, including six stalls with carved poppyheads, misereres, with foliage, and angel corbels. The chancel roof is modern, but the nave roof, with traceried spandrels resting on carved cherubs and shields, has been here since Chaucer's day. The church is rich in piscinas, of which it has three. The font, with angels round its stem, must have been splendid 500 years ago, as the stone seats in the chancel still are, with their vaulted canopies and pinnacles. There is a deeply splayed lancet, and the sculptured archway by which old Sir John mounted the rood stairway is still here, but the peephole to the altar has been filled up. A portrait brass in the chancel, with the kneeling figure of Richard Saunders, who died in Shakespeare's day, has facing it one of the quaintest things of the kind we have seen, a stone hand carved on the wall with the words "He lise just down thare," indicating the tomb of a 17th century rector, John Virgin. Among the church possessions are a Tudor chalice, a chained Bible, a poor-box which has begged for 400 years, and an ironbound Tudor chest.

He Saw All the Stuart Kings

OAKLEY. Spread over a valley at the foot of the hills, it has Jacobean farms and cottages nestling in the trees. A 14th century tower with a tiny spire rises over a church which still has Norman work as its treasure. In the churchyard is the only example in the county of a tomb under a canopy in an outer wall. A medieval door opens for us into a nave with Norman piers supporting 14th century arches. There is a long peephole, fashioned to allow the 14th century lords of the manor to see from their transept the altar in the new chancel. In an aisle are two old coffin lids. Corbels 500 years old, some finely carved with grotesques, support the modern roof. The altar table is Jacobean. There is still here the barrel organ which accompanied the singing in the 18th century. In the transept sleep the Tyrrells, of whom one (Sir Timothy), saw the passing of Raleigh and Milton and all the Stuart kings. One of Timothy's 12 children was James, a friend of Locke; he has a wall monument showing a trumpeting figure holding a tablet on which we see two books he wrote, a History of England and The Laws of Nature. He was one of the Justices who refused to support James the Second's Declaration of Indulgence.

BUCKINGHAMSHIRE

William Cowper's Village

OLNEY. A pleasant little market town on the Great Ouse, it is for ever known as the home of William Cowper in the happiest years of his troubled life. Here he lived 19 years and here he wrote nearly all the poems and all the charming letters by which he will be remembered. Olney without Cowper would have as its only distinctions its fine massively spired church and two curates who ministered there (unless we count the tapering monolith in the marketplace to 62 men whose names live for evermore); but Cowper peopled the place with his friends, and described the neighbourhood and its yearly round of life and weather in his poems and letters. What can be seen of this period that brought fame to Olney is centred on the church and on the home of the poet, now preserved as a museum.

The church is mainly 14th century, with a pinnacled tower from which rises a sturdy stone spire, rare in this countryside and 600 years old. The tower is in four diminishing tiers, each with a gabled window. The pinnacles have grotesque heads, and under the parapet of the 14th century chancel are many other heads showing types of joy and sorrow. We come into the church by a porch with two storeys, rebuilt with the old stones. The nave has five bays on each side and is as Cowper saw it, but the church is not in detail the church in which Cowper worshipped and John Newton preached, for it has been much refashioned, while the pew in which the poet sat has been removed to the museum.

On the walls is a memorial tablet to Stanley Hipwell, touchingly recording an act of sacrifice which cost him his life, for after leading a raid in the Great War he waited to see the last man safely back and then returned to No Man's Land to search for a comrade. Another tablet, a little mysterious, shows a woman in a black blouse and a red skirt, leaning on an anchor, the inscription saying it is in memory of John Thompson who died in 1819.

In the churchyard lies John Newton, for 16 years curate here, and during the last 13 of these one of Cowper's most intimate friends. At the end of that time Newton became rector of St Mary Woolnoth in London. There, after 27 years, he died and was buried, seven years after Cowper's death. More than 80 years later all the bodies were removed from the vaults of that city church for burial at Ilford, and

Olney made a claim for the relics of the curate who had left it 113 years before, and whose association with Cowper had echoed the name of Olney through the world. So it is that the coffins of John Newton and his wife now lie under a massive granite monument in Olney churchyard, and his coffin plate mounted on the wall, close to the pulpit in which he preached in London. The pulpit is interesting because it went from St Mary Woolnoth to Northampton prison, and came from there to Olney. It is probably the only pulpit in England which has escaped from prison.

There has been much controversy as to the influence of John Newton on Cowper. Newton, a converted captain of ships carrying cargoes of slaves from Africa to America, preached a terrifying theology, and Cowper, the most tender-hearted, lovable, and humorous of men, was subject to lapses into melancholy insanity. It would seem to us that perhaps they might have been better mated. But Newton was a sincere friend, and helped to concentrate the energies of the despondent poet. He it was who arranged for Cowper's settlement at Olney with his friends the Unwins, in the house which is now the Cowper Museum.

Cowper was then 35. He had made some translations and written some verses which showed his pleasure in writing but were of small account, and his shyness and want of self-confidence had proved his incapacity for business. Also his brain-storms had made it necessary that from time to time he should be placed under control.

Yet everyone who knew him well saw in him, when his mind was clear, a most lovable nature, keen sympathy, high principle, all with a charming strain of humour, and his friends, men and women, were many and loyal. Olney was the place where these friends gathered round him through 19 years, and, notwithstanding his lapses into mental instability, enabled him to win a place in the literature of his country as a poet of great feeling, embracing both human and animal life. He introduced a simple unaffected love of the outdoor world that the more formal poets of that time had missed. He touched poetry with the glow of humanity and human nature, and scorned the dominating dullness of such men as Pope.

The house in the market square where the poet lived, and where now are gathered a number of things associated with him, has its rooms named after the most faithful of his friends. There is the

BUCKINGHAMSHIRE

John Newton room, the William Bull room, and rooms recalling the friendships with Mary Unwin, with whom the poet boarded for 31 years; her son William (through whose acquaintance at Huntingdon he was first attracted to the family); Lady Hesketh (Cowper's cousin), and Lady Austen, who suggested to him subjects for his writings and a freedom in style which made him popular. These were his most intimate friends, who safeguarded him and brought happiness into his chequered life. In one of these rooms are many remembrances of Mrs Unwin—her workbox, her bobbin-winder, and the manuscript of Cowper's poem to her, My Mary.

Cowper's own bedroom is called the John Gilpin room because in it he wrote that most popular humorous poem after hearing the story from Lady Austen; but it might well have been given another name, for here he wrote the poem on the loss of the Royal George, Toll for the Brave. He did not know that the great ship had sunk because her timbers were rotten and that brave Kempenfelt and his 800 men had been murdered by official neglect.

In the parlour, where his greatest poem (The Task) was written, we may see the sofa which gives the title to its first canto, his walking stick, and other personal relics. In this room he wrote the poem which has been sung all round the world, God Moves in a Mysterious Way, and many more of the 67 hymns which, with 281 written by Newton, made up the Olney Hymns. Newton's armchair is still in the kitchen. In the hall we see the porthole through which Cowper admitted his hares, Puss, Tiny, and Bess, to gambol on the Turkey carpet in the evening, and to be made famous in verses that have kindled much sympathy with animal life. Here, too, is the shutter from the poet's cottage at Weston Underwood, on which he wrote perhaps the saddest of his lines:

> *Farewell, dear scenes, for ever closed to me:*
> *Oh, for what sorrows must I now exchange ye!*

When he was 55 Cowper, for the sake of his health, moved with Mrs Unwin to higher ground at Weston Underwood, and there he lived nine years. There Mrs Unwin's health failed, and Cowper, so long and so lovingly cared for by her, now became her helper. Eventually friends removed both of them into Norfolk for a change, and Cowper felt forebodings that were sadly fulfilled. There were further health failures, and first Mrs Unwin and then the poet died, both being buried in the churchyard of East Dereham.

The garden at the back of the Olney house, which became the museum at the centenary of Cowper's death in 1900, is much smaller than in the poet's lifetime, and, one of his favourite resorts, the summer house, has become detached but may be visited; on its walls are the signatures of many men of letters. Here it was that Cowper's stimulating friend William Bull, the Independent minister who came over fortnightly to visit him from Newport Pagnell, spent many genial hours; we may lift one of the floorboards and see where Mr Bull kept his pipes and tobacco for these visits. There are few memorials so intimate in spirit with the life they keep in remembrance.

Above the Vale

OVING. Poised on the crest of a high range, with fine views over the Vale of Aylesbury, it is fronted by North Marston against a background of trees, with its own charms and graces, and a manor perhaps four centuries old. The best part of the church came together 700 years ago. We pass, by a door made before the kings rode to the Field of the Cloth of Gold, through a south doorway which admitted men and women born as serfs to the lords of this manor into the nave these serfs would know; but two of the arches are now claimed for a vestry, in which are two little old chests. The font at which the babies of these serfs were christened is here today, low and without a pedestal. The chancel in which they heard mass is a fine example of 13th century architecture. One window, the gift of 14 priests, shows Melchizedek, the priest king of Salem, in red and blue, a man with a sword kneeling before him.

One of the aisles has a small window piercing the top of an arch, its glass showing an angel with a trumpet. Part of the old rood stairs and the upper doorway remain. The roof, with carved bosses now the worse for time, was carved in the days of Henry the Eighth; and there are four carved benches on which worshippers sat wondering and aghast as, six times in succession, they were bidden to acclaim his marriage. The altar cup came when Queen Elizabeth ordered the renewal of the sacred plate wrested from Protestant churches in Mary Tudor's Reign of Terror.

BUCKINGHAMSHIRE

Here Fell a Hundred Men

PADBURY. It has timbered cottages looking old enough to have been here in those Civil War days when the Royalists in battle killed over 100 Commonwealth men at Padbury; but it is for the peaceful charms of the 13th century church, with its Jacobean tower and its quiet background of fields, that we come today. Students of architecture are drawn to ponder and sketch the beauty of the 14th century windows in the clerestory. The arcades are rich in sculptured heads, vigorously carved corbels, and little faces of graceful fancy. One of three piscinas has 13th century foliage, and a second has a wooden shelf 600 years old. A fading 14th century painting shows St Catherine with her wheel, and an old consecration cross still glows vividly red. On a beam in the chancel roof is a head of Christ, and on another a little man with a shield, both the work of a medieval craftsman. A massive Jacobean table with angels at the corners has the names of the nine men who gave it.

The Family of William Penn

PENN. From this remote spur of the Chilterns (600 feet up among the beech woods), where houses, fields, church, and a much-loved family share the same name, links run out across the wide sea. Here lived the ancestors and some of the descendants of the great Quaker who stamped a continent with his ideals. It is a place where "peace comes dropping slow," by the pond on Tyler's Green, through the long row of elms. It is a place of historic charm, where a church stands which was given as a wedding present by Henry the Eighth to Sybil Penn who had been Elizabeth's governess.

In the village are 17th century cottages and a house refashioned in that period, when it was already 200 years old; it is called Putham place and is now divided into homes for farm labourers. It has the old chimney stacks and windows, and the great hall can still be traced.

The villagers boast that from the 14th century church tower they can see a dozen counties. When we stood in the churchyard we noted five ridges of hills rolling away to the south. In the medieval church are many treasures, the oldest being a 13th century stone coffin with a cross on the lid and the round base of the font, which was probably once part of a Norman pillar. We stand in wonder before the font, which is of lead. Its date is uncertain. It is scratched all over with the initials of silly people as long ago as 1626, but the font is obviously older than that. It is one of about 30 lead fonts now left in England, and is the only one which is quite plain, the only one with a rounded base. The bowl is three inches thick, about a foot high, and about six feet round.

In contrast with this simplicity is a 17th century chest, elaborately carved, standing beneath a window showing Catherine of Alexandria in a green cloak and Margaret of Scotland in blue. Both chest and window were given to the church in memory of Lucy Shepperton, who died in 1928.

Penn remembers some shining heroes in its new windows. The Black Prince and Joan of Arc stand in one, with a little picture of Bethune at their feet to remind us that Colonel Hugh Hill, DSO, was buried there during the Great War. A picture of a medieval attack on the Moors is under the figures of Godfrey of Bouillon and Ferdinand of Castile in another window, which is set in honour of Captain Derek Pawle, who fell in the Cameroons in 1915. Angelina Pawle who died in 1931 is remembered in the beautiful new east window, where we see the Adoration of Christ, with the archangels Gabriel and Michael in shining splendour among the heavenly host.

Near this window is a pair of misereres with four panels of figures, and with winged heads below the seats. They are at least two centuries younger than the magnificent nave roof, which is left as the 15th century builders made it, with tracery in the spandrels and trefoil-headed arches, the timbers standing on stone corbels shaped to the heads of bearded men and angels with shields. On the floor of the south chapel, under which lie the earliest of the Penns, are their portraits in brass, among them a curious picture of Elizabeth Rok, whose face peeps out of her shroud. Elizabeth is one of the five people in Buckinghamshire who were engraved in their shrouds. She died in 1540, and her inscription on a separate plate has a beautiful flower border. The oldest Penn portrait is of John and his wife; their six sons, all in ruffs, have a plate to themselves. John died in 1597. Next comes William Penn, who died in 1638, his wife, one son, and two daughters; he looks odd with a beard and moustache

Marlow — Suspension Bridge and Church

Taplow — Cliveden and its Glorious Woods

BUCKINGHAMSHIRE BY THE THAMES

Lathbury — Norman Carving

Lavendon
15th Century Font

Marsh Gibbon
13th Century Capital

Aylesbury
The Norman Font

Stantonbury

The Norman Chancel and its Rich Carving

THE WORK OF THE ANCIENT CRAFTSMEN

above his suit of armour. The finest family group is John Penn's, who died in 1641. His wife, the five sons and five daughters, drawn in varying sizes and postures, make a delightful picture. John's mother-in-law, Lady Drury, keeps her daughter company, in her best gown, with her coat-of-arms on a shield and a little greyhound leaping above it. Some grandchildren of the famous William Penn, who died at Ruscombe in Berkshire and is buried at Jordans, lie under the nave, where there is a stone speaking of William as the Proprietor of Pennsylvania.

The Curzons, who brought to this church the 18th century pulpit, with its spiral stair rails, from a chapel in Mayfair, are remembered in several wall tablets. To Assheton, Lord Curzon, who died in 1820, is a memorial with two mourning figures and a medallion. A delightful brass inscription on the tower arch tells how clever little Patricia Cuthbert was. The one-handed clock in the tower, made in 1715, had been stopped since 1910, and in 1925 Patricia, 13 years old, made it work again.

But the great medieval treasure of the church has been brought to light in our time. During the restoration of the church in 1938 a number of oak panels covered with broken plaster were removed from the wall above the chancel arch, and were being carted away as rubbish when a wise workman detected paint beneath the plaster. An expert was called in, the boards were cleaned, and a superb medieval painting of the Last Judgment was revealed. There are many of these Doom paintings fading away on our church walls, but few painted on oak, and none richer in colour than this. It comes from two periods, which gives it further interest, for it was begun about 1400 or soon after, and it would appear that it needed repair towards the end of its first century, and then was completely painted over. The work is done in oils and is remarkable for the richness of its red, orange, and yellow tones. Our Lord is sitting on a rainbow with angels trumpeting about Him and other angels carrying symbols of the Passion. The Twelve Apostles are grouped below with the Madonna. These figures, in richly coloured robes, flank the sides of a green slope, at the foot of which two souls are seen rising from their graves. The painting is 12 feet long and more than half as high in the middle, and it has now been happily placed in the south aisle so that it is more easily seen than most brasses.

The Admiral's Flag

PENN STREET. Two pines stand sentinel at the churchyard gate, guarding a 19th century church with a spire of oak shingles rising above the beech woods. It springs from a central tower with eight sides and eight gargoyles. The church has two possessions which have come from famous places: the banner of Sir William Howe, which hung for a long time in Westminster Abbey, and a huge copy of Raphael's Transfiguration which was once the altarpiece in Curzon Chapel, Mayfair, and was brought by Earl Howe in 1905 to this church, which the first Earl Howe had built. The banner, now hanging on the chancel wall, has three dragons with red tongues out. The most beautiful of the Howe memorials is a simple open screen with a frieze of foliage in dark oak.

In the grounds of Penn House, the home of Earl Howe, has been planted the great mast of the ship of Admiral Howe (one of Nelson's gallant band of brothers), from which his flag is flown every year on "the Glorious First of June."

A Rare Survival

PITCHCOTT. It has views across the Vale of Aylesbury to inspire a poet. Timbers from trees which were in their prime in Queen Elizabeth's day strengthen the upper part of a 15th century tower, but the south door looks as old as its 14th century doorway; the porch is 1662. Our three chief building centuries are represented in the narrow little church, but the nave has much that the Normans left. The 13th century chancel, with a modern arch, has a window of glowing colour, with scenes from the life of Our Lord, a chalice of 1569, a low piscina, and an ancient locker.

The most interesting thing we found here is one of those rare survivals, a 13th century stone book-rest in the splay of a chancel window, from which the priest read and spoke to people who were not allowed to enter the church.

Ancient Timbers

PITSTONE. A little place on the Chilterns, with Pitstone Hill as a background, it has a post windmill, and a church remote in the fields with sombre cypresses about it. The church was built by the Normans; we found some of their simpler ornaments and two grotesque carved heads on a window ledge. Their font remains, beautiful as when they carved its bowl with fluting, separated by a cable roll from a band of arches. Over all this is a wavy design, and on one side are lovely flowers.

The chancel floor has tiles 600 years old, some with Latin inscriptions, some with signs of the Zodiac. The columns between the chancel and the chapel have carved capitals. The nave, with its roof and its handsome columns, was built 500 years ago. In a corner of the chapel is a piscina beautifully carved with foliage.

The most ancient timber is a 13th century chest, but there is early woodwork at the end of one of the 16th century pews, among which are two sturdy examples of the box type, in which worshippers may have mourned the death of Queen Elizabeth. Whatever its age, no other woodwork in the church can compare with the fine Jacobean pulpit, its canopy carved with pendants, its six panels with bosses and mitres, the standard with handsome scroll work. It is the treasure of this little church which Time has left alone in its green solitude.

Norman Church in Saxon Village

PRESTON BISSETT. It lies remote, but the Normans found it and built a church in this Saxon village. Of the thatched cottages which lead to the church, that at the churchyard gate has the curious name of Old Hat: the Old Straw Hat, some of the boys call it. There is a low 15th century tower to the 14th century church, with a weird company of figures on the outer walls, all distinct and individual; among them we noticed a monkey, a jester, and Satan. The interior, with a tower arch so low that we touched the top, has part of a Norman capital inserted in a wall of the chancel, which, with its arch borne on the backs of crouching grotesques, has fine 14th century priest seats. There is a monument in memory of a rector's son who was killed by a tiger in the Indian jungle.

The Old Camp

PRINCES RISBOROUGH. It is a pleasant little town of many gabled and timbered houses, looking up from Aylesbury Plain to Bledlow Bluff and to the great cross gleaming on the hill at Whiteleaf. To one side of the church lies the Mount, earthworks supposed to have been a Saxon camp, now protected by the National Trust.

On the other side is the fine old manor house, with pilasters of mellow brickwork reaching almost to the eaves. Within it, rising from floor to attic, is a Jacobean staircase, with pierced scrollwork instead of balusters. There is a quaint market house, a square building with arched entrances, remade a century ago.

The Norman church, rebuilt in the 13th century, waited until our own time for a spire to its 15th century tower. One Norman window remains, but the richest possessions are in an aisle with founders' tombs under four medieval arches. In the wall above is a triple lancet with graceful shafts, two standing unattached in the wide splay. Beautifully carved canopies span the sedilia and the piscina, which has a tiny head set a-tilt. In the chancel is a handsome window showing Christ in majesty between the archangels Michael and Gabriel, and a charming Madonna and Child between stately angels swinging censers. The modern reredos, vivid in rich red, blue, and gold, shows the shepherds and the wise men. The pulpit, handsome with panels and arches, was carved in Restoration days.

Cromwell Calls

QUAINTON. It has treasured literary memories and the essentials of our perfect English scene. Here is a spacious green with a pond and the ruins of a medieval cross; a grand old windmill; Tudor cottages with old companions; a rectory with the mark of centuries in its walls; gabled almshouses with fine chimneys, porches, and heraldic shields; and a fine 14th century church graced by tall trees, with a yew growing by the porch.

The church, like the cross, is supposed to have been built by the Knights Hospitallers, who until the Reformation had a hospice close by. Standing between the rectory and the almshouses, a picture of charm and serenity, it is an attractive shrine. Its 15th century tower, with battlements and parapet, has a sundial, and from its corners peep queer grotesques. The height and boldness of the great nave bays, lit by a lofty clerestory, are impressive. Behind the pulpit is a peephole like a lancet. The font is about 500 years old. Only one stall-end preserves its ancient carving, a lion; but in the north aisle is part of a screen whose paintings of four saints with books, the work of Tudor artists, are still clear.

There are ten portraits on six brasses, the earliest of which, a small figure of Joan Plessi, a girl with streaming hair, is believed to be the oldest in the county; its date is 1350. Kneeling in his cassock is a rector of Agincourt days; a rector who died as the Wars of the Roses ended is wearing a cope; Margery Inwardby is with her four children, brought here to rest in 1509; a 16th century portrait of Richard Inwardby shows him in a fur robe; and there is a small brass of a woman in a ruff.

Monuments of great literary interest are the painted alabaster figures of Richard Brett and his wife, kneeling at a desk with their four daughters. He was rector in 1595, and had a foremost part in translating the Bible, being one of the 42 men who made the Authorised Version the most beautiful book in the world. He served here 42 years and sleeps in his chancel, with inscriptions in Hebrew, Greek, and Latin.

There are several monuments to the Dormer family, the earliest to Fleetwood Dormer who died before the Civil War, to his son John, and to a second Fleetwood Dormer, the marble tomb having weeping cherubs by two large urns. A second monument of the same century is to Sir John Dormer and his wife, two busts. On the third monument is Sir Robert Dormer, with long curls, wearing his judicial robes, with his weeping wife and his son, sculptured by Roubillac, and cherubs in the clouds. Sir Robert, a gifted lawyer, was for the last 20 years of his life a judge. His only son dying at 30, the heartbroken father followed him to the grave.

Here on a great tomb, wearing a wig and knightly armour, with his wife by his side, lies Richard Winwood, who built the beautiful old almshouses over 300 years ago. A son of the Secretary of State to James the First, he lived at the manor house; and it is said that one day, while he was out hawking, he was joined by Cromwell, who, on his triumphant ride from Worcester, broke his journey to London and spent an hour or so enjoying the sport. The Colossus of the church is the 17th century tomb of Sir Richard Pigott and his wife, an immense monument with a huge urn and three cherubs at the top. The Pigotts lived from the beginning of the 16th century at Doddershall Hall, a fine moated manor with delightful chimneys.

One of the most interesting tombs is in the churchyard, that of James Lipscomb, an 18th century sailor and surgeon. He was the father of one of the county's worthiest sons, George Lipscomb, who, born at a cottage still standing near the green, called the Magpie, was doctor, lawyer, preacher, soldier, author, but above all was the historian of Buckinghamshire. His history was the absorbing passion of his life, his glory and his ruin. He went everywhere, saw and read everything, and gave years to his book, admirably written and nobly illustrated. The book did everything but pay. It broke his health and exhausted his resources, and in 1846, as the last pages were going to press, he died, not amid the scenes he loved, but in a London garret; and only by charity was he saved from a pauper's grave.

Beauty and Fine Possessions

RADCLIVE. Lying in a sharp bend of a valley rich with elms, where the Ouse receives a stream which comes down the slopes from Gawcott, it has much beauty and many cherished possessions. Between the church and the river the gabled manor house, with handsome chimneys, has a fine old oak screen, whose columns support a moulded cornice with carved spandrels; and the original staircase, with ornamental sides like pierced parapets, still runs up to the attics. On the other side of the church is the timbered Grange, with an avenue of beautiful trees ending in a delightful garden, shaded by a copper beech and a giant cedar.

A battlemented tower which has watched the slow tide of change for 600 years looms over a Norman church with a beautiful English doorway. The Norman font remains. In the porch we found two 15th century benches with elaborately carved poppyheads. A chancel arch 500 years old rests on Norman capitals, the round columns set in a framework of chevrons. Above the arch, under original stones reset, the lion and the unicorn rest on corbels which once supported the rood screen. Two double lancets in the sanctuary are interesting examples of the style immediately before the beginning of tracery. A nave window has fragments of 14th century glass, showing under golden canopies a careworn Madonna carrying the Child, with an Apostle. The most notable woodwork is the altar table, actually a 16th century chest, its boldly carved panels set between uprights carved with figures. Among them are two bearded heads with halos, one with the hair arranged like the rays of the sun. Rich and elaborate carving covers this extraordinary chest. Another chest, occupying considerable floor space under the tower, is of mahogany, with drawers and brass fittings, a rare piece of 17th century work; and to the same period belong the altar rails, with their pierced banisters, and the plain canopy of the modern pulpit.

Two Hamlets

RADNAGE. Snug in a valley of the Chilterns, it embraces two hamlets: a tiny group of cottages called Town End, and another group which calls itself the City! Backed by a fine beech wood, the Norman church and the yew-hedged rectory make a charming little hillside picture. There are two Norman doorways, and a Norman tower divides the nave and chancel. The chancel has three Norman windows, and the goblet-shaped font is probably as old as the Conquest. There are traces of 13th century painting on splays of windows and on the walls of the tower. A 15th century brass has portraits of William Este and his 12 children. Supreme among the old work is the magnificent roof of the nave, 500 years old and having great tie-beams supported by enriched brackets with traceried spandrels. The church still keeps the massive bier on which from 1699 the villagers have been borne to their last rest.

Sleeping with the Great Seal

RAVENSTONE. It is an endearing little place far from the high ways of traffic, with a tremendous chestnut in the churchyard and almshouses glowing with colour against the grey stone of the church and farm. The founder of these cosy almshouses was Lord Chancellor Finch, who gave the village much but would have taken from his country more, for he was a narrow-minded Royalist who would have hanged John Milton. It is the memory of the better side of him that dominates the village, as his tomb dominates the church.

He lies in splendour in black and white, wearing a robe with lovely lace embroidery, resting on his elbow with his wife at his side. The Finch chapel has a tiny oak screen made in his day, and most of the woodwork here is from that time: the chapel doors, the panelling, the tower screen, the pews, and the magnificent three-decker pulpit with its lovely canopy. The chancel arch is Tudor, painted in the 19th century. There is Norman herringbone work still showing in the walls of the nave, and the south arcade has its original bell-shaped capitals; they are 13th century. The font is 700 years old with a 17th century cover.

In the shadow of the 13th century cross is a stump of a cross older still, by which lies Thomas Seaton, the rector who founded the Seatonian Prize for sacred poetry at Cambridge.

But it is Lord Chancellor Finch who is the most notable figure here. Fatherless at 16, he had reluctantly to leave Oxford and take up the law. During the Commonwealth he built up a practice without let or hindrance. When Cromwell died, and the Convention Parliament, of which he was a member, was about to dissolve, Milton was a prisoner in the custody of the Sergeant-at-Arms, and the House ordered his release. The Sergeant demanded his due £150 in fees, and the sum was raised by the poet's friends, though Andrew Marvel stoutly urged that the sum should not be paid. Finch was Speaker at the time and fiercely opposed Milton, saying that he had been Latin secretary to Cromwell and well deserved hanging! His last speech in the House of Commons was in support of the right of the Crown to exact supplies without redressing the grievances of the nation, which meant a reversion to the dark ages of tyranny. At 54 he was Lord Chancellor and used to sleep with the Great Seal under his pillow.

Queen Anne's General

ST LEONARDS. Its chief possession is its 15th century church, a charming little building with a pyramidal bellcot crowned by a weathervane. Once a cell of Missenden Abbey, it fell into ruin, and Hampden may have seen its bare walls. It was Cornelius Wood, one of Queen Anne's Generals, who restored it. In the chancel are two stone seats for priests, angel corbels support the 16th century beams of the roof, and on a wall is a monument to Cornelius Wood, showing him larger than life, with his hair sweeping his shoulders, against a background of cannon-balls and cherubs with golden trumpets. Here are his gauntlets, and the great crested helmet he wore. The beautiful glass in the sanctuary window to a lady who died in 1918 illustrates Humility by the Annunciation, Truth by a figure of Christ standing on a green dragon, and Courage by a red-cloaked David wielding his sling at Goliath.

The Seven Village Boys

SAUNDERTON. We liked the remembrance of the Seven Heroes of Saunderton on the simple cross in the churchyard, *To the boys of this village*. It faces the quaint thatched buildings of a farm which look across to a tiled church with a little bell turret, all remade last century from materials 500 years old. A knight and a lady greet us as we come, both worn away by centuries of weather, probably as old as the fleur-de-lys carved round the font 700 years ago. There is a screen with open tracery made from two 14th century screens, and medieval woodwork still holding up the bellcot. The floor of the vestry has medieval tiles with foliage and other designs, but perhaps the most attractive possession of the church is the 500-year-old brass portrait of Isabella Saunderton; it shows her head and shoulders.

The Lamp of Memory

SHABBINGTON. Across the Thame from here is Oxfordshire; on this side of the river a few cottages line the road beneath the low mound on which the Normans built their church. At the entrance to the churchyard, shadowed by a stately elm, is a lamp in memory of Arthur and Harold Bros, father and son, who ministered here from 1876 to 1923. Both doorways and the chancel are impressive 14th century work, and in the porch is a coffin lid with bold Gothic lettering, still sharp and legible, cut when Chaucer was writing his poems in the same style.

The oldest work here is Norman, herringbone and stones in the nave bearing the impress of the Conqueror's architects. The pulpit is Jacobean, but below the plaster roof of the nave are great tie-beams which were put up while the Wars of the Roses were still raging.

The Portrait of Dame Susan

SHALSTONE. The fertile soil of the Ouse valley has produced regiments of trees for Shalstone. They line the lane; they form an avenue of magnificent chestnuts leading over the fields to the church; they run to the manor house, set in great cedars and copper beeches, its wall hidden by a lofty box hedge. The church itself is reached between two towering hedges of yew and holly, with a triumphal arch of yew before the porch.

Sir Gilbert Scott, born not far away, made the church new last century, and lavished on it a wealth of decoration inside and out. It has heads, flowers, sprays of yew and other ornament on the capitals, and attractive adornment everywhere. Much 15th century work remains, with monuments of great interest, the most notable a 16th century portrait brass of Dame Susan who, at the death of her husband, John Kyngeston, vowed herself to life in a religious community. Her brass is of rare beauty, showing the widow with her hands clasped in prayer, a ring on her finger, and a long inscription telling the story.

For over three centuries the beautiful manor has been the home of the Jervoise, Purefoy, and Fitzgerald families, and there are many monuments to them, one reaching almost to the roof, erected in her lifetime by Elizabeth Purefoy, with a bust of herself as a girl. Born in the days of Charles the Second, she lived under seven sovereigns, dying at 93. On the walls are monuments by two of the fashionable sculptors of their day. One is a tablet with an urn, carved by Nollekens in memory of a rector, George Jervoise, who died a few days after Trafalgar. His widow lived to rebuild part of the church, and died at 90, a Westmacott sculpture showing her with her hand on a Bible. A second Westmacott work is a tablet in the sanctuary to two of the Jervoise children, the little girl resting her head on her brother's shoulder. But much more attractive than the conventional marble is the lovely figure of an angel with outspread wings, carved in oak about a foot high, kneeling on the poor-box.

The Toot

SHENLEY. It has two corners a mile apart, both close to Watling Street: Brook End with the green and the brook and a few pretty cottages, and Church End where is gathered the beauty with which Nature and Man have endowed this place.

The church has still some of the stones built into it by the monks who came from Normandy when William Rufus was king. Its 15th century tower rises between Norman transepts, a Norman chancel and a 14th century clerestoried nave. There are Norman windows and two mass dials from those early days, with stately doorways, a fine porch, and rich 13th century carving on capitals. The stone seats for the priests are 13th century, the font is 15th, and the pulpit has Jacobean panels. On a great monument with many painted shields lies Thomas Stafford in armour and ruff, he with four sons and his wife with three daughters. He died a few years after Queen Elizabeth, and all wear Tudor costume. It was his son who built the gabled almshouses in the village street.

By the church is the old Georgian rectory, divided from the

churchyard by a lovely yew hedge and with a great cedar on its lawn. Close by is Shenley House, approached by a splendid avenue of limes. At Shenley Wood is a mound 120 feet wide, with a wet moat round it and seven acres of defences; it rejoices in the name of the Toot.

The Window in the Buttress

SHERINGTON. There were more acres than houses as this old place settled down to be a village, and the houses, many of them thatched, still have ample space about them. The scene is dominated by the splendid church, from whose high ground we see the beautiful slopes of Woburn. By the lychgate are two immense chestnuts, and in the churchyard two lofty pines.

The only church in England dedicated to St Laud, a sixth-century French bishop, it has a noble central tower begun by the Normans. In one of its buttresses is a 14th century window with a wide splay, through which a watcher may see the altar from the churchyard. In the 15th century porch is a door with a curious handle which, attached to the shaft by a hand, is engraved with two shields of the arms of a medieval rector. Thanks to the 16th century clerestory, to the great west window of the 15th, and to the beautifully traceried sanctuary window of the 14th century, the church is a temple of light, sharply revealing the carving on the 700-year-old piers, the ornate tracery on three fine medieval stone seats, and the worn figures of saints on the 15th century font. A modern window has a striking St George, with St Hubert in a blue cloak.

Between the Waters

SIMPSON. Lying between a river and a canal, it has a tiny green with a thatched cottage on one side and, down a short lane, a delightful little timbered house. The big church, with its central tower and transepts, tells of higher tides of life than we find here now. Although the porch, with its crowned head and two other heads critically watching the coming and going of worshippers, was added when the Tudors were nearing the throne, the main part of the church is of the 14th century, which gave it the chancel, the transepts with their handsome arches, and the traceried windows with carved heads. The low arches and two curious peepholes suggest rare chances of hide and seek in medieval days, when players as well as parsons had their stage and their hour in our churches, and laughter ran like a silver thread through nativities, moralities, and miracle plays. The oldest thing in the church is the font, to which children of baron and serf were brought 700 years ago. The font is low, but John Bacon's 18th century monument to Sir Walden Hanmer reaches from the floor to the full height of the chancel roof. Carved in a great circle of white marble, a woman representing Justice presides over this huge sculpture, sitting with a pair of scales.

John Kemp of Kent

SLAPTON. Round about it stretch fair fields, and by it runs the River Ouzel. A 15th century tower rises over the 13th century church, and in a porch are the original stone benches. From the first church there still remain the plain font and the chancel arch, on which we found traces of ancient colour.

In the chancel are two portrait brasses, one of Reginald Mauser, a 15th century rector, and another showing Thomas Knyghton in the rich robes he wore in the time of Henry the Eighth. Another brass shows one of Henry's servants, James Tournay, a dumpy little man with two wives and 14 children. His posterity endures, for the peace memorial on a wall bears his name, his descendants still living here. In the chancel floor are twenty 14th century tiles; brightly coloured fragments of the 15th century screen remain; and on the doors is ironwork wrought before the first sword was drawn in the Wars of the Roses.

The village still benefits by a charity founded 400 years ago by good parson Knyghton, but it has no memorial of its most illustrious rector, John Kemp, the man of Kent who passed from here to the bishopric of Rochester, to become Lord Chancellor, Primate, and Cardinal, and to stand like a lion against Jack Cade.

Out of the Slough of Despond

SLOUGH. It seems to have been named after a field, in the days when it began in the small village of Upton, and the name which puzzles many people is pronounced to rhyme like Now. It is growing into a great industrial town, born of two national tragedies of our time—the War and the Depression. We may say, perhaps, that its modern prosperity has come out of the Slough of Despond. During the war the Government used hundreds of acres here for storing machinery and motor vehicles, and with the coming of peace this vast area of unwanted stores became a byword. It was one of the rubbish heaps of the Great War, and a company was formed to take it all over and establish light industries on 600 acres. Since then factories have been set up by the score. The provision of houses and schools gave the local authorities grave problems to consider, but they have been well met, and when the Depression struck the big industrial areas of the North thousands of idle men were able to find work and homes at Slough. More than a million of money has been spent on this scheme, and the population has multiplied by four. It is good to know that the town has nearly 300 acres of playing fields.

The long wide street of Upton, where the coaches used to stop on their way to Bath, has grown into this lively place, and the heart of it all is still the lovely churchyard of St Lawrence at Upton; we can well understand, as we stand by the ancient yew and in the shade of these hoary elms that Upton folk claim this churchyard as the inspiration of Gray's Elegy. Certainly the poet would know it well, and must have thought of it in writing his masterpiece.

On three sides of the old church of St Lawrence lies the park of Upton Court, which belonged to Merton Abbey before the Reformation. Built into the walls is a 17th century hiding-place, reached by way of the chimney in the great hall. Light falls through 16th and 17th century windows, painted with the Abbey arms, on to rare woodwork a hundred years older. Another old house is Upton Dairy; it has a thatched barn with heavy timbers in the walls and roof, and is 17th century.

Several curious inscriptions catch the eye as we walk round the churchyard, in which lie descendants of our great astronomer Sir William Herschel, who lies here himself not far from the scene of his great discoveries. On the stone of a famous jockey is written "It is the pace that kills." Charles Baker, who had the title of Second Yeoman of his Majesty's Cellars, is much praised on his grave as a perfect and blameless man:

> *His virtues walked their tranquil round,*
> *Nor made a pause, nor left a void,*
> *And his Eternal Master found*
> *The given talents well employed.*

On a stone close by this we are told that "praise on tombs doth but ambition feed." Not far away lies Sarah Bramston, spinster of

Eton, of whom we read that she was "a person who dared to be just in the reign of George the Second."

We pass through a Norman doorway with chevron moulding and carved capitals into the little church, which rose, it is believed, on Saxon foundations within 50 years of the landing of the Conqueror. At the beginning of the 12th century the builders first set up the nave and tower, and in 1160 the chancel was added and the nave lengthened. When the 19th century arrived the tower had been struck by lightning and the church was in a ruinous state until Slough saved this venerable spot, added the south aisle and gave a new roof and parapet to the tower.

Glancing eastward as we enter, we are struck with the fine design of the tower arches and the wonderful roof of the chancel. The two arches are modern in Norman style, but the two bays of the low stone vaulting in the chancel are perfect examples of Norman craftsmanship. They rest on round scalloped capitals springing from a Norman stringcourse.

The original tower arch is now in the east wall of the modern aisle. The Normans actually built three arches, but only the centre one remains as they shaped it, the two side ones being enlarged in the 13th century. One of them, through which the organ pipes now peep, contains one of the rarest devices to be found in any church in England, for it is made of oak with round pillars and carved capitals. The arch has four depths, each separated by bands of ornament, and is a remarkable piece of early woodwork, 700 years old. The roof of the nave is 15th century and is in four bays, with kingposts and heavy beams. In the south doorway of the tower hangs an oak door made at the same time, and the light comes into the tower from a window just above it in which fragments of the old glass remain. Older than all these is the arcading round the bowl of the font, the work of a Norman craftsman who may also have carved the pillar piscina with a beaded edge.

Among the treasures of the church is a curious 16th century almsbox with three locks, and on the wall of the tower is a remarkable little alabaster Trinity with traces of colour still left on it. It was probably carved at that wonderful centre of art in medieval England, Chellaston in Derbyshire. The head has been broken away from the figure of the Almighty on the throne, but the small figure of the Son on the Cross, set between the draped knees of the Father, is as it was finished by the sculptor 500 years ago.

One relic of the rich days of the old church has found its way to St Mary's, the new church built last century; it is a piece of the ancient screen, shaped in leaves and tendrils and now gilded so as to make a lovely frame for the Ten Commandments.

In the aisle are brass portraits of the Bulstrodes, the earlier owners of Bulstrode Park. The oldest is of Agnes, who died in 1472 and kneels in a shroud; an inscription belonging to someone else is nailed beneath her portrait, saying in Hebrew, I know that my Redeemer liveth. Next comes Edward Bulstrode, with a sword and in the armour he wore as esquire to Henry the Seventh and Henry the Eighth. There are portraits of two of the royal servant's three wives and his twelve children, who are drawn in two groups. Another Edward is in armour with a sword, engraved with his wife and ten children in Elizabethan dress.

As we walk away from this wonderful old church, and note the little turret for the sanctus bell, we think of another bell in the tower which rang out merrily in the happy days of Charles Stuart, and again when Pamela, the heroine of Samuel Richardson's novel, was married. Such stories were new in those days when the novel was coming into being, and the drawing of character and the presentation of incident in Pamela were so vivid as to make the story seem alive. Richardson wrote it in two months and people have been reading it ever since. It was the first best-seller, and was commended from the pulpit, and ladies would wave their copies of it to each other at public assemblies. The poor read it as eagerly as the rich, for Pamela was a daughter of the people, a beautiful girl in the service of a man whose approaches she withstood until by her goodness and charm she so completely won his admiration that he married her. People joined together to buy copies of the book, which were passed from one to another, and here at Slough the blacksmith read the story each night to the villagers in the firelight of the forge. As they listened they were so transported by the eventual triumph of Pamela that they ran in a body to the church and insisted on ringing the wedding bells.

Perhaps it will seem to many travellers that the best possession of Slough is its distant view of Windsor Castle; it should be preserved for ever. We remember that Queen Victoria came from Windsor to Slough in her carriage to make her first railway journey, taking the train to Paddington. She declared herself quite charmed with it, though she had been for years afraid of the new-fangled invention which many people imagined would be the destruction of our countryside. Prince Albert would take the train to London on the rare occasions when he travelled alone, but at times he would send a message to the driver, "Not quite so fast next time, Mr Conductor, if you please."

Queen Victoria travelled from Slough in the first eight-wheeled coach ever made, part of a train in which the carriages were roughly fastened together with crude couplings. Questions were asked in Parliament about the queen taking such a dangerous journey, but it appears that great precautions were taken, the illustrious Brunel being in the cabin, and Sir Daniel Gooch, one of the greatest designers of railway engines, being the driver. On the footplate was the queen's favourite coachman, who insisted on being there to look after her Majesty's interests. A new coach was built for the queen in 1850 with a disc and a crossbar signal on the roof which the queen could operate herself, a servant riding on the tender to look out for her Majesty's signals. Even 20 years after that the queen wrote a letter to the railways begging them to be careful about accidents.

The Famous Herschels

IT was at Observatory House in Slough, delightfully set on a lawn among the trees, that two of our greatest astronomers, Sir William Herschel and his son John, made their home. With them lived Sir William's sister Caroline, who not only helped with the making of the telescopes, but would feed her brother as he worked and make notes for him on the roof during winter nights till the ink froze on her pen. She herself also discovered five comets not known before, and she must be remembered as rightly sharing their fame. King George the Third gave Brother William £50 a year extra for Sister Caroline.

William had made his wonderful discovery of the planet Uranus while he was an organist at Bath, a feat which brought him to Slough as astronomer to George the Third, enabling him to give up the life of a musician and to devote his last 36 years entirely to the study of the skies. It was here that many of his most famous researches were

The Chancel and the Tower

The Rare West Doorway
STEWKLEY'S MAGNIFICENT NORMAN CHURCH

Stewkley　　　　　　　　The Splendid Norman Chancel

carried out. More than a century after his death the reflector of his 40-foot telescope, which had been lost for nearly 60 years, was discovered built up in its iron case behind the staircase of the cottage joining the house. It weighed half a ton, was four feet in diameter, and retained the beautifully polished surface he and Caroline had given it. One end of the telescope is now in the garden, the reflector being in the house.

Sir John Herschel, William's only son, inherited his father's great gifts, and after a brilliant career at Cambridge applied himself to chemistry and astronomy, publishing at 30 a revision of his father's catalogue of nebulae and star clusters, with over 500 which his father had missed. In 1834 he visited the Cape to examine the southern hemisphere, and completed the survey of the heavens begun over 20 years earlier. A high authority on sound, light, meteorology, physical geography, and optics, he had the distinction of following Sir Isaac Newton as Master of the Mint, as well as in the range of his studies. Here he lived until 1840, when he moved to Hawkhurst in Kent, working over his father's results and his own, helping to advance the new science of photography then coming into being, and building up a great bequest of knowledge for posterity. He died in 1871 and sleeps in the Abbey.

The Abbot Hanged on an Oak

SOULBURY. It stands at the head of a tiny river setting out on its journey to the Ouse, a delightful little place with a pond on its shaded green. For six centuries the Lovetts lived in its beautiful 400-acre park, a remarkable example of a house famous in the countryside for 600 years after the Conqueror, lords of their village during the reign of nearly 30 sovereigns, but producing no man prominent in national affairs. One Aylesbury Lovett was Master of the Wolf Hounds to the Conqueror, and their crest is a wolf's head. Liscombe House, in which they lived, was rebuilt in Tudor days and has been altered since, a modern corridor now uniting it to a beautiful 14th century chantry, with fine traceried windows having shafts and carved capitals.

The church, which rose with the first house in the park, has kept step with it through the centuries, and was repaired in Tudor days, when it received its tower, its clerestory, the spacious windows and the fine arcades, and the porch with an embattled parapet. The Tudor roofs of the nave and aisles rest on oak angels holding shields, on one of which is the pastoral staff of Robert Hobbes, who, as Abbot of Woburn, was spiritual head of Soulbury. Having acknowledged Henry the Eighth head of the church, he saw Sir Thomas More beheaded, and then he too followed Becket's example and declared the Pope supreme. In 1538 he paid the penalty, being hanged on an oak at the gate of his own abbey. Many a time he must have seen his staff and his initials on the corbel here.

The richest monument is to a Lady Lovett who died six years after Queen Elizabeth; she is kneeling face to face with Sir Robert, he in splendid armour, she in black robe and farthingale, their two daughters behind. The costumes and arms have been repainted, and the monument is as magnificent as when it was carved. Sir Robert, widowed in 1609, married again a year later, lived until 1643 and was buried at Sparsholt in Berkshire. His son sleeps here in an immense marble tomb, with a cherub bearing a crown between two cherubs who weep, while doves rest on the summits of the columns, the whole presided over by a dog or a wolf. Another of the Lovett tombs shows the figure of an Irish lady, mother of the only baronet in the family, who placed this beautiful memorial here. There is a 16th century portrait brass of Alice Mallet and eight daughters.

Deserted in the Fields

STANTONBURY. The growth of its neighbour Wolverton has drawn away the people from this ancient shrine and left, melancholy and deserted in the fields by the silent Ouse, a church with some of the finest Norman carving in the county.

There is no tower, and the little porch is a stripling of four centuries, but it has a seat on either side 700 years old, made from stone coffin lids. In the nave are the walls the Normans built, the masonry rough-hewn, under a roof whose worn queen-post was carved by men who may have shaped bows for Agincourt. Between the nave and the 13th century chancel is a magnificent Norman arch of three orders, the outer having chevrons, the middle one grotesques of birds and animals, the inner one characteristic mouldings. The shafts are splendidly carved, one of the capitals with foliage, the others with animals and heads, grim and grave. A medieval table has survived all the ravages of time; the pulpit has the panels and frieze carved when Elizabeth was queen: and, forlorn on a chancel bracket, are the helmet and gauntlets which may have been carried at the funeral of Sir John Temple in the 17th century.

The Verneys and the Chaloners

STEEPLE CLAYDON. It was given to Catherine of Aragon by Henry the Seventh, and here she was long remembered and her birthday kept as a festival, for she it was who introduced the lace-making for which Buckinghamshire became famous.

Here also is remembered a great scholar to whom Mary Tudor gave the manor, Sir Thomas Chaloner, servant of two kings and two queens. He lives in a glowing page of Hakluyt's Voyages, which show him wrecked in Algerian waters, where, swimming till his hands and arms entirely failed, he saved himself by gripping with his teeth a cable hanging from another ship. His successor, the second Sir Thomas, was tutor to Prince Henry, Charles Stuart's brother, and was lord of 420 servants. It is to Thomas Chaloner that the village owes its most interesting secular building, still a centre of social life. He built a school with a clock, fenced and planted waste land about it, and, creating a trust which still exists, left a generous endowment for a schoolmaster. Thomas was one of Charles Stuart's judges, and signed the death-warrant.

His school flourished and decayed in turn, the playground becoming an arena for bull-baiting, and it was left to Sir Harry Verney to restore it to its use last century. He extended it and maintained it as long as he lived, with the help of his wife, Florence Nightingale's sister. His son Edward added the hall and, first to adopt the Free Libraries Act, opened the Chaloner Library, to which Florence Nightingale gave £50 for books. The library has Florence Nightingale's cheque framed on a wall, and it has on its gable a shield with the fine motto, Liberty is the Best of All Things.

Over the 14th century church rises one of the county's few spires, which, built by Sir Harry Verney and his brother in memory of their father, is now a famous landmark. The chancel is 14th century, the nave and the font are 15th century. There are seats which were old before Catherine of Aragon was a bride; and the pulpit is that from which the parson preached to the Chaloners. One of the 18th century

Chaloners has a tablet telling us that "a lieutenant in the Navy above 30 years, he showed his courage in ten expeditions in eastern, western, northern, and southern seas." A hero of our own war has a window with St George, a green-eyed dragon, and St Michael with glowing red wings. There are busts of Sir Harry Verney and his first wife, daughter of one of Nelson's captains, Admiral Hope. An ardent reformer and a model landlord, Sir Harry was closely associated with the work of Lord Shaftesbury and Florence Nightingale, and one of the founders of the Royal Agricultural Society.

The County's Norman Crown

STEWKLEY. It is the Norman crown of the county, with a church which brings to mind the famous little church at Iffley outside Oxford. Jacobean cottages flank the long street. Dovecot Farm has a beautiful Tudor window; the manor house, with gabled wings and its original chimneys, has a Queen Anne dovecot.

The church was built when Henry the Second was king and Becket was a rector in Kent. Norman architecture was rising to its culminating majesty and luxuriance of ornament, and here for a hamlet was raised a temple like a miniature cathedral, a marvel of lavish decoration. Save for the modern porch and the vestry, and for the pinnacles and gargoyles of 600 years ago, the church is still as the Normans left it. Time has spared and man has respected it, and it remains unspoiled.

The magnificent central tower has on each face a beautiful arcade, above which are little gargoyles, with bigger ones at the corners, from where a lion and a cowled monk seem about to spring. Round the outside runs a zigzag moulding, and above it are the corbel tables to carry the Norman roof-beams. The west front is a picture of Norman splendour. The wonderful central doorway has two shafts at either side, the inner ones with spiral ornament running up to richly carved capitals. The main doorway is flanked by two blind arches, each carved with chevron, and with birds and animals on its columns. The great arch has a singular tympanum, its face carved with three dragons. The north doorway is enriched with animals and by the south doorway are three mass dials.

The interior is a very enchantment of beauty, with sculptural splendour everywhere. From the west we look through the two great central arches supporting the tower, a harmony of strength and gorgeous decoration. Each arch is of two depths, the outer order with chevron, the inner one carved with an astonishing variety of beak-heads, cat's-heads, and 40 other decorative devices.

From the arches the eye is carried to the chancel, to the altar, and to its deeply splayed window, elaborately framed in zigzag. Round the whole interior runs a line of intricate moulding, and every window is bordered with chevrons. The amount of carving is almost bewildering in its opulence and variety.

The Norman font is plain with a tapering bowl. The piscina was new when the church was a century old, but a quaint corbel head at the back of it seems Norman. Beside it is the seat of the priest who first used it 700 years ago.

In the sanctuary wall are five medieval tiles, and above them a gem of 16th century alabaster, showing between two red-winged angels the crowned Madonna, her hair as golden as her crown. Beside this group, perhaps part of a reredos, is a figure who may be Joseph, his hair and beard gilded, a long strap securing his purse.

STOKE GOLDINGTON. Standing high amid clumps of yew of neat and various designs, the church has for its companion an ancient manor, now a farmhouse, the two forming a grey group.

The Normans looked out on the green hills not far away, and here they built their church. An embattled tower of the 15th century replaces theirs, but their nave remains, and traces of their diapered work are visible over the chancel arch. Theirs, too, is the plain font. For the rest, the work is mainly 13th century, when the curious worn head over the south doorway was carved, to be enclosed a century later by a porch through which we follow nearly 20 generations of worshippers. In the porch is an old stone coffin lid. New piers in the 13th century succeeded Norman work in the nave, and the roof they bear still has tiebeams cut in the 17th century from trees in the valley.

Long Lost and Found Again

STOKE HAMMOND. Prettily situated above the valley, through which runs the Grand Union Canal, it has thatched and timbered cottages, and a 17th century inn with fine chimneys. In the churchyard, which has an avenue of limes, are two yews planted in 1687. Here are tombs of the Fountaine family from 1802 to 1908, continuing the record of a great stone in a transept, on which are recorded the deaths of eight members of the house between 1650 and 1709. The tower was added 600 years ago to the original 13th century building. The font and its pillars are 14th century; so are the finely carved sedilia and piscina, which, long lost, were discovered last century embedded in the chancel wall. The roofs of the aisle, nave, and chancel, are all 15th century.

Among the wall monuments to the Disney family one of the 17th century has five kneeling figures in its pediment. In the tracery of a window are four prophets and two bishops in 15th century glass, and in a 20th century window is an interesting touch of realism, views of the church, of the bridge by which we have just crossed the canal, and a canal barge drawn by a patient horse on the towpath. The altar table is a masterly piece of work of Jacobean days, and the pillar almsbox has kept it company most of the time.

John Hampden's Farm

STOKE MANDEVILLE. It struck one of the sparks that lit the train that blazed up into the Civil War, for Moat Farm (with three sides of its moat remaining) belonged to John Hampden, and it was on this farm that a Ship Money tax was imposed in 1635. Hampden refused to pay it, and at the courts five judges supported him; but there were seven against him and the decision outraged public feeling and made the conflict between king and people inevitable. It was the beginning of the end of Charles Stuart.

The Norman church in which its people gathered then stands solitary and decaying in the meadows, with something of the 17th century tower and the old arcades, but unroofed except for the chancel with its Norman arch. The new church has something of the old, the delicately carved 15th century font, with a high oak canopy, a Tudor chest with three locks, the eagle lectern, and a beautiful Elizabethan panelled marble monument of the three children of Edmund Brudenell, showing a young girl, her head resting on one hand and two babies lying with her.

England's First Sunday School

STOKENCHURCH. The Oxford road, breasting one of the highest spurs of the Chilterns, runs by its lime-shaded common past a few old cottages and a church of ancient grandeur. The south doorway has an arch enriched with carving, and another 12th century arch resting on Norman columns with zigzag capitals divides the Norman nave from the 14th century chancel, where, through an old opening to the roodloft, we can see a beam of the roof built over the nave 500 years ago. The roof has five bays, tie-beams, and carved spandrels. Its timbers rest on corbels cut alternately with human heads and angels. The worn head of a forgotten king still remains in the rebuilt arch of the transept, where is a charming little canopied piscina. The ancient font has an oak cover shaped in the 17th century. In the chancel is another 14th century piscina, and in one of the chancel windows is a fragment of old glass. There are brass portraits of Bartholomew Tipping and his wife, the lady very grand in a wide-brimmed 17th century hat. Bartholomew Tipping the younger has two memorials, a stone one in the church with a weeping cherub on one side and a cherub on the other side blowing a trumpet; and a grammar school which he endowed before he died in 1680. On each side of the chancel arch is a brass portrait, each in armour and each bearing the name Robert Morle; one died in 1410, the other in 1415.

Here, in a simple grave, lies the founder of Sunday schools, a great friend of John Wesley. The credit of founding the first regular English Sunday School belongs, not to Robert Raikes, but to Hannah Ball, who has been sleeping at Stokenchurch since 1792. She was born at High Wycombe in 1734, one of a family of 12, and educated by an Uxbridge uncle and by her own exertions. An earnest Christian, she prayed that she might become a mother in Israel, and unwittingly prepared for her work by looking after the children of a cousin for five years, and then after the children of a widowed brother at High Wycombe. At 31 she was attracted by the preaching of John Wesley, with whom she maintained a warm and interesting correspondence. She kept a diary for a quarter of a century, full of fine feeling and generous philosophy. She established her little Sunday School in 1769, about 11 years before Raikes founded his at Gloucester. The building is now a humble chair factory, but in the town is the Wesleyan chapel she built from plans sent her by John Wesley. There are still preserved the table at which she sat, the clock by which the services were timed, the diary she wrote, the entries made in one of her books as a girl of 15 setting forth her prayers and aspirations. In her chapel is a Hannah Ball Parlour, and at the second centenary of her birth the whole town honoured her memory.

The Sunday School she founded has continued from her day to ours, the pioneer of a movement attended by momentous consequences, for at such Sunday Schools many of the poor obtained all their learning until education became national and compulsory. A woman of broad but independent views, she took her scholars one Sunday to a church service at which the preacher asserted that if any Arminians entered heaven the angels would cease to sing. She rose from her pew, gathered her little flock about her, and marched indignantly out of the church with them, never to return.

Curfew Tolls the Knell of Parting Day

STOKE POGES. It is the whole world's place of pilgrimage. From every land they come to see a simple English churchyard. It has no great thing to show and yet from here there has gone out into the world a picture of our countryside that stirs men everywhere. Here in the shade of this great yew sat Thomas Gray listening as

> *The curfew tolls the knell of parting day,*
> *The lowing herd winds slowly o'er the lea,*
> *The ploughman homeward plods his weary way,*
> *And leaves the world to darkness and to me.*

Here, all about us, the rude forefathers of the hamlet sleep, and Thomas Gray sleeps with them.

It is probably true that hardly any village church has so many nationalities in its visitors' book as Stoke Poges, and they come to tread the paths the poet trod, and to read, on a plain cracked gravestone set on an altar tomb of mouldering bricks, the incomparable epitaph he wrote for his mother:

The graceful, tender mother of many children, one of whom alone had the misfortune to survive her.

They laid her to rest with her sister in 1753, and 18 years later the grave was opened for Gray himself. A small stone in the wall records his burial.

It is all the monument there is to him here, but we pass one in the road, a huge sarcophagus under the trees at the edge of a field. It was put here by William Penn's grandson in 1799, and now belongs to the National Trust. One more pleasant remembrance there is of him in his old haunts, for the room in which he used to write has been kept as it was at Stoke Court, known in his day as West End Cottage.

Two lychgates bring us into the churchyard of the famous Elegy, with the fine sweeping roofs of the church against a background of the great trees round the manor house. It was in this house that Charles was held a prisoner by the army, and, long before, Sir Edward Coke entertained Queen Elizabeth here; there is a high column in the park crowned by a statue of Coke, who looks down from a height of 68 feet on his old home. In a meadow by the church is a Garden of Remembrance in which burials take place without gravestones, the ground being laid out with a lake, a fountain, and a rose garden.

A splendid timber porch 600 years old brings us into the church, and we are back at once in ancient days for the round piers were set up by the Normans and crowned with pointed arches by our first English builders. The north wall of the chancel has herringbone work 800 years old, and in the chancel is a 14th century tomb recess crowned with a handsome finial. From those days of long ago is a mass dial set in the wall.

In the little brick chapel opening off the chancel lies Edward Hastings, a man of great account in the terrible reign of Mary Tudor. Ordered to raise 4000 men in Buckingham to set Lady Jane Grey securely on the throne, he declared instead for Queen Mary, who made him Master of her Horse, so that he held her horse's bridle from the Tower to the Abbey on the day of her coronation. So he ushered in the bitterest reign of our great Tudor dynasty. With Lord Howard he escorted Princess Elizabeth to London from her captivity in the great house of Ashridge in Hertfordshire, and when Elizabeth came to the throne he gave up the glory of being Lord Chamberlain and retired to Stoke Poges, built this little chapel, and died in the manor with no son to succeed him. He has no monument, and his chapel is cluttered up with an 18th century gallery, its best possession being a very fine coffin lid carved with a cross 700 years ago.

The Penns, who followed the Hastings at the manor house, preferred to sit in the little chapel under the tower, where we may look through a 13th century arch across the church. A cloister leads from this side of the church to Stoke Park, and in its windows are shields and fragments of Flemish glass. They are interesting rather than beautiful, one fragment showing a satyr blowing a pipe as he sits on a clumsy-looking velocipede, one of the first examples in any window of a bicycle.

There is only a plain tablet to the Penns, and among the other memorials in the church is a seated figure of Nathaniel Marchant, the artist; he is in a relief by Flaxman. There are three brass portraits, one 500 years old of Sir William Molyns in armour, and one of 1577 showing Edmund Hampden and his wife. There is a 600-year-old font, three piscinas older still, and a curious treasure kept in a glass case which was the bronze base of an old processional cross. In a beautiful window in memory of two old boys of a local school are St Michael and St George and Gray's line beneath them, The path of Duty is the way to Glory.

The Poet of the Country Churchyard

THOMAS GRAY was born in Cornhill in 1717, son of a business man of obstinate and brutal temper, whose violence drove his wife away after she had borne him 12 children. The poet was the sole survivor of her family, and on him she lavished all her love, he returning her affection in abundance.

Mrs Gray, a dressmaker, had two brothers among the assistant masters at Eton, and the boy left the Burnham home of one uncle to enter Eton at 11; and at Eton his other uncle, William Antrobus, watched him with careful eye, particularly with a view to his instruction in the use and composition of homely medicines.

Gray was reserved and studious, and detested games, yet he made lasting friendships. At seventeen he went to Peterhouse, Cambridge, as a pensioner, but disliked the life, kept much to himself, and regarded his existence as like that of a pendulum, swinging from chapel and hall to his rooms and back again. Yet it was with a pang that he left it, four years later.

Returning to his father's house, he accompanied Horace Walpole to France, Switzerland, and Italy, quarrelled with him and returned alone, always remembering with a shudder the sight of a wolf carrying off Walpole's lapdog as they crossed the Mont Cenis. Inheriting money under the will of his father, Gray installed his mother and her two sisters at West End, Stoke Poges, and himself returned to Cambridge, where he took a law degree and made his home for life. The summer vacations, however, he spent here with his relatives, and in

1742 he began his immortal Elegy. For seven years it was incomplete, and was not resumed until 1749, when, under stress of emotion occasioned by the death of an aunt, he finished it amid the scenes which had inspired it.

The Elegy was an immediate success, running through four editions in two months, and spreading Gray's fame throughout Europe. The honour was his, the profit was the publisher's, for the poet was too sensitive to accept payment for his poems. Translated into all familiar languages, the poem was on the lips of Wolfe before the heights of Abraham as his boat dropped down the St Lawrence. "I would rather be the author of that poem than take Quebec," he said. Gray's reputation was now so high that he was able to refuse the office of Poet Laureate. In 1753 he lost his mother, and tenderly mourned her to the end. At 52 he was appointed professor of modern history in his University. It was at Cambridge that the rest of his poems were written, and there, in the summer of 1771, he died. He was brought here to sleep beside his mother, realising the wistful beauty of the lines he had written more than 20 years before:

> *Here rests his head upon the lap of earth*
> *A youth to fortune and to fame unknown:*
> *Fair Science frowned not on his humble birth,*
> *And melancholy marked him for her own.*
>
> *Large was his bounty, and his soul sincere,*
> *Heaven did a recompense as largely send:*
> *He gave to misery (all he had) a tear,*
> *He gained from Heaven (twas all he wished) a friend.*
>
> *No farther seek his merits to disclose,*
> *Or draw his frailties from their dread abode,*
> *(There they alike in trembling hope repose),*
> *The bosom of his Father and his God.*

Here he lies, within hail of the woods he loved, whose gentle slopes were to his vivid fancy mountains and stark precipices.

The Splendid Font

STONE. The relics of its ancient past are in the museum at Aylesbury, where we see the jewellery, weapons, and implements of Saxons and Romans who made their homes here. A chapel has been built on a Roman site. That far-off past has no visible monuments here, but thatched cottages and red-tiled barns preserve much of the ancient charm of the village, and the Norman church is founded on an artificial mound, tall pines and the impressive 14th century tower adding dignity to the beauty of the scene. Supporting the tower parapet is a corbel table of masks with a grim gargoyle projecting from the centre of each row. Over the original doorway of the tower are a king and a bishop.

The Norman doorway of the church has zigzag on the centre of its three depths of moulding, and the Norman arcade is still in the nave. The font is one of our accepted Norman treasures, a work rich in beauty, with carving all round the bowl. One man is confronting a dragon with his sword while thrusting his left hand into another dragon's mouth, a big dove pecking a dragon as if to help him. Spiral ornament and beading run in all directions, framing fishes, lizards, snakes, a prancing goat, and grotesque heads. Whatever its origin, the font has had strange adventures. Ejected in favour of a modern one from the church at Hampstead Norris in Berkshire, it was removed to the rectory garden in the 18th century, reached London, passed from one church to a second, and, being at last recognised as a work of antiquity, was brought here. Ancient lancets light the transepts, and the modern chancel has its 13th century arch.

The Gurneys, who lived here for 500 years, are represented by portrait brasses. One shows Thomas Gurney, who died in 1520, with his wife, and their six sons and three daughters. This is a palimpsest for on the other side of Thomas Gurney's brass a portrait of a 15th century lady is engraved. The other brass here shows Agnes Gurney in 15th century costume, and the shrouded form of her husband who has lost his head.

In the floors of nave and chancel are a number of 14th century tiles, and there are Tudor bench-ends and carved poppy-heads attached to many of the modern seats.

A group of men of science have found a happy retreat in this charming village. There is a wall tablet in memory of Admiral William Smyth, who claimed descent from Captain John Smith, founder of Virginia. A devoted astronomer, on retiring from the Navy he built an observatory at Bedford, and made valuable contributions to the Royal Astronomical Society, of which he was a gold medallist.

There is a brass inscription to Sir William Flower, a son of Shakespeare's town, who won fame as an Army doctor in the Crimea and still greater renown as Director of the Natural History Museum. It is to his enthusiasm that we owe the magnificent display in the great central hall at South Kensington.

In the churchyard lie two vicars who contributed to the scientific learning of their generation. Joseph Bancroft Reade discovered important data respecting the radiant properties of light and heat, and furthered the science of photography, of which he was a pioneer; and James Booth, presented to the living by the Royal Astronomical Society (to whom it belongs), was a famous mathematician and advocate of popular education who wrote much on his favourite subjects, and founded the Journal of the Society of Arts.

The Little Princes

STONY STRATFORD. It is the home of cock and bull stories, for the Cock and the Bull inns stand side by side in a narrow street and it is said that the famous phrase began with them. Here, in any case, innumerable cock and bull stories have been told, though one of the inns is famous for something more, a magnificent wooden doorway with carving worthy of the workshop of Grinling Gibbons.

The village has heard many stories and seen many sights, for from the days of the Romans Stony Stratford has been a stage on the road to London. Here have been found plates shaped like leaves and dedicated to ancient gods; we may see them in the Roman rooms of the British Museum, with enamelled horse trappings found here. Here halted the sad cavalcade with the body of the queen of Edward the First, and here they set up one of the beautiful crosses of which the last gave its name to Charing Cross. Here the blood-stained Richard Crookback seized the little King Edward and carried him to London on the pretence of crowning him there; it is the Archbishop of York who comforts Edward's mother in Shakespeare, looking forward to the meeting which was never to take place:

> *Last night, I hear, they lay at Northampton;*
> *At Stony Stratford do they rest tonight;*
> *Tomorrow, or next day, they will be here.*

So this market town on Watling Street, where it crosses the Ouse into Northants, has the memory of the foulest crime of one of our foulest kings, the beginnings of the cruel murder of the princes in the

Tower. It has the memory also of a tragedy of its own, for twice in the 18th century were terrible fires at Stony Stratford, the second destroying half the town and one of its churches. On the corner of a house is a sundial set up between these two fires with the inscription "Time and Fire destroy all things." Close by this house is an elm under which John Wesley preached.

The medieval tower of the burned-down church survived the fire and stands a melancholy ruin with its battlements and gargoyles. The tower of the existing church is from the same 15th century, the rest of the structure being 18th. Over the doorway is a statue of a hermit with a wounded doe. There is a 15th century chest, a Jacobean Bible box with dragons carved on it, and the snake of Aesculapius carved on the pulpit, which was given by soldiers of the RAMC who worshipped here during the war.

There are 18th century shops and houses in the streets, and in the walls of some charming almshouses are stones from a religious house destroyed by Henry the Eighth. The Baptist Chapel by Horse Fair Green has a table, a wooden window, and the wooden candlesticks brought from a chapel founded in 1657, the year in which John Bunyan was called to be a preacher in a church farther down the Ouse.

A Marvellous Spectacle

STOWE. A wonderful place it is to come upon, even in our countryside of wonder, for it has that famous house to which so much genius has paid tribute—Sir John Vanbrugh, Sir John Soane, Robert Adam, and Grinling Gibbons; and it is a rich experience to come to it by the three mile avenue from Buckingham or the avenue with broad green verges from the village of Water Stratford.

If we come from Buckingham the stately arch designed by Lord Camelford brings us into the park of 800 acres with classical buildings dotted about—an obelisk in memory of General Wolfe, an ornamental bridge across a lovely lake, a column with the prows and sterns of Roman galleys projecting from it and a Roman lady crowning it. On a small hill is what is known as the Queen's Temple, now restored in perfect taste as a temple of music, with a fine Roman mosaic eight feet square in the floor.

Stowe House has saved itself from the disaster of these days by becoming a great public school, in many ways one of the luckiest in

BUCKINGHAMSHIRE

England, for it has no space problems. Its front must be about a quarter of a mile long, and its gardens (in which Capability Brown learned gardening) seem to have no end.

The house is impressive on either side and marvellous indoors and out. On both sides are great colonnades and sculptures; on one side a statue of George the First and on the other a central colonnade of six huge columns is approached by 30 steps, guarded by a lion. Great columns flank windows to right and left, and everywhere are statues and sculptures and plaster reliefs. The colonnade leads us into an immense round hall, impressive with columns of coloured marble. Above them runs a frieze with hundreds of figures in a triumphal Roman procession, and above this rises a dome with diamond-shaped panels. To right and left of the hall are the common rooms of the school; where the society gossips of the Georges whispered scandal, we find today a splendid library, a great reading room, and dining halls. On the walls are portraits by Peter Lely and Godfrey Kneller.

A little apart stands the chapel designed for the school by Sir Robert Lorimer, creator of the national memorial in Edinburgh to the Scots who fell in the Great War. The west front of the chapel has four great columns, and over the door is a square tympanum with a relief in wood of David killing the lion. The lofty interior has fluted columns on each side, with stalls between them richly carved and bright with painted shields. Here is panelling from the old chapel, some of it originally from the home of the Grenvilles in Cornwall, and let into the panelling are some little masterpieces of Grinling Gibbons. Every chair on the floor is carved with the name of a scholar. High on the walls are angels in stone, all looking to the altar, and high above the altar is a small round window glinting with rich glass.

Surprising, it seems, to come upon a medieval church in this great park, but here remains the 13th century shrine at which worshipped the village folk of Dadford, Boycott, and Lamport, hamlets round the park. The tower is 14th century, and over its doorway is a 14th century crucifix. We come in through a 15th century porch guarded by a statue of a man removed from a tomb and set up here on his feet.

It was in the 16th century that the owners of Stowe built their chapel here. In it is a lovely altar tomb on which lies Martha Penystone, with her feet resting on a hound appearing ready to spring.

On a shelf at the foot of the tomb, her small hands loosely laid on her dress, her mouth about to break into a smile, lies Martha's little daughter Hester, born in the summer of 1612 to die in a few short weeks. The portrait of another little child, an Elizabethan boy, shows him in complete Tudor costume as if he were grown up, and the brass is curious for its inscription which tells us that he was born on October 31, 1592, and died on January 1, 1592. It is quite correct for New Year's Day was then in March. On another brass is Alice Saunders in the butterfly headdress fashionable about 1480.

Above the altar of the chapel is a window in memory of the last Duke and Duchess of Buckingham, who passed away towards the end of last century. The light of the window falls on to a reredos standing out with all the beauty given to it by a Jacobean craftsman; it appears to have been an overmantel, and has two arches carved with bearded figures having cloaks over their shoulders.

The Procession of Life in a Great House

STOWE has seen a remarkable procession of men within its walls. It was Sir Richard Temple who built it, the forgotten inspirer of a never-forgotten line in English poetry. Who but for Pope would ever recall him now? To his own generation (he died in 1749) he was a sturdy patrician, turning from peace to war, and from war to government, with brave integrity. Today he owes the fact that he is remembered to the poet he housed and befriended at Stowe. As a wealthy young baronet he shared in the campaigns of Marlborough, and distinguished himself in battles of which posterity, like little Peterkin, asks what they were all about. He deserves to be held in remembrance for having revolted against the corruption of Walpole's ministry, for having endured dismissal from high military command, for demanding the prosecution of the ring-leaders of the South Sea Bubble, and for having lifted up an unappeasable voice against the subservience of British interests to the Hanoverians, and the sending of English soldiers to fight in Hanover's quarrels.

All this tumult and vexation happened in 1733, which explains the significance of the date set out in heavy type above the dedication of the first of Pope's Moral Essays, inscribed to Temple. The dull but fiery poet had a genuine affection for the soldier-statesman, and added to his own reputation by having so considerable a national

The Gateway near Buckingham

The Impressive Colonnaded Front
STOWE HOUSE

Stony Stratford — The Market Place and Wesley's Tree

Taplow — The Thames Valley from Taplow Court

figure among his intimates. The political storm passed, and Temple was made Viscount Cobham and a Field Marshal and died beloved and widely mourned. The public memory is short, and the Cobham of social and political history receded into oblivion, so that today it is only in Pope's lines that we remember him:

> *And you, brave Cobham! to the latest breath*
> *Shall feel your ruling passion strong in death.*

Of the three Dukes of Buckingham who lived at Stowe the first two exhausted their resources in collecting treasures, bringing about a bankruptcy for the third to redeem. Richard Grenville, elder son of the Marquis of Buckingham, was born in 1776, and for a quarter of a century was known as Earl Temple, by which title he sat for 16 years in the House of Commons, sometimes supporting and sometimes opposing his cousin Pitt. He married the only child of the third Duke of Chandos, and at 46 was created Duke of Buckingham and Chandos. He poured out wealth on pictures, statues, books, and manuscripts, entertained the royal family of France with princely munificence, and impoverished himself so much that he had to seek seclusion abroad. Returning after two years, he wrote an account of his travels, became Steward of the Household, and spent his declining years among his treasures, grieved at having to sell many of them to keep the wolf from the door.

His son Richard Grenville was the second duke, known for many years as Marquis of Chandos. He so consistently opposed Free Trade as to gain the title of the Farmer's Friend. The rent-roll of his estate was £100,000 a year, but the property was deeply encumbered; yet he continued to buy land, and to entertain like a prince. While owing his creditors over a million, he added to his liabilities by prodigal hospitality to Queen Victoria; it was on a visit here that the Queen first met Disraeli privately. Two years later bailiffs took possession of the house, and dealers from all parts of Europe attended the 40-day sale of pictures, china, plate, and furniture. The library was dispersed, the manuscripts were sold, and the duke was censured by The Times as a spendthrift. He died in 1861.

The third duke, an upright and honourable man, laboured to repair the ruin of the family fortunes, and succeeded in paying off the bulk of the debts. He was a humane and brilliant Governor of Madras during a period of terrible famine, a successful railway chairman, and chairman of committees in the House of Lords. He died in 1889.

Nelson and His Friend

SWANBOURNE. The county has few prettier villages than this, with its fine Tudor manor house, its delightful black and white cottages, and the splendid silver birch gracing its peace memorial. The 13th century tower has one of the rare old clocks with stone faces. In a splendid 13th century doorway hangs the door which has been opening and shutting 500 years. A Tudor clerestory of three small windows lights a 13th century nave. The plain font was in use 300 years before the Reformation. The old chancel, renewed after 600 years, has still its original double piscina; but of the 15th century wall paintings only traces remain. The oak lectern and the altar table are 17th century. The oldest memorial is a 17th century portrait brass of Thomas Adams, a freeman of London, with his wife and four children bereaved by a tragedy of long ago, for poor Thomas

> *In prime of youth by thieves was slain,*
> *In Tiscombe ground his blood the grass did stain.*

Over a door is a tablet to James Askew, who lived under both Cromwells and six sovereigns, dying at 94. Many members of the Fremantle family sleep here, and there is a brass tablet to the most famous of them, Admiral Sir Thomas, one of Nelson's band of brothers, who, accompanied by his indomitable wife, sailed in the Seahorse on the expedition against Santa Cruz. Separated from Fremantle, Nelson, in trying to land, received the wound which cost him his right arm. He was rowed out of the fight while Fremantle was still in the thick of it, and was borne to the Seahorse and told that he might die unless he went aboard and had his wound dressed. "Very well," he said, "I will die rather than alarm Mrs Fremantle in this state when I can give her no tidings of her husband." Eventually Fremantle was carried aboard wounded, and Lady Fremantle had two maimed admirals on her hands, for Nelson sailed with his friend for home. During the slow voyage the devoted woman restored both her patients to convalescence. Fremantle, who was in the council of war with Nelson the night before Copenhagen, followed him so closely at Trafalgar that only one ship divided him from the Victory when Nelson broke the enemy's line.

BUCKINGHAMSHIRE

His son, born seven years before Nelson died, was made Baron Cottesloe in the year of his golden wedding, in memory of which the fine east window was erected here. It shows the Marriage at Cana and the Last Supper. Lord Cottesloe died at 92, and there is a marble tablet to three of his remarkable sisters, aged 90, 88, and 66. It would be hard to find a group of people in any little church with such a record, five people with 430 years of life between them.

The Splendour of the Thames

TAPLOW. It stands magnificently on the Thames, facing Maidenhead at that point where the river, flowing north to Cookham, reveals a scene of indescribable beauty to those who sail on it, the woods rising to crown the cliffs 300 feet above the river. In the distance are the glorious woods of Cliveden, with Lord Astor's home peeping over the treetops. The old house here was built by the Duke of Buckingham, the evil genius of Charles the Second and was the home of Frederick Prince of Wales. It is remembered as the place where Rule Britannia was sung for the first time, coming into a masque of James Thomson, which was performed here in 1740. Lord Astor's house, one of the splendours of the Thames, was built by Sir Charles Barry, architect of the Houses of Parliament. It has a terrace 430 feet long looking over the valley of the Thames, one of the glories of England's greatest river.

Also set in woods by the river is Taplow Court, so long the house of Lord Desborough, with a long avenue of cedars of Lebanon and a site famous a thousand years ago. Here was a Saxon church and the home of a Saxon nobleman. Some of his possessions are now in the British Museum, for the old churchyard in the park has yielded up gold brooches and silver armlets, a gold buckle and an iron sword, glass vases, drinking horns, and small things tipped with silver which may have been used for games.

The Saxon church has vanished, and Taplow's church stands now at a meeting of the roads, a handsome 20th century structure with a copper spire peeping above the trees. Its stately arcades draw the eye to a chancel arch filled with a stone screen, with angels in the tracery and the Madonna and St John standing by the Cross. There is a Norman font from the old church, but it is a group of ancient brasses that brings the pilgrim here. The oldest of them all is from the time of the battle of Crecy and shows a small figure of Nichole de Aumberdene with flowing hair; he is exquisitely engraved in the head of a floral cross resting on a quaint dolphin, he having been a fishmonger. Richard Manfeld is here with his sister Isobel, her hair falling over her shoulders, and with them is a sorrowful boy in a shroud; they are a 15th century group. A Thomas Manfeld in Tudor armour is with his wife on a brass which had been used before their portraits were engraved on it. An inscription brass to Ursula Denny, who died in 1564, tells us that, though her husband served King Henry and his three sovereign children, she suffered imprisonment for her faith.

A brave and familiar name comes to us in a little chapel with 17th century panelling and a window representing Faith and Fortitude. It is the Grenfell chapel, and in it a window brings to mind two names we see on the peace memorial, Julian and William Grenfell.

These sons of Lord Desborough spent their boyhood by the river with which their father's name is inseparably linked. The first Lord Desborough, a Harrow boy and a Balliol man with marvellous feats to his credit in his youth (swimming Niagara and stroking an Eight across the Channel) won for himself in our time the name of the Father of the Thames, by his work as Chairman of the Thames Conservancy, and it is fitting that he should have one of the noblest homes on the banks of the river.

Two sets of Grenfell brothers the Great War took from England, both of whom we come upon in this county which was their home. Both pairs of brothers were young and filled with affection, Davids and Jonathans in their love for one another. Francis and Riversdale Grenfell we come upon at Beaconsfield: they were the sons of Field-Marshal Grenfell. Julian and Billy Grenfell, whose names are on the peace memorial here, were the sons of Lord Desborough, distinguished through life as athletes and sportsmen and equally conspicuous as scholars. They were marked down from boyhood as notable men, for the charm of their personalities, not less than their characters, was inescapable.

Of Julian Grenfell it was said, as of Sir Lancelot, "he was the gallantest man I have ever known, and the gentlest." Julian left ample evidence that he had poetic vision, as well as a fine humour that flowed easily into rhyme. Before he fell in France he wrote a witty "prayer for the young men of the Staff," but in his serious moments he could rise to this:

> *The fighting man shall from the sun*
>   *Take warmth, and light from the glowing earth;*
> *Speed with the light-foot winds to run,*
>   *And with the trees to newer birth;*
> *And find, when fighting shall be done,*
>   *Great rest, and fullness after death.*
>
> *The thundering line of battle stands,*
>   *And in the air Dearth moans and sings;*
> *But Day shall clasp him with strong hands,*
>   *And Night shall fold him in soft wings.*

That Billy Grenfell, too, could write verse was shown by his farewell to a fallen comrade of his boyhood:

> *O heart and soul and careless played*
>   *Our little band of brothers,*
> *And never recked the time would come*
>   *To change our game for others.*
> *It's joy for those who played with you*
>   *To picture now what grace*
> *Was in your mind and single heart*
>   *And in your radiant face.*
>
> *Your light-foot strength by flood and field*
>   *For England keener glowed;*
> *To whatsoever things are fair*
>   *We know, through you, the road;*
> *Nor is our grief the less thereby.*
> *O swift and strong and dear, Goodbye.*

All this was true of the two Grenfell boys. Lovely and pleasant were they in their lives, and in death they were not divided. Julian fell in May and Billy in the following July, both on the Western Front.

The Medieval Bridge

THORNBOROUGH. It slows us down to cross at snail's pace the only medieval bridge in the county. The boundary stone of Thornborough and Buckingham stands on it. The bridge is 165 feet long and 12 feet wide, with six arches through which runs the Claydon Brook on its way to the Ouse.

The church, standing by the 17th century manor, has small medieval tiles in its chancel floor, and herringbone rubble work in its walls put here by the Normans. There is also a little 15th century glass in the windows with a saint holding a spear, and a brass portrait of 1389 showing William Barton with his wife, both in gowns with drooping sleeves, and she with a veil. The chancel arch is 13th century, the nave arches and clerestory 14th, and the porch 15th. The porch has stone seats and an ancient roof; the roof of the nave is modern but has a head and Tudor roses of the 16th century.

Three Wives and Sixteen Children

THORNTON. Cottages, church, and hall are grouped in the splendid park, with its luxuriant avenues. Chestnuts march on either side of us as we approach one after the other the three bridges crossing the divided Ouse, beyond which lies Northants.

The 14th century church was transformed when the hall was built a century ago, but the old tower was saved, with one weird animal gargoyle creeping round the corner as if in quest of the grotesques beyond. The reconstruction left the building without a chancel, the two fine arcades ending at the east window, which is set in the old chancel arch.

Once united on a rich 15th century tomb, but now placed apart under the tower, are the fine figures of John Barton and his wife, she with two angels at her head and greyhounds snatching at her gown. On the floor by the altar is the famous 15th century brass of Robert Ingylton, his three wives, and their 16 children. He is a superb figure in armour, with a huge sword poised across his body; his wives, each with her own children, are below, dressed as they might have been to ride on pilgrimage with Chaucer. Over the group is a rich fourfold canopy, above which rise splendid shafts and spires. The engraving, full of beautiful detail, is in excellent preservation. In a second fine brass is one of Ingylton's descendants, the stately Joan St John in the costume worn by Elizabethan ladies.

Two memorials come home to the heart, the wooden cross from the grave of Sir William Kay who fell fighting with his regiment in the last great battle of the Great War; and the cross from the grave of Lieutenant Jackson. The one a general the other a young lieutenant, they were both only sons.

Portrait of a Rector

TINGEWICK. Its winding valley road touches the Oxford border, and the church, set between a thatched barn and fine gardens, crowns a little hill with a stream flowing round to the Ouse. At the churchyard gate a chestnut climbs as if it were on its way to the gargoyles of the 15th century tower.

The nave of the Normans is still here, the north wall immensely thick, and their zigzag carving clear on one of the arcades. There is Norman masonry in the windows, and the font appears to be Norman reshaped in the 15th century. The chancel, which has a dainty piscina, is 15th century. The plain altar table was made when our shipyards were building ships to fight the Armada. There is one notable brass, a strange portrait of Erasmus Williams, a Tudor rector kneeling on a tomb between pillars, on one of which is the owl of wisdom, and on the other a globe. The brass has a cluster of symbols, the sun, the moon, a string of books, painting materials, and astronomical instruments, with Biblical texts explaining. A rhyming inscription signed R. Haydock begins:

> *This doth Erasmus Williams represent,*
> *Whom living all did love, dead all lament.*

There are many tablets to the Risleys, one of whom was rector for 59 years of the last two centuries. The peace memorial to the 17 men who did not come back is a window in which Christ gives a crown to a knight in gold armour, over which is a rich blue cloak.

The Grim Secret

TURVILLE. A delightful village at the head of the Hambleden Valley, backed by a great hill with a black-capped windmill, it has dormered and timbered cottages looking out on its little green. Also it has a grim secret, and memories of two famous men.

Sheltered among pines and larches, the church, with a 15th century flint tower, has two Norman doorways with 13th century arches, a plain Norman font, stones with Norman carving in the chancel arch, and a closed Norman window. The rest is mainly 14th century, including the tower arch, which reaches the ground in one sweep. The surprising possession of the church is a massive stone coffin hewn from a single stone six feet long, and with a three-stepped cross on its lid. The coffin is known to have contained the body of a 13th century priest, but when opened in modern times it was found that the original occupant had vanished and that a woman had been put in his place, apparently some time in the 14th century. Here were her bones, and on one of them was the mark of a bullet. She was buried, according to law, "in woollen," but no man knows what dark tragedy brought about her end and the hiding of her remains in this coffin. The mystery of the priest exiled in death is the grim secret of this place.

Many old families have memorials here, the most interesting of them in an 18th century chapel, an altar tomb with an urn from which flames come. In the tomb sleep William Perry and his wife, heiress of the Earls of Leicester. In a window glow the Perry arms in vivid colours, with a muzzled bear and a porcupine.

Among the fine woodwork are the original kingposts and two beams of the 14th century roof, and medieval benches in the nave. The chapel has a neat oak screen, and on a wall is a stone frieze copied from a 14th century fragment displayed on a window-sill.

Turville Park, now with its own chapel, stands on high ground with splendid views. Built by William Perry in the 18th century, it was the last home of Charles Dumouriez, the great French General and Foreign Minister, who from his cell in the Bastille became at once the right hand and the dupe of Louis the Sixteenth, redeemed Holland from Austria, suffered defeat, fled to the enemy, and came to England as the secret enemy of Napoleon. Here he died in 1823, and he sleeps at Henley.

Later to the hall came another famous man, Lord Chancellor Lyndhurst, son of John Copley the American artist. Born in Boston when the town was English and Lord North was our Prime Minister, he was himself offered our Premiership by William the Fourth, but did not accept the responsibility. He was one of our greatest Chancellors, and his judgments have never been excelled. An odd little story is told of him. His second wife adored him, but she learned that he had been a bully when a boy, and "I can assure you (she said) I thumped him well at 80 for what he had done at 14."

Norman and Tudor

TURWESTON. This beautiful village with thatched cottages and a shaded green has a church which has seen eight centuries, gradually changing with them. Inside are two stalwart Norman piers capped with flowers and medieval arches. There are Norman windows at the west end and a medieval east window with tracery and rich modern glass. The roof is Tudor, but the chancel with its arch, and the south arcade of the nave, are 13th century.

In a handsome recess is the fine brass portrait of a priest in vestments of 500 years ago, and opposite is the tiny brass of a man this priest may have married to one of the two wives shown with him. On a wall monument are sculptured a couple from Stuart England, Simon Heynes and his wife, kneeling on blue cushions against a starry blue sky, their baby in a cradle beside them, and a golden cherub hovering over them. The font is new, in memory of Thomas Lukas, an airman killed in the war. It is carved with the Sacraments in its panelled sides and has statues of the Madonna and saints at the corners. In the modern stone reredos the Madonna appears with St John, who is holding a chalice with a serpent peering out of it.

Memories of Great Events

TWYFORD. It has a Norman treasure, and into its story come memories of great events. The 700-year-old church, with scratched mass dials at a window, has a 14th century tower overlooking the remains of a medieval preaching cross. Its most splendid possession is in the two-storeyed 15th century porch, which has a magnificent Norman doorway of two depths of moulding, the outer one decorated with beakheads and the inner with zigzag, the arch supported by round shafts with a capital on which two animals are fighting. Flanking the columns are Norman stones deeply cut to represent shafts of light radiating from suns. Here, with traces of ancient colour, a 15th century door still swings on its original hinges, and there is another old door in the 13th century doorway facing it. The arcades are 13th century, but there are more Norman beakheads and zigzag by the chancel arch. The carved font has been claimed as Norman, but is generally regarded as belonging to the generation after them. Corbel heads of women and priests sustain the 15th century hammerbeam roof of the nave, the medieval roofs of the aisles have corbel faces making extravagant grimaces. On an aisle floor among fragments of carved stones we found a curious figure of a man holding a heart.

The 14th century base of the chancel screen still has original white circles painted on its panels; a second screen, the pulpit, the altar tables, and the rails, are all Jacobean, but there are 22 seats in the nave and two in the chancel in which Twyford folk have been sitting for 500 years.

There is a worn marble figure of a nameless cross-legged knight, with a helmet covering his face, his Crusader's shield hanging from his shoulder, and near him, in a splendid 16th century altar tomb, sleep Thomas Giffard and his wife. On the immense marble top of the tomb is a finely engraved portrait of Giffard in elaborate Tudor armour, his mailed feet resting on a greyhound. Famous as a work of art, the brass has been used twice. Engraved in 1416 for William Stortford, treasurer of St Paul's Cathedral, it still bears on the back the expression of his hope that he might be buried in his cathedral crypt. The brass served its purpose for over a century, but in 1550 it was carried away, to receive the portrait and inscription that we see. A still older brass has an excellent portrait of John Everden, rector here in 1413. The vestments are perfect, the ornament on them beautifully wrought.

Twyford was the home of the Wenmans, whose wall memorials include one with cherubs, classical columns, and painted coloured heraldry to the most famous member of the family, Richard the first Viscount, with whom rest three of his four wives. After leaving Oxford he sailed as a volunteer under Essex and Howard, to help the French Protestants by a blow at Spain on her home front. His gallantry in the fight with the Spanish ships and at the capture of Cadiz won him a knighthood. The first of his wives, Agnes Fermor, brought him within sight of the scaffold, for she was found to have been in the company of men connected with Gunpowder Plot, and she and Wenman were arrested for complicity, so that the man who had risked his life for the Protestant cause was in danger of losing it as a Roman Catholic plotter. Happily, he cleared himself and she came triumphant out of her cross-examination. They lived on in peace.

Four Men

TYRINGHAM. It is a quiet little Eden, with nothing to tell us of its stirring story, but it has seen a thrilling day. While Shakespeare was writing his tragedies a man of his county, handsome as Apollo, strong as Hercules, and a Croesus of landowners, was one of four men walking in this lovely park. He was Robert Catesby, and with him was a kinsman, "strong and comely and very valiant," a travelled linguist, deeply versed in diplomacy, Thomas Winter. The other two were young Tyringham, owner of the hall, and his cousin, Sir Everard Digby, from Gayhurst House, across the Ouse, which runs through this park. All four were kinsmen, and two were leaders of Gunpowder Plot, talking over the grievances of Roman Catholics.

Tyringham escaped the fatal toils, but Digby was slowly involved in the web. Of these four men only Tyringham died in his bed. Catesby perished fighting; Digby suffered frightful barbarities. Winter, too, died on the scaffold, praying that he might suffer, not only for himself but for his brother Robert, another conspirator.

But there is neither sign nor hint of all this here today. The hall to which the conspirators came was succeeded in the 18th century by the stately house now in the park, built by Sir John Soane, who built the Bank of England of his day and lived in the house we can still see as he saw it in Lincoln's Inn Fields. His also is the classical bridge spanning the river here.

An architect of our own era, Sir Edward Lutyens, has added a new beauty to the park, a lovely domed temple of music with a series of magnificent marble columns. The same artist's work appears in the church, in as simple a peace memorial as we have seen, a plain marble panel with the laurels of victory.

The church, rebuilt last century amid these limes and beeches and chestnuts, still has its Norman base to the tower. It has two brasses of 15th century folk, one of Mary Catesby and one, with beautiful lettering, of John Tyringham, in a tunic under his plate armour, a great hound at his feet. In his day his family had been patrons of the church for 274 years; they remained patrons 414 years more, and no fewer than 30 sovereigns occupied the throne in the 688 years covered by this remarkable record. Joseph Tarver was rector for 54 years of last century, and the east window is to his memory, showing Peter and the Madonna.

The Marvellous Pulpit and the Ancient Song

UPPER WINCHENDON. Here is a rare treasure, an oak pulpit cut from a solid block and shaped with three sides on each of which is carved a traceried panel. We have seen old chests cut from the solid, but no other pulpit like this which is still used after 600 years. There are very few pulpits so old in all England and none so curious. It was beautifully made. The three sides look like traceried windows, all different; and an embattled ridge runs along the top. It is pitiful to see it so defaced by tacks and nails driven into it, a sad act of vandalism.

The pulpit adorns a stout little church with spiral capitals in a doorway which has stood in the fields on Winchendon Hill since the 12th century, a Jacobean manor house near by called the Wilderness and the great park of Waddesdon beyond. The porch has 600-year-old timbers set here by the men who made the pulpit. On the floor of the church, which is sunk four steps down from the Norman doorway, is a medieval chest; between the nave and chancel is a 15th century screen, its upper panels traceried, and over it a curious object hanging, the crest of a unicorn's head with a crown round its neck, set on a funeral helm of about 1600. The plain round font, probably Norman, has still a fragment of the padlock staple by which it was locked against witches, and has a cover made out of a pulpit sounding-board, with spiral foliage on its panels. In the nave are some 16th century seats grey with age, and the altar table and altar rails are 17th century. In the chancel wall is a stone corbel cut in the 12th century, and near it is a monument to John Goodwyn, his wife, and their 18 children. The memorial is decorated with shields showing lions, birds, and shells inset in brass below an arch with crinkled leaves in the spandrels. John died in 1558.

By the screen is the brass portrait of Sir John Stodeley, one of the men who preached in the little old pulpit. He died in 1502. In the aisle, where we stand to look through the round-headed peephole to the altar, is a pathetic little inscription: W. M. aged six weeks and one day, 1728.

Memories of a man who made a stir in his day cling to these quiet fields. Here stood the home of the Whartons, destroyed in the 18th century. The most famous member of the family was Thomas, the scapegrace lord whose proud boast was that he had sung a king out of three kingdoms. What this means is that he wrote the words of Lillibullero, which was set to music by Henry Purcell, the song being sung everywhere in England just before the flight of James the Second.

This rhythmical verse was much used by Irish Papists in their attacks on the Protestants in 1641, and Lord Wharton's use of it in his song caught the fancy of the soldiers and is said to have had a great effect in bringing about the revolution of 1688. Never did so slight a thing have so great an effect, an old writer says, as this refrain which was sung perpetually in city and country by army and people:

> Lilli bullero, lilli bullero bullen a la
> Lero lero, lilli bullero, lero lero bullen a la,
> Lero lero, lilli bullero, lero lero bullen a la.

For three years, while this songwriter was Lord Lieutenant of Ireland, a man immortal in our literature worked as his secretary, the scholarly Joseph Addison. Wharton was a forcible man and made many enemies, one of the hardest judgments passed on him being that of the irresponsible Dean Swift, who said that Wharton was "wholly given up to vice and politics." We need not believe the dean.

The Stone Giant

WADDESDON. For a generation its name has been familiar to art lovers in Europe. It has fine views over the rolling country of the Vale of Aylesbury, charming houses old and new, eight trim almshouses, an old inn with fantastically shaped yews, and, high over all, the manor house with an 800-acre park made from the fields and hedgerows of half a century ago. Modelled on a French chateau, the house was built by Baron Ferdinand de Rothschild, who formed here a magnificent collection of books and manuscripts, jewels, carvings, armour, and silver dating back as far as the great days of Greece. He left the collection to the British Museum, where it is widely famous as the Waddesdon Bequest, in a room of its own.

The palatial chateau rose swiftly, but the centuries have shaped the battlemented church, to which we come down an avenue of great chestnuts. It is a noble spectacle. The tower is 15th century, but we come through a doorway built by the Normans, sheltered by a porch with a 14th century recess in which is a little statue of St Michael in memory of a rector's son who died for us, H. C. Farmer. There is a window to him in the lady chapel, with St Michael, the Madonna, and a saint. The architectural glory of the nave, drawing the eye at once as we come into it, is in the three nave arches, made new 600 years ago from the original materials of the old church. They keep their richly carved Norman capitals, with bays of the 13th and 14th centuries carrying on the serial story of the architecture. The three arches of the Normans are among the best Norman sculpture left hereabouts; they are a charming trinity, with dainty heads between two of the arches. An oak screen adorns the lady chapel, in which, with the worn coffin-lid of a priest 700 years ago, is a piscina carved before Richard the Second lost his crown. There is a font 600 years old, and two tiles in the sanctuary with pelicans which have been tramped on through the centuries.

But perhaps the most impressive possession of the church is the stone giant lying at the entrance to the chancel, a knight in armour about seven feet long, his hand on his sword and a lion at his feet. He is believed to be Sir Roger Dynham, whose last fight was fought 700 years ago. We know little of him; but another Sir Roger, of the 15th century, appears in a canopied brass, showing him with folded hands, his head on his helmet, his feet on a stag. For four centuries he lay at Eythorpe and then, his coffin and brass being discovered in the ruins of his chantry, both were brought here.

There is a brass to a rector who just outlived Henry the Eighth, engraved with his grim shrouded skeleton—an early result of the morbid feeling which began to find expression in brasses and monuments at that time. Another 16th century portrait brass shows Richard Pygott and his wife, he virile in armour; and a tablet to a rector during the Napoleon wars tells the pathetic story of his seven children, who all died as babies. A fine high-backed canopied chest was made by French craftsmen whose fathers may have fallen at Agincourt, and with it is much charming modern woodwork in the canopied stalls, with misereres of angels holding books, winged lions, eagles, and unicorns. Corbel heads and stone angels 500 years old look down from the roofs.

Little Elizabeth

WALTON. Its 14th century church, with its thick-walled tower, stands by the meadows with the little River Ouzel running past. The porch has admitted worshippers to it for 500 years, and the roofs of nave and chancel sheltered congregations born under Queen Elizabeth.

There is a touching brass inscription in Latin and English to a child of 11 of Shakespeare's day, the English beginning pathetically:

BUCKINGHAMSHIRE

Elizabeth, the daughter dear
Of William Pyxe, here lies interred.
O! that her death for many a year
Almighty God would have deferred.

A delightful wall monument of the 17th century shows Bartholomew Beale and his wife face to face, with a lovely cherub below; and there is a medallion bust by Nollekens of Sir Thomas Pinfold, a 17th century lawyer, and a tablet to Charles Pinfold, an 18th century Governor of Barbados.

Waiting for the End of the World

WATER STRATFORD. Little change the years have wrought in this pretty nook in the valley of the Ouse. The charming manor house, with its dark roof descending low over the walls, has grown with the generations, but has kept its Tudor character, and the old cottages are thatched as they were centuries ago. The church is delightfully situated among sycamores and chestnuts, and its noblest features have been preserved, not only the 14th century tower (with a pyramid roof in place of the original cap), but the two splendid Norman doorways, one for priest and one for people. It is ranked among the small places of which the country is proud. The south doorway, with chevrons and grotesques on its capitals, has a magnificent tympanum, its beautifully finished sculpture wonderfully preserved, showing Christ with hand raised in blessing. The figure is encircled by an oval supported by the outstretched hands of kneeling angels. The feathers of their widespread wings, like their ample robes, are carved with extraordinary delicacy and fidelity. This rare tympanum rests on a lintel enriched with tiny arches with much charm of detail.

Over the narrow priest's doorway is another tympanum of surprising beauty, with a lamb before a cross, standing out from a background of dainty quatrefoils, resting on a lintel of dragons with tails entwined and heads turned as if wondering at this tangled skein.

There is a striking 17th century wall monument, with a cherub above and heraldry below, to Mary Franckyshe, who is resting on a canopied bed. At her feet stands her husband in a rich robe, while six girls kneel at the side, with a baby in its cradle before them and two boys behind. They are presumably the grandchildren of this honoured dame, who, born before Elizabeth was crowned, outlived her and saw the beginning of the sorrows of Charles Stuart. She may have dropped her alms into the oak plate still in use; she would hear the bells still ringing in the tower.

In all the long annals of this place nothing compares with that period of turmoil and terror arising from the wild prophecies of its rector John Mason, that he was to die, rise again, and bring the world to judgment. His predictions aroused a scene of religious excitement amost unparalleled in our history, credulous folk coming from far and near to dwell in barns and tents, awaiting for 20 years the end of the world. Except that the rector sleeps in its midst, there is but scanty record of those delirious days.

John Mason, born midway through the 17th century, was one of the earliest hymn writers, whose hymns, influenced by George Herbert, left their mark on men as unlike as Pope, Wesley, and Watts. He came here in 1674, with 20 years to live, but advancing years brought acute nervous affections, leading to nightmares and delusions. His condition worsened after the death of his wife, and he was consumed with a conviction that the Day of Judgment was at hand, and that it was here Christ would first appear. His wild messages spread through the countryside, and hosts of people sold their goods, left their homes, and came here to await the dread day. The great encampment of Mason's disciples was called the Holy Ground, where all lived on terms of equality. Their religious services were marked by extreme hysteria, dancing, shrieking, and clapping of hands, with cries of "Appear, appear!" When the rector died and was buried in the church, in May 1694, his followers would not believe that he was dead, and the excitement continued unabated, so that his successor had the body exhumed and exhibited to satisfy the mob. Still many were unconvinced, and in the end the camping ground was cleared by force.

Richard Baxter in a Grinling Gibbons Pulpit

WAVENDON. It is one of the villages in which we may still see women sitting at their cottage doors making lace, a custom introduced to the county by Catherine of Aragon. An old lady had just passed away when we called who had made lace at her doorway for 85 years, Rachel Rust, laid to her rest at 94.

Across the valley are the magnificent pine woods above Woburn

Turville — A Tranquil Village Scene

Walton — The Meadows by the Ouzel

From the Slopes of Coombe Hill

Old Cottages in the High Street
WENDOVER IN THE CHILTERNS

Sands; facing them here stands the embattled 15th century tower of the 13th century clerestoried church, the nave with four bays carried on slender pillars. The roof is modern but the stone angels supporting it have done duty for 500 years. The chancel has a double piscina, and an arcade with stone seats for priests recessed in the wall. In the tracery of a window is some 15th century glass with the head of a saint. A 17th century brass shows Richard Saunders and four wives. An oak chest with three locks was nearly a century old when the Armada took the seas.

But the glory of the church is its pulpit, a magnificent example of the work of Grinling Gibbons, with cherubs, pendants of fruit and flowers, and rich inlaid panels. Gibbons carved it for St Dunstan's Church in Fleet Street, London, where it succeeded pulpits in which William Tyndale and John Donne had preached. In this stood the famous Richard Baxter, one of the most remarkable men of the Puritan era and author of The Saint's Everlasting Rest. While he was preaching in St Dunstan's one day there arose a cry that the church was falling. Baxter was silent for a moment and then said solemnly: "We are in God's service, to prepare ourselves that we may be fearless at the great noise of the dissolving world, when the heavens shall pass away, and the elements melt with fervent heat." From this pulpit the old author William Romaine preached to such great congregations that Fleet Street became impassable.

St Paul's Thirty Miles Off

WENDOVER. It is clad in the beauty of the Chilterns, with the Roman Icknield Way as its highroad, with Boddington Hill on one hand, Backham Hill on the other, and crowning all, 845 feet high, Coombe Hill, from which on fine days, across glorious undulating country, St Paul's Cathedral may be seen 30 miles away. On this hill is an obelisk in memory of Wendover men who fell in the South African War.

The manor was owned by the family of John Hampden, and there are many timbered houses and ancient cottages here that he must have known. His cousin Cromwell is said to have stayed at the Red Lion inn, where much that he would see remains. Nearer our own time Robert Louis Stevenson visited the same house and celebrated it in enthusiastic prose.

The old timbered Bosworth House, once splendid, has been divided so that one part of it is now the post office, next to which an arch still shelters a 15th century pillar piscina. In the house a splendid series of 16th and 17th century wall paintings has been brought to light, to be shared between the Aylesbury museum and the Victoria and Albert, leaving here only two, with the timber framing of the others still showing colour.

The manor house and the church are neighbours down a pretty lane, with a stream at its side. A bold 14th century tower rises over a church girt about with tall chestnuts, sycamores, and limes with two yews flanking the churchyard path. Nearly 20 generations of worshippers have passed through the porch, with its richly carved arch. There is much 13th century work in the church, which has a triforium, and 14th century arcades on earlier pillars, the capitals of some carved with vivid animals, one with a figure kneeling in prayer, others with flowers. The chancel moulding ends in jolly little heads.

A quaint portrait brass shows William Bradschawe with his wife and their nine children kneeling, each child named, with the word "dede" to indicate those no longer living when the brass was made. Below the children's names are those of 23 grandchildren, a family tree of three generations, with 35 people who flourished under the Tudors, some owning Catherine of Aragon as lady of the manor.

Wendover sent Hampden to represent it in five Parliaments, and was later the seat of Burke and Canning, but it has given famous men as well as receiving them. Its most notable son was Roger of Wendover, who takes his place in literature as one of our first historians with his Flowers of History. The book, whose authorship was a mystery until the original manuscript was found centuries afterwards, dates from the creation to 1235. Although the earlier parts are valueless, the record of the half century before Roger's death in 1236 is an important document.

Roger had two great contemporaries, both Richards. Richard de Wendover, Bishop of Rochester, died in 1250, and the second Richard of Wendover, combining medicine with theology, became a canon of St Paul's, and physician to the Pope. In one generation this little place was the cradle of three men who, after seven centuries, still make it famous by having been "of Wendover."

Little of the Wendover they knew remains outside the church, but not far away Wellwick farm has still the charming gables and chimneys of the year when Shakespeare died.

The Vicar's Sons

WESTBURY. Secluded in the valley of the Ouse, it has old thatched cottages and a 17th century manor house made new, in a richly timbered 100-acre park. At the end of a lane we come upon a delightfully balanced group, the red and white 17th century vicarage, a thatched cottage, and the church, with a yew as high as the new saddleback roof of the 13th century tower. The churchyard is a rare summer scene, with flowers glowing in pedestal vases which look as old the 17th century tombs about them. The nave is Norman, with 14th century arcades. The 13th century chancel has painted walls with Bible scenes in memory of a 19th century lady. Two modern windows have St Nicholas in gleaming robes, Christ giving blessing, and a resplendent archangel.

There is a pathetic memory of five sons of a vicar, three of whom died for us in the war. Here for us to see are the swords of two of them and the wooden cross of one. Two other wooden crosses come from some corner of a foreign field that is for ever England.

Old Door and Old Bell

WESTON TURVILLE. It has something of the Roman Empire under foot, an inn at which wayfarers rested before Columbus was born, and a bell which was rung when the Wars of the Roses ended in the union of Red and White. It has another spectacular distinction, a reservoir half a mile long.

The 15th century tower looks down on the clerestoried church transformed 300 years after the Normans left it. The fluted Norman font is still here, banded at the top with ornament, its stem rich with cable moulding and even the base decoratively chiselled. The font and the plain chancel window are the chief possessions of the church, for in the centre of the window is a tiny treasure of medieval art, a lovely Madonna and Child, both crowned, in white against a blue background.

The medieval chancel has its original piscina, and one of its walls has Norman carving: a group of soldiers, probably from an Easter sepulchre, fragments of a capital, and a carved stone six feet long. One of the aisles, whose 14th century doorway has a door which the village has been opening for 500 years, has still the windows made when Wycliffe was beginning his work; and all the roofs, except in the south aisle, are by 15th century craftsmen. Under the modern roof of the south aisle is an oak screen of the days of Henry the Eighth, and there is Tudor panelling in the altar table. The pulpit, carved with vines, comes from the days of Cromwell; so do the two carved chairs in the chancel, one convertible into a table. There is a chest still older, and in one of the aisles is a cupboard seven feet high, its handsome doors painted with an apostle and a king holding a lamp and a casket. The 13th century gave the church one of its arcades and the 14th gave it a second and added a piscina.

Cowper's Farewell

WESTON UNDERWOOD. Cowper thought it one of the loveliest villages in the kingdom, and it still is: changed since he spent the last and happiest of his Buckinghamshire years in it, but still with the long views of the valley so dear to his heart, and so faithfully pictured in his poetry. The stone arch through which we enter the village is part of Weston Manor, many of whose limes, beeches, elms, and chestnuts the poet must have seen. His own home is still here, a pleasant two-storeyed house with dormer windows on the village street.

The most intimate association with the poet has been removed to the museum at Olney; it is the shutter of one of his windows, on which he wrote his melancholy Goodbye to the scene of his happiness:

Farewell, dear scenes, for ever closed to me;
Oh! for what sorrows must I now exchange ye.

To enjoy a view which so delighted him, from the south side of the church, we mount steps in the wall to enter the churchyard, where a grand yew hedge 15 feet high has the company of two old beeches.

The church has three bays begun by the Normans, to which English pointed arches have been added, touches of colour still on their round piers. The fourth bay and the aisles were added 700 years ago, and the chancel is of Chaucer's century. The font, with its traceried base, is 15th century, its cover having been added after the Reformation.

The treasure of the church is the great chancel window, which has not only its ancient tracery but ten of its 14th century stained glass lights, with Christ ascending in glory, angels on either side swinging censers and a company of saints; Peter with the keys, Laurence with his gridiron, and John the Baptist with a lamb in his arms and a sheep at his feet. The rich backgrounds are yellow, gold, and black.

The chancel floor has a portrait brass of John Olney and his wife, whose years were declining when Henry the Fifth was in the heyday of his youth. A second brass shows a group with Elizabeth Throckmorton and her five children, a fine engraved group marred by the absence of the lady's head.

The Throckmortons, an ancient family long established at the vanished hall, were still there in Cowper's time, among the dearest of his friends. It was to Lady Throckmorton that he wrote a courtly Ode on her beautiful transcript of Horace and a long lament on the death of her bullfinch which was devoured in the night by a cat:

> *The tree-enchanter Orpheus fell,*
> *His head alone remained to tell*
> *The cruel death he died.*

Around Elizabeth and her children are wall monuments of her descendants, among them a 17th century baronet, and a record of the fact that the heart of his son, a boy of 16, was placed here. The woodwork is mainly 18th century, the pulpit with its beading ornament and the box pews; but there is a chest which was in use when John Bunyan was in prison not far away, writing Pilgrim's Progress.

Church Extraordinary

WEST WYCOMBE. It is not to be missed, for even if it were not so beautiful the golden ball high on its hill would make it known. Fortunately it is ours for all time, perhaps the only village in England which truly belongs to the nation, for the public spirit of the Royal Society of Arts bought West Wycombe from its owners and gave it to the National Trust. It is worthy of this act of generous courage, for it is a lovely place, its delightful cottages overhanging the Oxford Road from London. The decaying beams of the ancient cottages have been preserved, an old inn has been turned into a village centre, and signboards of an apple orchard and a dramatic St George and the Dragon give charm and colour to the street.

It will probably be agreed that the gem of the village is the church loft with its upper storey corbelled over the pavement, forming a long room with an open roof of 15th century beams. The church itself is high up and far away, but in this room medieval travellers from Oxford to London would rest as the church's guests. At one corner of the tiled roof rises a bell turret of the 17th century, and a quaint clock hangs over the pavement.

It is through an archway under this room that we begin a long climb to the hilltop crowned by the church, 600 feet above the sea. It rises on a spur of the hill in a prehistoric camp of three acres. We pass on our way to it the ruined walls of a 19th century church and a great chalk cave. At the top of the hill stands the old church which Sir Francis Dashwood (Lord le Despencer) refashioned, with his great mausoleum beside it. He was Chancellor of the Exchequer in 1762, a man of great vanity and one of the notorious Medmenham gang of wild fellows, though he had the courage to try to save the life of Admiral Byng when the King, the Prime Minister, and the mob were all clamouring for his blood. He found an ancient church on this hilltop and made it what we see, a remarkable-looking building with its 14th century tower raised higher and glorified by an immense gilded ball which will hold ten men inside it. From its parapet is one of the greatest views in the county, for three long valleys meet at the foot of the hill.

The nave of this strange church is like a great hall with 16 columns in its walls, linked by festoons of plaster flowers. The painted ceiling of the nave has a gold star on a blue ground in the centre, and the ceiling of the chancel has a sentimental Last Supper. Fine oak columns form an arch behind the altar, and there are cherubs carved by Grinling Gibbons on each side of the east window. The priest has three Chippendale armchairs to sit in, but neither reading desk nor pulpit. The font bowl is of silver gilt set on a thin post encircled by a serpent and with a dove clinging to it.

For those who climbed up to this place long ago there was a stable attached to the west wall of the tower, a brick building still here. The rider who had put up his horse could stand on this hilltop by the Despencer mausoleum and look down on the Despencer home in the park. The mausoleum is a lofty six-sided building open to the sky, built of flint with plastered columns supporting a frieze on which great vases rest. Through iron bars we see the pedestal tomb of Lady Despencer on the rough grass, and behind it a monument to two kneeling women. In one of the walls was enshrined the heart of Lord Despencer's friend Paul Whitehead, an 18th century poet.

WEXHAM. A quiet and modest place, it borrows a reflected glory from its vision of the stately towers of Windsor Castle. Where a priory once stood is now a farm. The Norman church is that to which the old monks came chanting; it was enlarged 600 years ago, when the bell turret was added, still supported by its original timbers. There is a Norman window through which the light still comes, and another with zigzag, now blocked up. The nave doorway is six centuries old, with a nail-studded door which 12 generations have opened into this place. The tower and the yew-shaded porch have both their ancient timbers. The 14th century chancel has in the floor 14th century tiles with roses and fleur-de-lys.

On the Roman Plateau

WHADDON. It stands on a plateau where the Romans camped, with three delightful woodland acres (Thickbare, Thrift, and Broadway) which are all that is left of the medieval forest now known as Whaddon Chase, in which kings had hunted since the Conquest. Few manors have had a more varied career. Among crowding details we remember that Elizabeth visited here, and that Browne Willis the antiquarian, who lies at Fenny Stratford, here pored over his books in a house which has been much altered.

A row of red almshouses lies behind the church, whose tower is one of the clearest landmarks of the northern half of the county. It has a 17th century clock still working. The builders who set up this tower in the 14th century made a niche where a statue might stand looking toward Buckingham, but there is no statue. They had just rebuilt the nave (which has a north arcade of four bays and a south arcade of three) putting back in place the round Norman columns whose capitals, adorned with flowers and little grotesques, we admire so much today. The clerestory was added in the 16th century, a notable feature of it being two windows in the east wall, one over each side of the chancel arch. An odd shape keeps them company, a dog's head adorning the bracket of the 17th century font cover. The round font, resting on four ornamented shafts, was made in the 13th century. Two curious and unusual little objects hang on the wall, alms shovels made of oak and dated 1643, one bearing the initials of a churchwarden during the Civil War. The altar rails and the table with six legs and moulded rails are both admirable 17th century work. There are two oak chests, a small one and a big one, both 300 years old.

Some precious bits of the 14th century glass shine in vivid yellow and ruby in the tracery of an aisle window; we see two angels swinging censers, and below them is a small brass portrait of Margaret Myssenden, who died in 1612. She is in a high crowned hat, kneeling, and below her is engraved the skeleton of her son.

There lies in a 600-year-old chapel, still with its original roof, Thomas Pygott, a Sergeant-at-Law who died in 1519; he is on an elaborate canopied marble tomb with his two wives and their ten children. The tomb is panelled and decorated with tracery and shields, and the canopy enriched with flowers and crowned with a cresting of foliage. Thomas and his two wives kneel in brass on the wall at the back of the tomb, he with tippet and hood and the wives with pedimental headdresses. Behind the first wife are two sons and three daughters, and behind the second are three sons and two daughters, all in brass. Lord Arthur Grey de Wilton, who died in 1593, shares with his wife Jane Sibill a plain tomb over which is a canopy carved with squares and circles.

Over the altar of this chapel is a modern reredos with a relief of Christ and two angels above it. In front of the altar is a Madonna and Child in memory of Richard Selby Lowndes, who died in 1930. Other memorials of this family are on their graves in the churchyard; and over two of them rise bronze figures by Frank King, one of a girl with sheaves of corn, the other of the Archangel Gabriel. Little Billy Selby Lowndes, who died when he was only two (in 1926), lies in a grave marked by a white cross and these pathetic lines:

Sweet little flower, thou grief nor sorrow knew,
But came to win a parent's love, and then to Heaven withdrew.

The Oldest House in the County

WHITCHURCH. Inspired by fine views over the Vale of Aylesbury, it has proudly maintained a high level of comeliness in its thatched and timbered houses; there are two noble examples in the lane to the church. A massive 14th century tower with many niches has an elaborate sundial which has recorded all the bright

The Old Church and Mausoleum on the Hill

The Church Loft in the High Street
WEST WYCOMBE

Olney · The Cowper Museum

Weston Underwood · William Cowper's Home

Slough — The Old Church of St Lawrence

Wing — Saxon Church and 14th Century Tower

Whitchurch   White Walls and Thatch

Winslow   Cottages near the Church

hours since George the Fourth was king. The windows are all clear glass but one, the exception being a sanctuary window with blue and red glass made for it 600 years ago. Through it falls the tinted light on the piscina, in which the priest would wash the altar vessels after praying for a blessing on the parents of our first English king, Richard the Second.

The walls have two strangely dissimilar features, one a 15th century painting of St Margaret and her dragon, the other a ridiculous marble tablet showing the cloaked figure of John Westcar, with a sheep and a bullock proclaiming his calling, for, profiting by the famous Creslow Pastures hereabouts, he fattened sheep and cattle for the butchers and here claims the plaudits of posterity.

The oldest monument is the tomb of Sir John Smythe, a lord of the manor who, Chief Justice during the anxious years of Charles the Second, had the good fortune to pass out of office just before the still more perilous days of James the Second. A modern tablet recalls the life of Charles Spencer, for 40 years doctor here, and the latest tablet we found had the noble words, Live thou for England: we for England died.

The poppyhead stalls in the chancel were here when the Te Deum was sung for deliverance from the Spanish Armada. The carved oak pulpit, the altar table, the reading desk, the poorbox, and the parish chest are from oaks felled in Queen Elizabeth's England; but in the north aisle are a painted cupboard and parts of a screen which were in use long before her.

Near this delightful place is Creslow, a storied hamlet which has decayed at the touch of Nemesis. Today it counts for its good repute on the virtues of the pastures to which it gives its name; once it had a stately Norman castle, of which the ruins lie beneath their mounds. Here we find the oldest house in the county, a farmhouse with an ancient octagonal tower, mullioned windows, a superb cellar with a vaulted roof, and, crowning wonder of all, a stable with a splendid Norman doorway. It is a 14th century manor which, until the Dissolution of the monasteries, was owned by the Knights Hospitallers. The cellar was their crypt, and the stable their chapel. Theirs was the great Creslow Pasture, theirs the cattle and sheep fattening there. When they fell only the pastures remained precious here, feeding-grounds of animals for the Court table, royal acres indeed.

THE KING'S ENGLAND

Richard and His Rod

WILLEN. It has much of the charm of our countryside and an abiding memorial to one of the greatest teachers of his age, Richard Busby. As headmaster of Westminster School for more than half of the 17th century, it may be said of him that he birched knowledge into the youth of England. Destined to own the manor here, he was a poor scholar helped by charity to a distinguished career at Oxford. He left the University a perfect instructor, but a Spartan; a Royalist who without compromise held his position at Westminster during the Commonwealth, and after the Restoration grew rich on royal rewards. His austerity was notorious, but he was more than a flogger, for boys who grew to fame under his teaching loved him. Among his illustrious pupils were Dryden and John Locke, and at one time 16 of his old boys were bishops.

It was Busby, Birch, and Benevolence that did the business. According to Dr Johnson, he used to call the rod his sieve and say that whoever did not pass through it was no boy for him. The story is probably true that when Charles the Second visited the school Busby kept his hat on, explaining that he dare not let his boys believe there was a greater man than he.

Pious and generous as well as severe, on coming here he built this church (from designs by the scientist Robert Hooke, an old pupil of Dr Busby and a friend of Christopher Wren), installed a library in it, furnished it with plate, and left an endowment for the regular conduct of services. His library is in the village still, at the vicarage.

Red brick gateways guard the churchyard, over which rises a tower crowned with pineapple pinnacles, and approached by steps with a doorway which has fine ornamental ironwork. The roof, resting on quaint figures, has carvings of flowers and fruit, and in the centre of each bay is a huge boss. The font cover is beautiful; the pulpit, altar, rails, and sanctuary chair are rich and good. There are singing cherubs in the spandrels of the organ.

The Saxon Church

WING. It has a great thing, the finest Saxon church in the county, an impressive structure crowned by a 14th century tower and with a clerestoried nave, but with the Saxon walls of the nave and chancel and the Saxon crypt below, a wonderful glimpse of England before the Conqueror.

From the churchyard are seen the shallow arcades of the Saxon apse resting on narrow pilasters, each pilaster set on the walls of the crypt. The heads of three crypt arches appear above the grass, two built-up and one still giving light.

We come into the great nave by a doorway 600 years old, guarded by a comic lion and a curious goat. One of the aisles as well as the nave is Saxon and one 14th century. We rise by steps into the Saxon chancel under a splendid Saxon arch, above which is a double-headed window framed in Roman tiles and divided by a Saxon pillar. The wonderful crypt below the chancel is among the most interesting Saxon survivals, strangely designed and wonderfully preserved after 1300 years. Remains have been found of a peephole through which the interior of the crypt could be seen from the nave. The walls are built of rough flint with immense strength, and inside is a small chamber surrounded by a passage through which it communicates by three arches, the priest being able to reach the crypt from this passage without passing through the church.

The crypt was lost for ages and was opened up last century; it was probably closed when the church was refashioned 500 years ago. They gave the nave a magnificent roof, with grotesques carved on the bosses, angels on the wall plates, kings or saints on the end of every beam, and angels over all with outspread wings. From the same medieval craftsmen comes much of the screenwork with its carving of birds, squirrels, and dragons; two of their fine doors are still hanging, their seats are still in the nave, and grim dragons from their chisels are on a poppyhead. The pulpit is Jacobean. The font is 15th century.

There is a little glass 600 years old with a man and a woman and a tree between them, and brass portraits of the time of the Wars of the Roses showing an unknown civilian and his wife. On another brass is Thomas Coates, kneeling with the key, staff, and high hat worn by a Jacobean porter, for he was porter at Ascott, the pleasant gabled house in the park, home of the Dormers. Their monuments show them from Tudor days. Sir Robert of 1552 is sleeping under an elaborate canopy with Corinthian columns, with a sarcophagus decorated with heads of oxen, and scratchings on the tomb showing an extraordinary picture of a man swinging from a gibbet, as if to remind us that one of the rectors here, the notorious Dr Dodd, was hanged at Tyburn for forgery. Above this tomb are Sir Robert's gauntlets, resting on his helmet.

On a richly canopied tomb in the chancel, glowing with heraldic colours, lies Sir William Dormer in Tudor armour, his wife on the shelf below with a leopard at her feet and a ruff round her neck, and below them both a son in armour, three grown-up daughters, and three babies in cradles. Another Sir Robert and his wife kneel with their six children, all richly painted, and on the wall is a bust with cherubs weeping for Lady Anna Dormer of 1695. It was the Dormers who gave the village the four dormered almshouses, built in 1569 the reign of Elizabeth, and still the most attractive group in this village of Tudor and Jacobean cottages.

A Beacon for Six Centuries

WINGRAVE. It was built on its hilltop when the lowlands were undrained, and for six centuries its church has stood as a beacon. The modern tower stands on 13th century walls, and the church has much Norman work. There is a remarkable little chancel, surprisingly narrow for a church so high and light, with Norman arcading under two sanctuary windows, and a Norman doorway leading to a tiny 12th century chamber through the north wall. The chancel has three ancient stone seats, and four odd recesses by the altar. Two capitals with Norman carving are built in the sanctuary wall, and the Norman font is still in use, a plain bowl on a new base. The chancel arch, like the nave arcades and the aisles, is 14th century; the clerestory, with lights of tinted glass, is 17th; the stately tower arch is the survivor of the old 13th century tower.

There are linenfold panels from a carved 15th century screen in the tower with a huge old bell resting on the floor, to ring no more. The modern roof of the nave, borne on 15th century heads, has 12 figures holding books, and the chancel has a new roof of oak panels with bosses, but keeps part of its 15th century cornice. One of the aisles has still its 15th century roof, with angels and shields. The carved panels on the organ are Tudor, and there is Tudor panelling in the vestry, where we found a chest with the names of 17th century churchwardens on the lid. On a Sunday in June every year the floor of the church is strewn with hay, cut from half an acre left to the church by an old lady long ago.

Here Came Offa

WINSLOW. Proudly placed above a fertile vale, it was one of the homes of the kings of Mercia, and when the first Saxon church was rising, 12 centuries ago, here came Offa. Inspired by what he saw he planned the great St Albans Abbey, and gave it Winslow as part of its revenues.

Carrying its years with easy grace, Winslow has winding ways, and charming thatched cottages which were here when strolling players whom Shakespeare knew would come to the inn in the market square and act in the barn, which is still here and has still the ancient stables for company. The hall, built from the plans of Inigo Jones, keeps its beauty and the memories of its first owner, an 18th century Secretary of the Treasury. We were told that curfew has been rung here every night since 1068. The strokes must have sounded from successive towers, for this one, handsome and battlemented, dates from the 14th century and has a Tudor top. There is a small sanctus bell in the church which has been ringing out for more than three centuries.

Hopeful young yews line all the paths of a churchyard rich with flowers in summer, with a memorial cross in memory of the heroes of the war and the stump of a medieval one. The splendid 15th century porch leading us into the clerestoried church has St Lawrence in a pinnacled niche, grotesques on either side, and a fine oak ceiling of the same age, carved with angels and bosses. The inner doorway has two heads, mitred and crowned.

Within the north wall is a peephole through which many generations watched the elevation of the host by priests who sat in these stone seats, stored their vessels in this old aumbry, and cleansed them at this canopied piscina. Here is their richly carved chair. On a wall are two medieval paintings reduced to patches, one of St Christopher carrying the Child, the other showing the death of Thomas Becket. By the altar are two brasses, one of Thomas Fige with his wife and their seven children, engraved in Shakespeare's day; the other a portrait of Dorothy Barnard, in flowing gown with clasped hands, who died in the next generation. A brass tablet links two centuries:

John Abbott, who died in 1860 after being 29 years parish clerk, was succeeded by his son for 43 years. Very different is the record of Lieutenant Vaisey of the Royal Air Force, to whom there is a tablet telling us that, although mortally wounded in a battle with three planes, he brought his machine and its observer safely home, himself to die. The peace memorial chapel, plain in rather sombre grey, has a good screen, a triptych of the Crucifixion, and a handsome chair. The font, with a pinnacled oak cover, is the gift of the children. The pulpit is the richly carved upper tier of a Jacobean three-decker, with birds on the book-rest. One aisle has a 17th century altar table; the other has books of Queen Elizabeth's day.

Winslow has a chapel of much interest for its age, built by the Particular Baptists in 1695, a little difficult to find, at the back of the cattle market.

From Saxon Mound to Traffic Signs

WOLVERTON. We may wonder if we could not write half the story of our land round Wolverton, from the Saxon mound to the traffic lights at Oxford Circus. Certainly it has a very great story for this age of ours, and it comes out of the far past when the Saxons threw up the mound by the church.

The church, with two fine cedars before it, throws its shadow over the mound and looks out into the meadows of the Ouse valley. There may have been a church here as old as the mound itself; we know there was a Norman church, for one of its carved stones is in the rectory, the patriarch of the village houses, with fluted Corinthian columns at the door and the arms of the Longuevilles on the pediment. The inner doorway of the rectory has grotesques in its spandrels and the head of a heraldic greyhound in its tympanum.

But the Saxon church has gone completely, and all that is left of the Norman church is the queer head carved by a Norman mason and a consecration cross which was fixed in the wall when the church was made new last century.

Of the medieval church the 14th century tower remains with its arches intact, and the grotesque Norman head is in its stair turret. There is a marble monument with one of our first baronets on it, Sir Thomas Longueville of 1685. But for the rest it is modern—a brass portrait of a vicar's son killed in his teens while flying in France

(Bouverie St Mildmay), a graceful font canopy with a golden eagle in flight as the pulley-weight, saints and angels on the reredos and Fathers of the Church on the pulpit, and a painting of Christ and the children above the tower arch.

But we think of Wolverton not for what we see here but for what has happened here in days that seem to us so very long ago yet are still in living memory. The great works of the LMS have here transformed a village into a busy town. It is halfway from London to Birmingham, and it happened that it was a convenient place in the early days for teaching railways traffic control. Strange it seems to us today, but in the early days of trains there were men on the lines giving signals. It chanced that there were an unusual number of signal-posts near Wolverton station, and here men came for training. Here they were taught to stand erect for a signal if the line was clear, to wave a red flag before the engine if there was danger, and to bring the red flag smartly to the shoulder as the engine passed. They are scenes from Wolverton's past which seem to give it a place of its own in the history of transport.

We have been able also to see copies of the private time-tables that were once used here, in the days before Greenwich had linked the country with its own time. Then they set times down in their tables in terms like these:

Arrive Wolverton:
  London time 10.25; Local time 10.20.

And so it is that Wolverton, beginning its story with the Saxon mound in the shadow of the trees, has not only something old and new for us to see, but something curious for us to know.

The Little Son

WOOBURN. With Bourne End on the Thames as a neighbour, it lies in a narrow part of the Wye Valley, with hills on either side. Near the church are black and white cottages, a handsome Tudor barn, and an inn with quaint Jacobean figures of an architect and a builder, wearing round caps and high boots. Tall limes and chestnuts shade the churchyard, which has been dominated for nearly 500 years by the massive tower of the clerestoried church, whose arcades are supported by bold Norman columns. In a chapel 600 years old is part of a 15th century roof with modern colour, and a chest which has stood on its finely carved feet for seven centuries. The elaborate and coloured chancel screen, with two archangels standing on wheels, is the fine work of Mr J. N. Comper.

There are brass portraits of John Godwyn and his wife, builders of the great tower; of Christopher Askowe and his wife in Tudor costumes; and of Thomas Swayn in the cope he wore as chaplain to a bishop in the days before the Reformation.

But most interesting of the brass portraits is that of the little son of Lord Wharton, inscribed:

> *Let an infant teach thee, man,*
> *Since this life is but a span,*
> *Use it so that thou may'st be*
> *Happy in the next with me.*

His father, a courtier who became a zealous Puritan and led his regiment to defeat at Edgehill, was a friend of Cromwell, who wrote to him, six years after the death of this child, congratulating him on the birth of another son, a mercy which he was sure "would not cause Wharton to plot or shift for the young baron to make him great." Remembering the little heir's mother, Cromwell added, "My love to the dear little lady, better to me than the child."

Wharton, who took no part in the trial of the king and survived the Restoration, sleeps here with his little one, whom he followed to the grave 54 years after.

A Bishop's Throne for Three Village Boys

WORMINGHALL. It has the distinction, probably unequalled by any other village in the kingdom, of having been the birthplace of three bishops. They were Robert King, a 16th century abbot who became Bishop of Oxford and sat at Cranmer's trial; John King, Bishop of London, whom James the First called king of preachers and Sir Edward Coke the best speaker in the Star Chamber; and Henry, John's son, Bishop of Chichester. In the fields by the church is Court Farm, still here as in their days, but of the great building these bishops knew as boys there remains only one Tudor chimney.

The Norman church, with its low 15th century tower, has a Norman doorway in its porch; the 14th century chancel has a Norman arch with carved capitals, and there are Jacobean seats in the nave. In the chancel is a Tudor brass with portraits of Philip

BUCKINGHAMSHIRE

King, his wife, five sons, and seven daughters, all wearing ruffs; a baby rests on a huge pillow at its mother's feet. On the brass, which refers to Philip's father Robert, is John, the future Bishop of London, to whose memory there is also a wooden tablet carved with Tudor roses. A further reminder of the Kings is the group of almshouses built here in 1675 by another John, Bishop of Winchester.

Henry was the most notable of this remarkable family. Author of excellent prose, and of the famous poem "Tell me no more how fair is she", he was on terms of affectionate intimacy with Ben Jonson, Izaak Walton, and the poet Donne. Walton celebrated him in his life of Donne, on whom King wrote an elegy lamenting that the dead poet could not himself compose the lines:

> *So jewellers no art or metal trust*
> *To form the diamond, but the diamond's dust.*

King's wife died when she was only 23, and as he was a Prebend of St Paul's she was buried in the old cathedral, he writing to her a most exquisite farewell in which these lines occur:

> *Sleep on, my Love, in thy cold bed*
> *Never to be disquieted.*
> *My last Good-Night. Thou will not wake*
> *Till I thy fate shall overtake.*
> *Stay for me there; I will not fail*
> *To meet thee in that hallowed vale.*

Donne made King his executor, and gave him a lifesize drawing of himself in a winding-sheet, made as he awaited death at his deanery. King had the drawing reproduced exactly in white marble, and, almost the only monument in St Paul's to survive the Great Fire, it is in the cathedral today just as Sir Henry Wooton described it: "It seems to breathe faintly, and posterity shall look upon it as a kind of artificial miracle." Remembering the fire, posterity does so look upon it, but who remembers that we owe it to the love and reverence of the bishop born here, who has been for nearly three centuries sleeping in his own cathedral at Chichester?

Here Lies a Man Who Sowed a Fateful Seed

WOTTON UNDERWOOD. For over 600 years the manor has been owned by the Grenvilles. Here was their home; the church is the temple of their dead. In it lies one of our Prime Ministers. A splendid mile-long avenue of elms brings us to the handsome 19th century house replacing the old one after a fire. Near the gate a second avenue branches off through the park to the cottages about the ancient church, where, on seats round two old elms, the villagers rest in grateful shade when the day's work is done. The embattled tower, with its copper spire and a wooden sundial at one corner, is modern, but in the doorway between the tower and the 15th century nave is a lintel carved by Norman masters.

A magnificent iron screen with foliage, shields, and other decoration guards the Grenville chapel, built by William Grenville in 1343 and largely made new by the last Duke of Buckingham in 1867. Here lie many generations of Grenvilles (who became the Dukes of Buckingham) in tombs arranged in named compartments, or in more graceful tombs standing apart. Under the original recess, with ornament carved by 14th century craftsmen of her own day, is the figure of Agnes Grenville, carved two centuries after her death. On brackets above, one at either side of the west window, kneel the 16th century figures of a man in armour and a woman in a ruff. Let into black marble are portrait brasses, engraved while Spain was preparing the Armada, of Edward Grenville in a long gown, his wife in a ruff, their infant son in his christening robes.

An elaborate wall monument is in memory of Caroline, who died in 1874, first wife of Richard Grenville, Duke of Buckingham. Her husband, last of the ducal line, also sleeps here and has an alabaster relief of two angels in flowing robes holding a crown for him. Born in 1823, he inherited estates encumbered by the extravagance of his father, one of the most notorious spendthrifts of the 19th century. By heroic effort he paid off the bulk of his father's debts, but his claim to gratitude is based on his successful work as Governor of Madras, where he organised relief for nearly a million people during the terrible famine of 1876.

The most famous Grenville lying here is George Grenville, Prime Minister and kinsman and rival of Pitt.

It is hardly possible to exaggerate the effect his life had on our politics and on the modern history of the English-speaking peoples, for he sowed the seed which divided the two English-speaking nations. Known as the Father of the Stamp Act, he was born at Wotton Hall in 1712, grandson of Sir Richard Temple of Stowe. His university career ended, he was elected member for Buckingham at

29, representing it until he died nearly 30 years later. For 20 years he was a devoted public servant who, as Edmund Burke said, "took public business not as a duty he was to fulfil, but as a pleasure he was to enjoy." He became Prime Minister and Chancellor of the Exchequer, Lord Bute nominating him in the hope that he would be a useful tool who could be used in the hands of George the Third and of Bute himself; but Grenville was independent, protesting against Bute's secret influence and so making himself hateful to the king.

Grenville and the elder Pitt were kinsmen, but acted apart. The crowning blunder of Grenville's career was his introduction of the Stamp Act. The Seven Years War had removed the last French foe from American soil, and the colonists were ordered to bear some share of the cost of "defending, protecting, and securing the British colonies and plantations." It was the first attempt to impose taxation on goods imported into the colonies, and the stamping of documents in America was a declaration of the right of the mother country to impose such charge. In spite of the protest of the colonists, the Bill was passed almost without opposition.

The colonies fiercely resisted any taxation save that imposed by their own assemblies, and Pitt, emerging from retirement, sternly denounced the measure, holding that taxation without representation was illegal. His attempt at repeal was defeated, however; the right of England to legislate for the colonies was maintained; and so was sown the seed of the war bringing into being the United States. When Grenville died, and was buried here, it was felt that he had been honest but narrow and obstinate, yet, as Edmund Burke said, if he was ambitious his ambition was of a noble and generous strain.

Ancient Carvings

WOUGHTON-ON-THE-GREEN. Set so delightfully in the valley of the Ouzel, it has beauty across the vale in its charming cottages, some of them as old as the 15th century tower which crowns the church. The church itself is 13th century, when the nave, the font, and the wide chancel arch were built, but it was the men of John Wycliffe's century who gave it the porch with its beautiful little niche, the aisle, and the fine carvings, of which the boldest is the lifesize figure of a priest lying with a dog at his feet in a great recess in the chancel. Two carved heads, one of a knight, are on the arch above him.

In the thickness of the wall run the steep roodstairs, with a canopied entrance on which are carved two lifelike faces. The lovely arch of a piscina in the aisle has elaborate pinnacles and finials, and on it are two delightful heads. In the nave wall is a crude carving of a man with his tongue out, apparently one of the corbels from the first church here. The altar was carved more than 300 years ago, and its companion, a richly carved and very solid chair, has kept it company all the time. Lying in the churchyard is an ancient coffin lid, and looking out from the doors and windows are queer creatures of humour and grim fancy, one on the north doorway appearing still capable of a ferocious spring.

The Eton Scholar

WRAYSBURY. With the green fields round it and the Thames running by the Farthest South of Buckinghamshire, it possesses in Ankerwyke, a charming low house in delightful grounds by the river, a link with Norman days. Here was a convent, and, beautiful with age in its robe of ivy, there still lingers part of the gatehouse by which the quiet nuns came and went. Near it stands a magnificent yew which knew their secrets, and more. Tennyson's Talking Oak, boasting its 500 years, talked of fashions a few generations since, but this yew would have talked to him of Runnymede and King John, whose hunting lodge was close by, some of its ruins being still on a farm.

In the 13th century church is the font at which the children have been christened 700 years, and a carved piscina which has also served since the church was new. A 15th century chapel has part of its old roof. The panelled pulpit, whose sounding board is now used as a table at the vicarage, is Tudor, and there is 500-year-old panelling in the south aisle. In the chancel floor is a stone to Edward Gould, a servant of Charles the Second, who died 20 years after his master's long exile had brought him back to the throne.

The remains of a rich canopy still shelter the brass portrait of a knight in armour who fought for the Tudors. A second brass portrait shows John Stonor in the garb of an Eton scholar of the 16th century, who rose at five in the morning, prayed as he dressed, made his bed, swept his room, stood in a queue to wash, and began his lessons at six. He talked all day in Latin, learned a little Greek, and went to bed by rushlight.

INDEX

This index includes all notable subjects and people likely to be sought for, and a special index of pictures appears at the beginning of the volume.

Addington, 11
Addington, Lord, 11
Adstock, 12
Aird, Sir John, 75
Amersham, 12
Ammonites, 123, 124
Andrewes, Margaret, 159
Ankerwyke, 276
Anne of Denmark, 196
Area of county, 1
Ashendon, 15
Aston Abbots, 15
Aston Clinton, 16
Aston Sandford, 17
Astwood, 18
Atterbury, Francis, 191
Aubrey, Sir John, 33
Austen, Lady, 63
Aylesbury, 18

Ball, Hannah, 130, 231
Barn, notable, 11
Barnes, Dr Philip, 127
Barton Hartshorn, 22
Bate, Dr George, 180
Batten-Pooll, VC, 92
Baxter, Richard, 13, 257
Beachampton, 22
Beaconsfield, 23
Beaconsfield, Lord, see Disraeli
Becket, Thomas, 37
Bedford, Earls and Dukes, 54–56
Beeches, Burnham, 42
Bekonscot, 26
Bellew, Henry, 95
Bells, notable:
  Bradenham, 35
  Bradwell, 36
  Lee, 164
  Slough, 223
Benches and Stalls:
  Brill, 37
  Buckingham, 41
  Edlesborough, 77
  Great Hampden, 107
  Haddenham, 117
  Haversham, 126

Hillesden, 133
Ivinghoe, 150
Lower Winchenden, 178
Monks Risborough, 193
North Marston, 202
Penn, 208
Pitstone, 211
Turville, 248
Twyford, 250
Upper Winchenden, 252
Waddesdon, 254
Whitchurch, 265
Wing, 267
Benet, Sir Simon, 23
Bentinck, Hans, 103
Bible, notable, 41
Bierton, 28
Bigg, John, 69
Black Prince, 65
Bledlow, 29
Bletchley, 31
Boarstall, 33, 72
Boddington Hill, 117
Booth, James, 237
Borton, VC, Colonel, 92
Boswell, David, 200
Bosworth House, 258
Boveney, 33
Bow Brickhill, 34
Bradenham, 34
Bradwell, 36
Brasses, notable:
  Amersham, 14
  Beachampton, 22
  Bletchley, 32
  Burnham, 43, 44
  Chalfont St Giles, 49
  Chalfont St Peter, 50
  Chenies, 53
  Chesham Bois, 59
  Chicheley, 61
  Clifton Reynes, 64
  Denham, 68
  Dinton, 70
  Drayton Beauchamp, 73

Drayton Parslow, 74
Edlesborough, 78
Eton, 89, 90
Hambleden, 119
Hedgerley, 128
Lower Winchenden, 177
Maids Moreton, 180
Middle Claydon, 189
Monks Risborough, 193
North Crawley, 200
Penn, 208
Quainton, 212
Shalstone, 217
Slough, 223
Taplow, 243
Thornton, 246
Tingewick, 247
Twyford, 250
Upper Winchenden, 252
Waddesdon, 254
Wendover, 258
Whaddon, 264
Wraysbury, 276
Brett, Richard, 213
Brill, 37
Brontë, Patrick, 145
Broughton, 37
Buckingham, 39
Buckingham, Dukes of, 240–3, 274–5
Buckland, 41
Bull, William, 198, 206
Bulstrode family, 223
Bulstrode Park, 103
Bunyan, John, 196, 197
Burke, Edmund, 24, 26
Burke, Richard, 24, 26
Burnham, 42
Burnham, Lord, 24
Busby, Richard, 11, 266

Cadbury, George, 26
Calverton, 46
Campbell, VC, General, 92
Campbell, John Henry, 94

279

INDEX

Cantelupe, Thomas de, 118, 120
Cardigan, Earl of, 118
Carrington, Earl, 194
Castlethorpe, 47
Catesby family, 122
Catesby, Robert, 258
Catherine of Aragon, 40, 175, 227
Catherine of Valois, 175
Chalfont St Giles, 47
Chalfont St Peter, 50
Chalgrove Field, 106
Chaloner family, 227
Chantrey sculpture, 149
Charles the First, 40, 65, 108, 160, 233
Charles the Second, 128, 160
Chaucer, Alice, 183
Chearsley, 51
Cheddington, 51
Chenies, 52
Chequers Court, 79
Chesham, 57
Chesham, 3rd Lord, 18
Chesham Bois, 59
Chesterfield, Lord, 116
Chesnut avenue, 125
Chests, notable :
  Beaconsfield, 24
  Burnham, 44
  Cublington, 66
  Fingest, 98
  Great Kimble, 111
  High Wycombe, 131
  Ludgershall, 178
  Moulsoe, 195
  Newton Longville, 199
  Penn, 208
  Pitstone, 211
  Radclive, 214
  Upper Winchendon, 252
  Waddesdon, 254
  Wavendon, 257
  Whitchurch, 265
  Wooburn, 272
Chetwode, 59
Cheyne family, 59, 73
Chicheley, 60
Chiltern Hills, 2
Chilton, 61
Cholesbury, 62
Chrismatory, 104
Cippenham Palace, 43
Claydon House, 188

Clifton Reynes, 63
Cliveden, 243
Coke, Sir Edward, 233
Coleshill, 15
Colnbrook, 65
Congreve, VC, Major, 92
Contour Camp, 111
Cook, Captain, 50, 67
Coombe Hill, 257
Cottesloe, Lord, 243
Cowper, William :
  Chicheley, 60
  Clifton Reynes, 63
  Newport Pagnell, 198
  Olney, 203-6
  Weston Underwood, 260
Crab, Roger, 58
Creslow, 265
Croke family, 62
Cromwell, Frances, 81
Cromwell, Oliver :
  Aylesbury, 19
  Buckingham, 40
  Chequers, 79
  Dinton, 69
  Newport Pagnell, 196
  Quainton, 213
  Wendover, 257
Crosses, notable :
  Aylesbury, 19
  Bladlow, 29
Crypts, notable, 20, 267
Cublington, 66
Cuddington, 66
Curfew, 269
Cymbeline, 111

Danes Borough, 34
Dashwood, Sir Francis, 186, 262
Datchet, 66
Dayrell family, 100, 165
Denham, 67
Denham, Sir John, 136
Desborough, Lord, 243
Despencer, Lord le, 262
Devonport, Lord, 187
Digby, Everard, 102, 251
Dinton, 69
Disraeli, Benjamin :
  Aylesbury, 18
  Bierton, 28
  Bradenham, 34
  High Wycombe, 129, 130
  Hughenden, 138-144

Disraeli, Isaac, 35-36
Ditton Park, 67
Doors, notable :
  Aylesbury, 21
  Brill, 37
  Cheddington, 52
  Dorton, 72
  Hanslope, 121
  Hardwick, 123
  Hillesden, 133
  Langley Marish, 158
  Lee, 164
  Maids Moreton, 180, 181
  Swanbourne, 242
  Twyford, 249
  Weston Turville, 259
Doorways, notable :
  Adstock, 12
  Bletchley, 31
  Bradenham, 35
  Dinton, 70
  Hanslope, 121
  Horton, 138
  Lathbury, 159
  Leckhampstead, 162
  Lillingstone Lovell, 166
  Little Hampden, 168
  Slough, 222
  Stewkley, 228
  Stony Stratford, 237
  Twyford, 249
  Water Stratford, 255
Dormer family, 213, 267
Dorney, 71
Dorton, 72
Drake family, 13, 14, 167
Drake, Sir Francis, 102
Drayton Beauchamp, 72
Drayton Parslow, 74
Dropmore, 74
Drummond, VC, Lieut., 92
Dryden, John, 67
Dumouriez, Charles, 248
Dunton, 76
Dunville, VC, Lieut., 92

East Claydon, 76
Edgcott, 76
Edlesborough, 77
Edward the First, 117
Edward the Third, 65
Edwards, Thomas, 78
Eleanor, Queen, 237
Elizabeth, Queen, 65, 134, 195, 233

INDEX

Ellesborough, 78
Elliott-Cooper, VC, Col., 92
Ellwood, Thomas, 48, 50, 152, 155
Emberton, 81
Eton, 82
Evans, VC, Colonel, 92
Evelyn, John, 43
Evesham, Epiphanius, 184

Faith, Saint, 199
Farnham Royal, 94
Fawley, 95
Fennell, Jane, 145
Fenny Stratford, 96
Finch, Lord Chancellor, 215, 216
Fingest, 97
Firmin, Saint, 200
Flags, historic, 88, 194, 210
Fleet Marston, 98
Fletcher, Walter, 88
Flower, Sir William, 236
Fonts, notable :
  Adstock, 12
  Aylesbury, 20
  Bow Brickhill, 34
  Castlethorpe, 47
  Clifton Reynes, 64
  Drayton Parslow, 74
  Fingest, 98
  Great Hampden, 106
  Great Horwood, 111
  Great Missenden, 115
  Haddenham, 117
  Halton, 117
  Hambleden, 118
  Hedgerley, 128
  Langley Marish, 156
  Leckhampstead, 163
  Linslade, 167
  Long Crendon, 176
  Ludgershall, 178
  Monks Risborough, 192
  Newton Longville, 199
  North Marston, 202
  Penn, 208
  Pitstone, 210
  Stoke Mandeville, 230
  Stone, 236
  Weston Turville, 259
  West Wycombe, 262
  Willen, 266
Fortescue family, 195

Foscott, 99
Franklin expedition, 122
Fremantle, Sir Thomas, 242
Frohman, Charles, 182
Fuller, Thomas, 161
Fulmer, 100

Gawcott, 101
Gayhurst, 102
Geology of County, 3
Gerrard's Cross, 103
Gibbons, Grinling, 257, 262
Gibbs, John, 197
Giffard family, 189
Glass, notable :
  Aston Sandford, 18
  Aylesbury, 19, 20
  Buckingham, 41
  Chenies, 54
  Chetwode, 60
  Clifton Reynes, 64
  Drayton Beauchamp, 73
  Edlesborough, 78
  Ellesborough, 79
  Eton, 91, 93
  Fenny Stratford, 97
  Hardwick, 123
  Haversham, 126
  High Wycombe, 131
  Hillesden, 133
  Hitcham, 134
  Horton, 138
  Ilmer, 147
  Lee, 164
  Linslade, 167
  Lower Winchendon, 178
  Ludgershall, 178
  Maids Moreton, 180
  Monks Risborough, 193
  Newton Blossomville, 198
  Oving, 206
  Radclive, 214
  Stoke Hammond, 230
  Stoke Poges, 233
  Weston Turville, 259
  Weston Underwood, 260
  Whaddon, 264
  Wing, 267
Goodall, Joseph, 89
Graham, VC, Captain, 92

Granborough, 104
Gray, Thomas :
  Burnham, 42, 43
  Eton, 87, 93
  Stoke Poges, 232, 234–5
Great Brickhill, 105
Great Hampden, 105
Great Horwood, 110
Great Kimble, 111
Great Linford, 112
Great Missenden, 114
Grendon Underwood, 115
Grenfell, Billy, 244
Grenfell, Francis, 24, 92
Grenfell, Julian, 244
Grenfell, Riversdale, 24
Grenville family, 241, 273–5
Grenville, George, 274
Grenville, Lord, 74
Grenville, William, 45
Grey, Sir John, 32
Gribble, VC, Captain, 92
Grocyn, William, 199
Grote, George, 43
Grove, 116
Grubb family, 136
Gunpowder Plot, 102, 251
Gurdon, Sir Adam de, 117
Gurney family, 236

Haddenham, 116
Hall, Timothy, 30
Halton, 117
Hambleden, 118
Hampden, John :
  Aylesbury, 18
  Great Hampden, 105–10, 112
  Stoke Mandeville, 230
  Wendover, 258
Hangman's Oak, 181
Hansen, VC, Major, 92
Hanslope, 121
Harding, Thomas, 57
Hardmead, 122
Hardwick, 123
Hare, Dean, 49
Hartwell, 124
Hastings, Edward, 233
Haversham, 126
Hawridge, 126
Hawtrey family, 79
Hay-strewing, 269
Hazlemere, 127
Hedgerley, 127

281

INDEX

Hedsor, 128
Henry the Fifth, 175
Henry the Sixth, 82, 83, 88, 91, 94
Herschel family, 221, 224
High Wycombe, 129
Hill, DSO, Hugh, 208
Hillesden, 132
Hitcham, 134
Hobart, Sir Miles, 164, 183
Hobbes, Robert, 226
Hoggeston, 135
Hooke, Nathaniel, 129
Hooker, Richard, 72
Horsemoor Green, 158
Horsenden, 136
Horse's tomb, 161
Horton, 136
Howe, Admiral, 210
Howson, George, 119
Hughenden, 138
Hulcott, 144

Ibstone, 146
Ickford, 146
Ilmer, 147
Ingoldsby, Sir Richard, 102, 125
Iver, 147
Ivinghoe, 149

James, George Payne, 182
Jeffreys, Judge, 50, 103
Jervoise family, 218
Johnson, Dr, 87
Jordans, 151

Kay, Sir William, 246
Keate, Dr, 84, 87
Kederminster family, 149, 157
Kemp, John, 220
King family, 272
King, Henry, 273
Knollys, Lettice, 177
Knox, John, 13

Lake, Viscount, 17
Langley Marish, 156
Lathbury, 158
Latimer, 160
Laud, Saint, 219
Lavendon, 161
Layard, Henry, 28
Lead font, 208
Leckhampstead, 162

Lecterns, notable, 30, 91, 118
Lee, 164
Lee, Sir Henry, 99
Lee, Robert E., 21, 124
Lee of Fareham, Lord, 79
Lenborough, 102
Liberty, Sir Arthur, 59, 164, 165
Library, Church, 157
Lillingstone Dayrell, 165
Lillingstone Lovell, 166
Lincolnshire, Marquess of, 194
Linslade, 167
Lipscomb, George, 213
Liscombe House, 225
Little Brickhill, 168
Little Hampden, 168
Little Horwood, 169
Little Kimble, 170
Little Linford, 171
Little Marlow, 171
Little Missenden, 172
Little Woolstone, 174
Long Crendon, 175
Loughton, 176
Louis the Eighteenth, 124
Lovett family, 225, 226
Lower Winchendon, 177
Ludgershall, 178
Luke, Sir Samuel, 196
Lupton, Provost, 84, 90
Lyndhurst, Lord, 248

Maids Moreton, 179
Malet, Sir Edward, 56
Marlow, 181
Marsh Gibbon, 183
Marsworth, 184
Martyn, Henry, 179
Mascall, Eustace, 94
Mason, John, 256
Mayflower barn, 152
Mayne family, 69
McKay, Alexander, 122
Medmenham, 186
Mentmore, 187
Middle Claydon, 188
Mills, Bertram, 49
Milman, Robert, 183
Milton, John, 47, 50, 136, 155
Milton Keynes, 191
Misereres, 22, 77, 208, 254
Monks Risborough, 192
Montfort, Simon de, 140

Morgan, William, 145
Mosley, Lady Cynthia, 69
Moulsoe, 193
Mulsho, William, 102
Mursley, 195
Museums :
  Aylesbury, 19
  Chalfont St Giles, 48
  Hambleden, 118
  High Wycombe, 131
  Hughenden, 139
  Olney, 204

Neild, John Camden, 201
Newport Pagnell, 196
Newton, John, 203
Newton, Richard, 162
Newton Blossomville, 198
Newton Longville, 199
Nightingale, Florence, 188, 227
Nine Men's Morris, 147
North Crawley, 199
North Marston, 200
Notley, Abbey, 51
Nugent, Sir Charles, 171
Nugent, Lord, 124

Oakley, 202
Offa, King of Mercia, 269
Olney, 203
Oving, 206
Owen, Sir Richard, 101

Padbury, 207
Palliser, Sir Hugh, 50
Pamela, 223
Pattison, Dora, 175
Peckham, family, 68
Penington family, 50, 152
Penn, 207
Penn family, 208, 233
Penn, William, 13, 152, 155
Pennington, Sir Isaac, 50
Penn Street, 210
Perceval family, 46
Pigott family, 213
Pinchard, Arnold, 43
Pineapple, first, 71
Pitchcott, 210
Pitstone, 210
Population of County, 4
Portland, Dukes of, 104
Preston Bissett, 211
Primrose, Neil, 187
Princes Risborough, 211

282

INDEX

Pritchard, Sir William, 113
Pulpits, notable:
  Bow Brickhill, 34
  Cheddington, 52
  Chesham Bois, 59
  Edlesborough, 77
  Fawley, 95
  Hedgerley, 128
  Ibstone, 146
  Ivinghoe, 150
  Newport Pagnell, 197
  Olney, 204
  Pitstone, 211
  Stantonbury, 227
  Upper Winchendon, 251
  Wavendon, 257

Quainton, 212
Quarrendon, 99

Radclive, 214
Radnage, 215
Ramsay, Sir William, 127
Ravenstone, 215
Reade, Joseph, 237
Reredos, notable, 104
Reynes family, 64
Richard of Wendover, 258
Richard the Third, 237
Richardson, John, 182
Richings Park, 147
Rivers, 2
Roger of Wendover, 258
Romaine, William, 257
Romans:
  Foscott, 99
  Hambleden, 118
  High Wycombe, 129
  Iver, 147
  Latimer, 160
  Lee, 164
  Stone, 235
  Stony Stratford, 237
  Stowe, 238
  Weston Turville, 259
  Whaddon, 263
Roofs, notable:
  Brill, 37
  Edlesborough, 77
  Fleet Marston, 98
  Great Missenden, 114
  Hartwell, 125
  High Wycombe, 131
  Ivinghoe, 150
  Ludgershall, 178

Maids Moreton, 180
Monks Risborough, 193
Newport Pagnell, 197
North Crawley, 200
North Marston, 202
Penn, 208
Radnage, 215
Slough, 222
Wing, 267
Wingrave, 268
Ross, Sir James Clark, 16
Rothschild, Ferdinand de, 253
Rule, Joseph, 152
Russell family, 54–56, 79

St Leonards, 216
Salden House, 195
Sandys, Hester, 161
Saunderton, 216
Savoy Farm, 69
Saxons:
  Bulstrode Park, 103
  Cheddington, 51
  Cholesbury, 63
  Hardwick, 123
  Iver, 147
  Lavendon, 161
  Princes Risborough, 211
  Slough, 222
  Stone, 235
  Taplow, 243
  Wing, 266
  Wolverton, 270
Schorne, Sir John, 200
Scott, Sir Gilbert, 17, 101
Scott, Sir Giles, 17
Scott, Thomas, 17, 101
Screens, notable:
  Bradenham, 35
  Colnbrook, 65
  Edlesborough, 77
  Eton, 88
  Great Horwood, 110
  Haddenham, 117
  Hillesden, 133
  Linslade, 167
  Maids Moreton, 180
  Middle Claydon, 189
  Monks Risborough, 193
  North Crawley, 200
  Quainton, 212
  Saunderton, 217
  Wing, 267

Wotton Underwood, 274
Seaton, Thomas, 216
Seymour, Jane, 182
Shabbington, 217
Shakespeare's Farm, 115
Shardeloes, 14
Shedden, Robert, 122
Sheldon, Gilbert, 146
Shelley, 181
Shenley, 218
Sheridan, Richard, 43
Sherington, 219
Shoemaker, Christopher, 115
Simpson, 219
Skilbeck, Clement, 30
Slapton, 220
Slough, 220
Smith, Captain David, 176
Smith, W. H., 118
Smith, Sir William, 134
Smyth, William, 236
Smythiers, Charles, 183
Somerset, Duke of, 159
Soulbury, 225
Spence, Joseph, 111
Springett, Gulielma, 13, 50
Stantonbury, 226
Steeple Claydon, 227
Stephen, James, 115
Stevenson, Robert Louis, 257
Stewkley, 228
Stoke Goldington, 229
Stoke Hammond, 229
Stoke Mandeville, 230
Stokenchurch, 230
Stoke Poges, 232
Stone, 235
Stony Stratford, 237
Stowe, 238
Suffolk, Duke of, 183
Swanbourne, 242

Taplow, 243
Temple, Sir Richard, 240
Thomas de Cantelupe, 118, 120
Thornborough, 245
Thornton, 246
Throckmorton family, 261
Tickford Abbey, 196
Tingewick, 246

INDEX

Todd, Henry John, 78
Towers and Spires :
  Amersham, 13
  Aylesbury, 20
  Beaconsfield, 23
  Eton, 84
  Fingest, 98
  Hanslope, 121
  High Wycombe, 131
  Lavendon, 161
  Long Crendon, 176
  Maids Moreton, 179
  Milton Keynes, 191
  Monks Risborough, 192
  Olney, 203
  Sherington, 219
  Steeple Claydon, 227
  Stewkley, 228
  West Wycombe, 262
  Winslow, 269
Toynbee, Dr Paget, 75
Turville, 247
Turweston, 248
Twyford, 249
Tylers Green, 129
Tylsworth, William, 14
Tyringham, 250
Tyrrell family, 202
Tyrrell, Sir Thomas, 47

Unwin, Mary, 205
Upper Winchendon, 251
Upton, 221

Verney family :
  Brill, 37
  Hillesden, 134
  Maids Moreton, 181
  Middle Claydon, 188-90
  Steeple Claydon, 227
Victoria, Queen, 224

Waddesdon, 253
Wall Paintings :
  Amersham, 13

Bledlow, 30
Brill, 37
Broughton, 38
Chalfont St Giles, 49
Chearsley, 51
Clifton Reynes, 65
Eton, 90
Great Hampden, 107
Hughenden, 141
Lathbury, 160
Leckhampstead, 163
Little Hampden, 169
Little Horwood, 169
Little Kimble, 171
Little Missenden, 173
Maids Moreton, 180
Padbury, 207
Penn, 209
Wendover, 258
Whitchurch, 265
Winslow, 269
Wallace, Edgar, 171
Waller, Edmund, 15, 25
Walton, 254
Walton, Sir John L., 78
Warham, William, 160
Waterside, 57
Water Stratford, 255
Wavendon, 256
Waynflete, William of, 83, 86, 88
Webster, Thomas, 34
Weedon, 124
Wellesbourne family, 140
Wendover, 257
Wenman, Richard, 250
Wesley, John, 238
Westbury, 259
Weston Turville, 259
Weston Underwood, 260
West Wycombe, 261
Wexham, 263
Whaddon, 263
Wharton, Lord, 252, 272
Whitchurch, 264
Whitehead, Paul, 263
Whiteleaf Cross, 192

Whitelock, Bulstrode, 96
Whitelock, Sir James, 95
Wilberforce, Bishop, 23
Wilberforce, William, 115
Willen, 266
Willis, Browne, 32, 96, 263
Wing, 266
Wingrave, 268
Winslow, 269
Winter, Thomas, 251
Winwood, Sir Ralph, 67
Winwood, Richard, 213
Wolfe, General, 239
Wolsey, Cardinal, 119, 199
Wolverton, 270
Woburn, 271
Wood, Cornelius, 216
Wooden arcade, 158, 222
Wooden monuments, 64, 110
Worminghall, 272
Wotton, Sir Henry, 89
Wotton, William, 191
Wotton Underwood, 273
Woughton-on-the-Green, 275
Wraysbury, 276
Wren, Sir Christopher, 95, 102
Wrighte, Sir Nathan, 102
Wycliffe, John, 178
Wycombe Abbey, 131

Yews, notable :
  Broughton, 38
  Chequers, 81
  Hedsor, 129
  Hughenden, 141
  Ibstone, 146
  Medmenham, 186
  Shalstone, 217
  Weston Underwood, 260
  Wraysbury, 276

heritagehunter

First published in 1940

This Heritage Hunter® edition published February 2016
Register for free at **www.heritagehunter.co.uk**
for a free ebook every month

ISBN 978-1523999354

Printed in Great Britain
by Amazon